War Baby is a riveting personal accoui
World War in a small hamlet in East S
existence of a young boy is suddenly broken by night time raids, dog
fights in the sky and preparations for war. The author's story deals
with the horror of crouching in a dug out shelter listening as
bombers drone overhead, to his evacuation to a remote hamlet in
the Welsh mountains, to being blown off a hayrick by an exploding
doodlebug near the end of the war.

The book covers the years 1938-1962 and describes his close family
life in post-war Britain and the author's problematic education and
turbulent adolescence as he successfully struggles to over-come his
dyslexia and succeeds in gaining the qualifications and experience to
become a College Lecturer. Mike Strange has an infectious sense of
humour, together with an acute understanding of the strength and
frailty of human relationships. Parts of his memoir will make you
laugh and cry at the same time.

War Baby
By Mike Strange
First published by CreateSpace in 2018
© Mike Strange
ISBN-13: 978-1983505591

A catalogue record for this publication is available from the British Library.

E-mail: strangedelacour@hotmail.com
Web: www.potterystalbans.co.uk

Front cover photo credit: Robert Sullivan

Author photo credit: Lisbeth de la Cour

NB: Where appropriate names of individuals and institutions have been changed.

Contents

Acknowledgements

This book is dedicated to my loving parents, Vera and Frank, and all the members of the extended family and friends that I grew up with during the war.

I would also like to thank all the members of the reconstituted family I now inhabit especially Lisbeth, Louise, Paul, Mark, Kian and Camilla, and our friends, Alex and Vivien, for all the help they have given me with my manuscript.

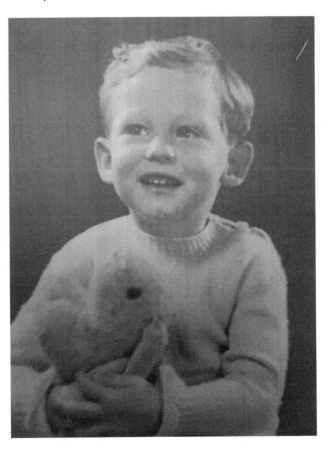

War Baby Mike Strange aged 2

About the Author

Mike Strange graduated from London University in 1960 and studied for an MSc in Politics and Sociology at Birkbeck College in 1976. He grew up in a little hamlet called Pound Green in East Sussex and later lived at a house on the edge of Ashdown Forest in Herons Ghyll. Mike has taught for most of his life in Schools and Colleges of Further Education. In the late 1970s he spent some time as a single parent and now lives with his second wife, Lisbeth, at the centre of a large reconstituted family, comprising five children and five grandchildren.

Apart from writing, Mike has built a large workshop and pottery studio at the bottom of the garden, where he and his wife make ceramics to sell at their annual Christmas Sale at their home and at a variety of art festivals and galleries. Mike also enjoys swimming, camping and walking with friends, and still makes the occasional Meccano model – a continuation of a childhood hobby referred to in this book.

Preface to My Story

I started writing this memoire over three years ago in 2014. The prospect of finishing a long and happy career in education filled me with foreboding and I wondered whether my interests in walking, swimming, camping, woodwork and making pots with my wife Lisbeth -- who is a very talented Ceramicist—would fill all the new leisure time which opened up before me.

It then occurred to me that being born in 1938 -- a 3 lb premature baby -- growing up during the war in East Sussex with the fear of imminent invasion -- when Brighton beach was mined and covered in a tangle of barbed wire, and villagers in Pound Green, where my family lived, were burying stashes of tinned food in our local wood -- being evacuated, and then returning home, only to be blown off a haystack by an exploding flying bomb -- meant that I had an interesting story to tell about my early life. I am now pleased that retirement gave me the time to do this.

To begin with, I intended the story to be just for my family and friends – something for the grandchildren to remember me by. However, although, in one sense it could be said that this is a "Diary of a Nobody" -- I am certainly no celebrity! I nevertheless agree with Mr Pooter, the fictional author of the original Diary published in 1892, who says at the beginning --:"Because I do not happen to be `somebody` -- why should my diary not be interesting?" Although I hope I avoid the moralising and boring minutiae of his account.

My story covers the period 1938 to 1962 finishing when I started my teaching career at St Albans College of Further Education. It is seen originally, through my eyes as a small child, and later deals with the vicissitudes of adolescence as my poor parents struggle to come to terms with my educational short comings resulting from my dyslexia, a condition which was not understood at this time. Their well-meant, sometimes desperate solutions -- ranged from "freedom schools" to a very conventional single sex boarding school. The bullying and conformist control I experienced in these institutions did little to prepare me for the demands of the outside world or heterosexual relationships at university.

My last chapter deals with my experience of working as a Graduate Trainee for the Central Electricity Generating Board in the early 1960`s which provided me with the necessary industrial experience, together with my work for the Workers Educational Association, for a meal ticket into teaching Liberal Studies and later Sociology and Politics in Further Education.

Although my story is told in the first person it is set within the context of a caring extended family. I was very fortunate to enjoy the loving support of my Father and Mother and Granny and Uncles and Aunts and the closeness and tribulations of our family, especially on my Mum`s side, are documented -- as are the mores of the time -- such as attitudes towards divorce and pre-marital sex. I have also tried to gear my account to changing views of class and race and to place my experiences within the political context of the immediate post-war era – such as the pernicious influence of Rachmanism in London`s bed sitter land.

War babies are now approaching their eighties, and some readers may be interested to read my first-hand account of these turbulent times before such memories are lost in the sands of history. At the beginning of my story I can remember crouching in our dug-out shelter listening to the wail of the sirens every night and dull rhythmic beat in the night sky as the raiding Heinkels and Dorniers flew overhead, blotting out the stars and the Milky Way as they headed towards London. The part of the Sussex Weald where I grew up is very beautiful – a patchwork quilt of wooded valleys, and small fields with twisting roads and meandering streams and the land rising towards the blue silhouette of the Downs in the far distance. House Martins nested under the eaves of our house and horses still hauled ploughs drawing brown furrows across green pastures. In harvest time, after the wheat had been scythed and stacked in stokes, there were rich pickings for the gleaners including my Mum and Gran and Me, as we gathered up the stray heads of corn and bagged them in sacks ready to feed to our chicken. In those far off days life seemed preserved in aspic and it seemed a crime against nature that it should be besieged by dog fights in the bright summer sky and the strafing of our village bus by a stray Messerschmitt....

Chapter 1
Evacuation

I was born on 5th July 1938 and I have no memory of life in Cousley
Wood, a small village in East Sussex, where I must have spent the first
months of my existence. There are a few sepia photographs, of course:
one of my Mum holding me in a long shawl outside a bungalow with
criss-cross leaded light windows; and another of my Dad, even then
wearing thick horned-rimmed spectacles. His brow is furrowed, and he
looks a little preoccupied, maybe he has just been listening to the
news of Hitler's military advances in Austria, or Neville Chamberlain's
deluded 'Peace with Honour' speech on the Home Service. My
understanding of this time is, of course, framed by lots of apocryphal
family stories often related – a kind of mantra which documents my
early precarious existence – the gist of which is that I am lucky to be
alive. My Mum was very delicate, and was rumoured to have suffered
from tuberculosis when she was young and even to have contracted a
mild form of polio. She was said to be very anaemic, and I can well
remember that relatively mild exertion would render her breathless.
Towards the end of her life I recall her suffering from very distressing
early morning coughing fits, probably the result of chronic asthma and
bronchitis. She was so delicate, apparently, that Frank, my Dad, had
been advised against marrying Vera, almost as if the excitement of the
wedding night alone might sprit her away to a more ethereal level of
existence. In any event, conception must have occurred, I calculate,
sometime around Christmas 1937. However, as a prelude to giving

birth, according to the family story, my Mum had to succumb to having her womb scraped and stretched. She was subject to homeopathic treatment at a clinic in Stonefield, near London, and, as far as I can gather, fed on a diet of fruit and nuts. I was born at a hospital in Blackheath, three months premature and weighing only three pounds – "Had your mother gone full term neither of you would have survived", so the siren voices echoing down the years have told me. "You, truly are, a miracle baby!"

Sometime in 1939 my parents must have moved to Buxted in East Sussex. We rented a substantial Edwardian house called The Hollies with a large rambling garden from the Hammersley family, who lived in a grand mansion at the top of the road. The Hammersley's also owned Toll Farm and we were friends with Farmer Ford and his family. The farm bordered the whole of one side of our garden and was raised up on a huge clay bank, topped by an unruly hedge with a ditch at the bottom, which flowed with brackish water and effluent, leached from the farm yard when it rained. Above the hedge silhouettes of various farm sheds, hayricks and straw stacks could be glimpsed, together with rusty entrails of long abandoned farm equipment, and the remains of old horse drawn carts. Farmer Ford was an obliging neighbour and let us have off-ration chicken meal for our hens. He turned a blind eye to my friends and we all used the farm yard, and surrounding fields and woods, as our very own adventure playground, a freedom we exploited to the full. For boys reared on the daring do stories in Hotspur, The Wizard and later the Eagle, the Hollies, with its one acre wild garden, afforded further opportunities for adventure. In front of the house Dad had made Herculean efforts to civilise the garden with flower borders and a small pond formed from an old kitchen sink. Beyond this, behind a pergola supporting climbing roses, he had carved the natural incline of the land into three level lawns separated by three grassy slopes. Making this "Capability Brown" statement in the Sussex clay and sandstone must have required hours of heavy labour with a mattock and shovel. Mum told me that mountains of earth were shifted in a rickety old galvanised wheel barrow, or literally rolled in an old barrel until it could be spilled out onto the required level to be tamped into place, and then rolled flat by a hand pushed Qualcast mower. Later in life, Dad developed a hernia – almost certainly a product of this gigantic effort.

Beyond the lawn, and behind another pergola, there was a kitchen garden where Dad grew peas and broad beans and celery, and, where I was given my first garden, where I can remember building an air-raid shelter for worms! And later on grew beautiful blue cornflowers. To the right of the kitchen garden stood a gnarled old apple tree which tempted one to climb to its highest branches in search of its bitter sweet fruit. On the left of the garden was an old deserted pig sty with a rusty corrugated roof which served as a key prop in many of our childhood games. A private place, away from the preying eyes of adults, it satisfied the cravings of our infantile imaginings from gangland lair to lady's bedchamber.

At the back of the house, behind a rickety asbestos garage, Dad, with the help of my Uncle Norm and Uncle Les, had constructed a makeshift shelter cut into the soggy clay bank separating us from Ford's farm. The corrugated roof, topped by more earth, was supported by old telegraph poles. The whole assembly looked rather like a first world war dug out. Access was by a narrow passage, flanked by old metal tanks filled with earth. Later on, while Dad was away at war, Uncle Norm carried out minor improvements including a shelf for candles and a hurricane lamp. We slept on canvas camp beds, and I remember preferring it to crouching under the stairs during air raids and doodlebug attacks, despite the rats, who, frequently foraged for scraps of cheese and spam left by us humans.

The rest of the back garden was fairly wild. Although for most of the war, when we were not absent during the evacuation, areas were fenced off to keep hens and ducks. At this time, with Dad away at the war, the garden had a dilapidated air about it -- a feeling of faded grandeur. Sometimes us kids would battle against the dense undergrowth and stinging nettles with sticks and bill-hooks exploring its hidden extremities. We found groves of "wild" currants and gooseberries which we fell upon like locusts. The tang of this newly discovered fruit bursting in our mouths and staining our lips and teeth.

Beyond the chicken-run the garden descended steeply towards the road. Here the "Orchard", as it was rather grandly called, boasted a rich variety of apple and damson trees. There were also walnut and almond trees that provided a rich harvest of nuts if you got there before the squirrels and weevils. Their straight springy shoots could easily be whittled into bows and arrows and catapults. This whole area of jungle fired our imagination for endless games of Cowboys and Indians.

Our house was a square brick structure with dormer windows. Its tiled roof was flanked at each end by large chimneys. It stood proud to the four winds. Climbing roses clung to its walls and enveloped a white wooden porch leading to the front door. Its east facing wall supported a battered old lean to green house. In the spring, house martins flew in from Africa and built their mud nests under the eaves and reared their broods of chattering chicks by my bedroom window. The house stood on high ground and commanded a distant view of Buxted Common lying in a wooded valley where John George Haig -- The Acid Bath Murderer-- is reputed to have buried the remains of his victims. Beyond, to the south, the land sloped up to form the beginnings of Ashdown Forest where A.A. Milne set the scene for Christopher Robin to stand on a bridge watching his "Poo Sticks" chase each other in the eddying stream. On a clear night, you could see a clump of tall pine trees on the horizon and the tall masks of the Kings Standing Radar Station winking their red warning lights. During the war we knew when the air raids were coming, minutes before the Dorniers droned over-head, when the lights went out.

I think my Mum regarded the house as rather ugly. It was certainly damp and I can remember, as a small boy, poking a stick through a crack in the floorboards and finding it coming up sopping wet from the from the stagnant water trapped by the clay beneath the foundations. There was no doubt that there were musty areas where our belongings were affected by rising damp. I can recall rummaging through the contents of a cupboard in our lounge and finding old copies of my Dad's Children's Magazine – a worthy periodical for children edited by Arthur Mee. I can vaguely remember that it had an early strip cartoon at the back featuring characters called Tiger Tim and Mrs Hippo. One article on the planets stimulated my early interest in astronomy. Dad also kept the entrails of an old crystal radio set that he had constructed before the war. The magazines near the floor were spotted by mould and most of their pages congealed together. Parts of Dad's old radio had turned bright green!

We had one radiator in the front passage fed by a coke boiler in the kitchen which also serviced the hot-water tank in the bathroom upstairs. There were fireplaces in the dining room and the lounge, and on cold nights, we would cluster around the flames in the grate - - our faces flushed and our backs too cold. As a small child, I can remember waking in the winter, to see diamonds of ice sparkling on the inside of the windows against the darker crosses of brown paper strips pasted on the panes, which The War Ministry told us would stop flying glass. Some days my Mum would push my pram the half mile to Hunters Farm where, near a rather sinister looking pond, there was a small wood where we collected rotten branches and twigs for kindling. The dried wood was put in a tiny room at the end of our kitchen, while sacks of coke and lumps of coal were kept in an old chicken shed outside the back door. We had electricity and Mum had a Belling Cooker, although we often boiled water and made soup on top of an oil stove whose wick was encased in glass and burnt with a friendly orange glow. In a room adjacent to the kitchen called, the scullery, there was a large black-leaded kitchen range with big heavy iron doors fronting an oven which we never used. I recall the room being rather gloomy with a couple pictures hanging on the walls of eighteenth century gents sagely drawing on clay pipes and pondering maps of military campaigns. I don't recall eating in this room which was used for more basic domestic tasks. But I can remember helping my Granny pluck chicken, in the build up to Christmas, prior to her moving on to the grisly part of removing their innards. I must have been singularly un-squeamish at this tender age as she used to cut off the chicken's legs with the tendons still hanging out, and Ian (my best friend) and I used to go charging around the house and garden scaring the life out of one another and our friends -- bowing out of secret places and clawing at them with animated chickens talons.

The scullery led on to a poorly illuminated passage leading to the two other rooms on the ground floor, the front door and the foot of the stairs. One of my first memories -- I must have been about two and a half at the time, is finding a coil of wire (probably used to reinforce chicken fencing) and twisting it into a spiral to trap my Granny with it in the dark stairwell. She decided to humour me and obligingly stepped into the device—attracting squeals of mirth from her deviant grandson.

I believe that when one approaches old age and wishes to divine some meaning or order to existence by writing a biography either, as a kind of stock-taking exercise—putting the books in order, or the vainglorious belief that –future generations will want to know something of my past. First memories assume significance because they are the moment when we come to understand that we are sentient beings. We are no longer bundles of reflexes -- obediently cooing, yelling, burping and smiling, in our prams -- to the bidding of fond aunties or indulgent friends. Suddenly, in a brief flash, we may appreciate our essential aloneness and vulnerability. I have two "first memories" I can recall. The first is rather mundane I am in the dining room on my own simply building a tower of wooden coloured bricks. As I add more and more bricks the tower becomes unstable and the bricks cascade to the ground. I think I must have cried out perhaps because I was elated at the effect my actions had on inanimate objects, because, suddenly my Mum was beside me laughing at my bewildered expression. The other "memory" is more vivid. I am walking with my Dad on a grass path looking for frogs in the pond he had made out of a sunken sink in the rockery. The sun is hot and the sky is bright blue – when suddenly there is the rata-tat-tat of gun fire and the shadow of diving planes above us and spent shells falling in the garden -- and my Dad flinging me to the ground and covering me with his whole body.

Because of the war I think that my early memories were an odd mixture of mundane experiences, spliced in with occasional moments of extreme excitement and sometimes terror. In 1940-41, just when I was becoming conscious of the world around me, the war was at its most intense on the Home Front and there was a genuine fear of a German invasion on the South Coast of England. Some of my memories reflect this. I dimly recall being loaded, as a baby, into a gasmask container designed for infants. The experience was terrifying and very claustrophobic. I remember the black hood with a perspex window and suffocating round filter at the front like a black and green gill. I can also recall being washed outside our air-raid shelter in a papier-mache tub. "Utility" my Mum said "part of the war effort" amazed it didn't leak!

My Mum and Dad loved living in the country and were firm friends with farmer Ford next door. We kept chickens and ducks and, despite the rationing, we always seemed to get enough "meal" from the farm, which we mixed with left over scraps to make a swill which kept them well fed. We collected our milk from the farm in a hand-churn every afternoon. The cows would be herded into the milking shed to be hand milked by the farm labourers. It was fascinating to see Ernie and Percy, and others, pulling at the udders and hear the noise of the milk being squirted into the metal pales between their legs, while all the time the cows plied their natural functions – pissing and shitting to their hearts content. At the end of milking, they would be released back into the fields and their dung would be piled in a steaming heap at the back of the shed ready for muck-spreading the next day. The milk was regularly transferred to the milk parlour next door and poured through a metal cooler before being ladled out to customers. It was considered a "treat" to offer some of the un-cooled milk directly to young children – a practice which revolted me. These un-hygienic practices sometimes led to outbreaks of brucellosis which caused my Mum to boil the milk "to get rid of the germs." – a practice which rendered it even more unpalatable. We had no fridge, and the milk would be deposited in the pantry, which led off from the scullery on the north-west side of the house, which was thought to be cooler. It was here that we kept meat inside a cone of wire mesh to ward off the blue-bottles. Mum prided herself on providing a "spread" when "family" was expected at holiday time. Freshly killed chicken and ducks would be hung up here "to mature." Occasionally, after Dad was invited by rich clients at the local branch of Lloyds Bank, to go shooting on their land, the odd pheasant or rabbit would also dangle from the hooks. My Dad always got on well with my Uncle Les, who was thirteen years younger than my Mum, and rather indulged by the family. Two 12 bore shot guns stood in the hall-stand by the front door and there were packets of red cartridges stored in draws, half hidden by hanging coats, which held a fascination for me, although I was warned never to touch them. Mum followed the Welsh tradition of not locking the back door, and I never imagined that the guns would be used in anger or defence. The war dominated my interpretation of reality. The threat, I dimly imagined, would come from the sea, I had seen bundles of barbed-wire entanglements on Brighton beach, where mines had been laid. Or out of the black sky one night when the lights went out at the Kings Standing Radar station. Dad would occasionally clean and oil his guns, breaking them open at the breach to draw gun cotton through each barrel. "You have to be careful with this one" he would say of his older prize gun "very light trigger." He spoke from experience. One day when he was out shooting with my Uncle when Les's gun discharged unexpectedly when he was climbing over a farm gate. The shot whistled over my Dad's head. "Bit close for comfort!" said my Dad always one for understatement. "Bit close for comfort!" This was standard repartee when the two of them got together after a good Sunday lunch and relaxed in arm chairs, drinking whisky, and smoking manikin cigars. Reminiscing and putting the world to rights.

I can remember ration books and ID cards, but I can never remember going hungry. Those living in the countryside followed the agenda of the seasons -- war or no war. Sometimes there were gluts and my

Mum and Granny struggled to bottle all the plums which fell and carpeted our little orchard, or find enough sugar to make jam from baskets overflowing with damsons or blackcurrants. The cows, oblivious of the war effort, continued to eat grass and make milk. Waste was abhorred! Left-over milk was whisked with the aid of a hand churn and turned into butter. There were no combined harvesters and harvesting was still very labour intensive, with the wheat being scythed by hand and gathered into sheaves of corn, that were then arranged in the fields to stand in stokes, which were later transported by horse and cart to stacks to await the arrival of the traction engine and complex thrashing machine to beat the grain out of the ears of corn. It was a wasteful process and villagers, including my Mum and Granny and Dad, before he went to fight, would go "gleaning"-- which meant gathering all the ears of corn left in the field at the end of the day. Putting them in sacks and taking them home to feed to our chicken. The annual arrival of the traction engine steaming down our lane, followed by the thrashing machine turning into Ford's farm is still vivid in my memory. As is, the super-human effort required to manoeuvre the two gigantic machines together, so that the main drive belt could be connected to the flange of the fly-wheel of the traction engine and the drive pulley on the thrasher. Once the whole contraption roared into life, men would stand on the carts as they arrived and pitch-fork bails of barley into the hopper where upon they would be devoured, as if by some alien beast, with much flapping of drive belts, shaking of sieves and whining of cogs! The noise, the smell of hot oil, the clouds of dust and steam, the blowing of chaff, and the swelling of the sacks of grain at the end of the machine were unforgettable. This was the climax of all the toil which had taken place in the fields at the end of summer. It united young and old alike. Children would roll in mounds of chaff. Youths, anxious to impress the experienced farm workers, would queue up to lead the carts coming from the fields with fresh loads to supply the elevators feeding the stack. And I would stand, for what seemed hours, marvelling at the great steaming colossus of the traction engine as the piston and valve gear thundered to and fro on the top of its boiler. And the spinning flywheel drove its great leather belt round and round against the back ground of hay carts, green fields, and blue sky.

Just before my Dad volunteered to join his artillery regiment and went for training in Chester he bought me a large collection of old Meccano. I was warned that I was really too young to play with it and, that must take great care with the nuts and bolts otherwise they would be sucked up by our new Hoover. I was indeed in awe of the set, which was mainly housed in neatly partitioned wooden boxes. I initially confined myself to looking at the well-produced pre-war Meccano Magazines which had beautiful coloured front pages featuring iconic pictures of steam locomotives pulling luxury Pullman carriages, or detailed plans of the Forth Bridge, or colour photos of blast furnaces. I gradually familiarised myself with some of the elementary Meccano instruction booklets and made some very simple tables and chairs from Meccano plates and strips featured in the "Set 0" manual. I was fascinated by all the beautiful brass flange wheels and gears and the blue Number 2 clockwork motor which I discovered, but considered these exciting pieces too challenging for my infant fingers. However, my fascination with thrashing machines and steam engines, and all the other exciting equipment which lay around Ford's Farm had fired my imagination, and I vowed that I would eventually build the models powered by engines and gearwheels featured in the more advanced manuals with a reassuring picture of an indulgent pipe smoking dad and two eager Meccano Boys on the cover.

Uncle Norm, my Mum's eldest brother, visited us quite often during the war. He was divorced from his first wife Edith, which was seen to be quite scandalous in the 1940's. He had to leave his position as Minister in the Congregational Church and, because he was a well qualified graduate, had managed to secure a job as a Factory Inspector in the Ministry of Labour. Uncle had been part of the Christian Left Movement, together with such leading lights as Dick Shepherd. I don't think he was a pacifist, at this time, although he did become a Quaker in later life. However, I imagine he was pleased that the Inspectorate was a reserved occupation, which meant he was excused war service. I think this led to a little friction between him and my Dad and Uncle Les, who experienced frightening events at Tobruk and Monte Cassino. Uncle Norm, however, could retort that living in Chiswick at the height of the Blitz, and inspecting factories in the East End of London, was hardly a cushy number! He had had to take responsibility for looking after my Mother --Vera, and his brother Les and my Granny quite early in life, when my Grandfather, Fredrick Chubb, who I never knew, died at an early age after his tailoring business in Swansea went bust during the great depression. He died of Bright's disease and my Mum thought that his early demise was brought about by heavy drinking. At this time the family lived at Killay a small village overlooking Fairwood Common on the Gower Peninsular. Norm was a bright boy who had secured a scholarship to the grammar school in Gowerton and then was accepted for training to enter the Congregational Church, eventually securing a first class degree in philosophy at London University. He was greatly influenced by the Christian Philosopher, John MacMurray, who emphasised the importance of human relationships, and this encouraged Norm to continue his studies after he was ordained. He eventually gained a MA relating to the work of Adler, Freud and Jung. The livings he secured in the Congregational Church, first at Hawkenbury near Tunbridge Wells, where he did his initial training, and then in a larger church in East Ham enabled him to look after his younger brother and sister and mother.

I think that having such responsibility at a young age, and the demands of running a church, must have taken its toll. My mother suffered very poor health and Les was still attending school. As the Minister, Norm was looked up to as the "officially good person" His sermons apparently, always the centre piece in congregational services, were very dynamic – a heady mixture of Christian Socialism and Freudian psychology! Young spinsters, I am advised by family folk-law, hung on his every word! My Uncle, I think, concluded that marriage to a "good woman" would stabilize the situation and fit well with his official role. He courted Edith, who I am told, was very spiritual and good at flower arrangement. They married at the beginning of the 1930's and my Cousin John was born in 1933. The union was not a happy one. I never met Edith, but I have a mental image of her as thin and gaunt and wearing thick lisle stockings!

The shame of separation and divorce for a clergyman at this time must have been immense. Families are notorious for taking sides and my Mum would relate incidences of Edith's frugality "She was so mean that at tea time even the tomatoes would be cut in half!" This frugality apparently extended to the bedroom-- "that woman was dead from the waist down!" poor Uncle. Denied the promise of Freudian Psychology! After the separation, Norm went to live in a flat in Chiswick and spent some time training to operate industrial lathes before he got the job as a factory inspector. Edith worked in a bank in Dorking and my cousin John was sent to a boarding school in Caterham, founded by the Congregational Church, at the very early age of 6. Because of the divorce I saw very little of him when I was a child. However, from reading his own biographic account of these times, I have come to appreciate how lonely and isolated he must have felt, both at school and at home, where the situation meant that he was left very much to his own devices. Uncle Norm's access appeared to have been limited to half-term meetings at his school. The sad truth is that I probably saw much more of my Uncle, who was something of a surrogate father to me during the war, than his own son during these formative years. Despite this, John always regarded his Father with great affection. Norm encouraged both of us, at different times, to build exciting models out of Meccano, which prompted John to study science and, in my case, helped me to sustain confidence in myself at a time when my early dyslexia threatened to parallelise my educational progress. I can remember him helping me to build a hand cranked gearbox – the cogs arranged so that the flywheel at the end of the drive train revolved at high speed.

Later, after the war, Uncle would borrow pieces of my Meccano to build models of faulty factory machinery so that he could prosecute bad employers. Norman was the only member of our family with a degree and he was good at leading by example. "Never say never boy!" He would say. In 1957 he encouraged me to apply for a late place study an external degree at Regent Street Polytechnic after I had failed 'O' Level French for the second time and was denied a place at Manchester University. He also helped John survive the first year at Birmingham University by paying for him to have extra tuition to overcome difficulties he was experiencing with maths at this time. This helped to set him on a path to becoming a research scientist and inventor.

We had a large free standing radio in the dining room. I can remember the shine of its walnut case and the round hole of its speaker, and the fact that you could glimpse the lighted valves through a grill at the back. It took a long time to warm up and was often difficult to tune in, although, it must have been a great improvement on my Dad's pre-war crystal sets. It was connected to a long aerial which was fed outside and led to an insulator on top of a pine tree at the back of the house. I can remember the family clustering around to listen to news bulletins on the Home Service and early comedy shows on the Light Programme like "Itma" with Tommy Handley, and a character called Colonel Chin-strap who was permanently inebriated. Sometimes we would listen to clandestine German propaganda broadcasts from someone people nick- named Lord Haw Haw. I can still remember his sing-song voice braying out entreaties for us to all surrender to the overwhelming power of the German Reith! Things must have looked bad at this time. I can recall my Mum saying that the villagers had carried sacks of tinned food over the fields of Ford's farm to bury in Waste Wood, where white enemies grew and we picked bunches of blue bells in the spring. Before he left for the war my Dad buried our own stock pile of tins in the soft peaty loam behind our garage, near the entrance to our dug-out shelter.

When the Blitz started in earnest, and the German bombers droned overhead night after night, we crouched on camp beds in Dad's makeshift shelter. Sometimes on an incoming bombing run, when the Heinkels and Dorniers headed towards London, we would stand outside and look up as formation after formation moved across the sky silhouetted against the black void of space, or the magnificent orb of the Milky Way. In the sleepy hamlet of Pound Green, between Buxted and Hadlow Down, in the middle of the Sussex countryside, we knew that we were not the target. The danger lay on the return run, when the bombers, who had failed to find a target, jettisoned their bombs to lighten the load as they made their way to the channel coast. Or from stragglers, weakened by Ack Ack fire or damaged in combat, falling prey to the waiting Spitfires and Hurricanes. One night, when my Granny went outside to see if the red lights had been turned on again at Kings Standing, across the valley from us, to indicate the end of the raid. When a huge box crashed on our lawn in front of her and "exploded" strips of silver paper all over the garden. (This technique, used by both sides, of scattering "chaff" in the sky to interfere with hostile radar signals) Although in this case, the whole box had been chucked out of an enemy bomb door to lighten the load for a homeward run! The incident happened so quickly that there was little time for us to feel fear at the near demise of my Granny! The happening was recorded as part of the verbal family archive of war-time experiences to be repeated down the years -- like the day time strafing of the village bus by a stray Messerschmitt, or the rounding up of German pilots who had crashed, by farm labourers armed with pitch forks. As the conflict intensified, gangs of older kids would proudly exhibit bits of twisted metal purloined from the growing number of crash sites dotted around the countryside. While others would collect bits of old iron "for the war effort". I had a wind-up Chad Valley tin plate bomber which trundled across the floor spraying sparks from its nose. And I contented myself by drawing lurid pictures of fighter planes and bombers with bullets flying between them, and death defying stick creatures floating to earth on parachutes!

Sometimes, at the height of the Blitz in 1941, my Mum and Granny must have decided to lock up the house and surrender the care of our chickens and cat to farmer Ford, and his wife, and go on a very "middle class" voluntary evacuation to South Wales. My Mum had kept in contact with some of the friends she had grown up with on the Gower Peninsular, and others who had worked in my Grandfather's tailoring business. The theory was that, as most of Swansea had been flattened in the war-time bombing, it would no longer be attacked. It was arranged that we would lodge with "Aunty" Ethel, who had worked for the Chubb family as a seamstress and lived in a working class part of the city called Pentrechweth. I have rather vague memories of the journey starting with me standing next to a large brown suitcase at Buxted station waiting for the train. And the excitement when it rounded the track billowing smoke as it passed under the bridge and thundered to a halt. I was fascinated by the big leather strap that was used to open the window, and being told I would get a smut in my eye if I looked out! On the journey I remember following the telephone lines as they appeared to rise and fall, as we passed each post and the rhythmic chatter of the carriage wheels on the rails. We must have changed trains a number of times, and I can recall a big London terminus, possibly Paddington, where there was a chance to look up into the towering cab of the engine and wave to the driver and fireman and glimpse their grime streaked faces under their peaked caps. Looking out of the window, as we journeyed across London, I witnessed an environment totally alien to my previous experience. Instead of the soft undulating pitch and fall of the Sussex Downs and green woods, I could see only cluttered back yards and the grey outline of identical houses topped by slate roofs. Sometimes, what had been houses, gave way to piles of rubble with gaunt blackened walls and blown out windows standing like giant tomb stones. On the way to Wales I wanted to go "wo wo" (my childish word for having a piss!) and Mum had to lead me along the corridor crowded with soldiers weighed down by all their kit. As we neared Swansea I saw men in cloth caps streaming out of factory buildings, rows and rows of terraced houses, kids playing in back alleys, and gigantic advertising boards, some on the side of buildings, others on hoardings rising out of ruined buildings, with slogans like "Players Please!" or "Guinness is Good for You!" When we got to Swansea it was late and I can't remember how we got to "Auntie" Ethel's. But I can recall my Mum and Granny being horrified at the devastation wrought by the bombing. As we passed down the main high street they gasped in wonder that the buildings that had been so familiar to them, including my grandfathers old shop, had simply ceased to exist.

Pentrechwyth comprised of streets of terraced houses housing workers employed in local industries lying to the north-west of Swansea. The front doors of each dwelling led straight on to the street and the step outside always displayed a liberal coating of "Red Cardinal" polish. Sections of the pavement leading to the entrance were religiously white washed. Auntie Ethel further reinforced her respectability with spotless net curtains at all the windows. Sadly, Auntie's fiancé had been killed in the first war and the front room was preserved as a shrine to his memory. This meant that, in effect, the house comprised one useable room and a small kitchen downstairs and two rooms upstairs and a washroom. There was no inside toilet and the lavatory was in a shed at the end of the tiny yard at the back. Needless to say, having my Mum, Granny and me to stay for an unspecified period made things rather claustrophobic.

I don't think we were billeted like "real evacuees" although, I imagine that some financial arrangement was struck. Initially we were made very welcome with much trilling of female voices and Welsh phases, like "that's lovely!" and "How are you bach?" "Auntie's" Sister Gladys, nick named "Gladdie," and husband (whose name I can't recall) lived next door, together with their two children Ken and Averil. Auntie's sister's family were always very hospitable and as their door was never locked. I remember spending as much time as I could with them. Averil had aspirations to be an opera singer and we would often gather around the piano in the evening, as she exercised her deep contralto voice, with my Mum and Gladdie taking turns to play. Mum, who used to play for male voiced choirs in the Welsh valleys, as a young girl, had a rare talent to "touch play" almost any tune that was hummed to her, was excited and in her element. The whole of the street seemed to behave like one great extended family. Most people were called either Jones or Evans or sometimes -- Evans the Butcher or Jones the Bread to denote their occupation. There was fairly marked gender demarcation with women staying at home, or working part-time after they were married. Men worked in local industries and were the natural bread winners. The community was very traditional and rituals were closely observed. When someone died all the blackout curtains would be lowered in the street during the day as a mark of respect. The family was all important for those who were old, ill or injured, looked after as a kinship duty. I don't recall "Auntie" going out to work, although she must had done when she worked as a leading seamstress in my Grandfather's tailoring business. Unusual, in a strong Labour voting area, she was a Tory. I fancied that she gave herself airs and graces. Although it was tragic that she had lost her betrothed, I fancied that there was something of the Miss Faversham about her. The hallowed front room, which held a kind of morbid fascination for me, was out of bounds. A sanction of course, I defied at every opportunity. It smelt of polish and church pews and purity. This was in stark contrast to Auntie's sanitary arrangements which required a run down a slippery path in all weathers to the "Lavvie" at the end of the garden. Where we held our noses and relieved ourselves as quickly as possible before wiping our bums with screwed up newspaper! On fine days, after hauling up my shorts, I would sometimes venture out of the back yard and walk down the road to look over a wall at engines shunting long lines of goods wagons in the railway marshalling yard below. The valley, where this happened, was always misty and grey with smoke and echoed to the clash of trucks shuddering into position. Above the valley, rose the green mountains, in places purple with heather, in others scarred by tips of spoil.

People were very friendly and I can remember a neighbour collecting some of my Granny's old wooden cotton reels and using his lathe to make spinning tops for me. Some of the kids in the street had bigger tops which they could whip with a cord on a stick to keep spinning. But I never mastered this. Nothing was ever wasted and Granny often busied her-self by un-picking old pullovers and cardigans in order to knit new garments. Sometimes, I would have to sit with my arms outstretched supporting a skein of old wool as she wound it into a ball. Having seen this, our friend said he could make me a French knitting machine. I then went to his workshop where he banged four small nails into the top of a cotton reel to which we attached strands of Granny's wool wound around the nails. By laboriously picking at strands of wool with a piece of bent wire, pulling them over one another, and then feeding a "worm" of platted wool down through the hole in the cotton reel a multi-coloured rope of wool could be produced. I was thrilled when I could finally pull a length of our new "French Knitting" out of the end of the cotton reel. I sat for hours at my Granny's feet humming to myself and manufacturing more and more of the magic rope, which, we eventually, stitched to a card to make a coaster which I insisted we use for years after.

For some reason, I think, towards the end of our stay in Pentrechwyth, a decision was made to send me to school. I couldn't have been very old and all I can remember is sitting at a wooden desk on a narrow bench next to a boy with an enormous bogey in his nose, listening to a language I couldn't understand (I was not a Welsh Speaker.) I can recall scribbling with a stub of chalk on a piece of slate, whiling away the time until my Mum came to collect me.

While we were in Pentrechwyth we made a number of trips to visit some of my Mum's friends in Gower. I can remember an exciting ride along the Mumbles on the top deck of a red tram (sadly this service was disbanded after the war) and visiting someone in Killay called Billie Tucker who grew up with my Mum on Fairwood Common. He was a butcher who sold meat in the Swansea market. He lived next door to his sister Connie who had a mentally disabled child called Johnny. Thankfully, he was never put in a home and was allowed to wander freely around Fairwood Common with the sheep and wild horses. We sat in the front parlour of Billie's house one afternoon and I noticed its spartan contents and faded wall paper patterned with roses, and the old gas lamps, which, although they had been converted to electricity, still illuminated the original cream bowl which hung by chains from the ceiling. Later, my Mum told me that he had never married because he feared the "bad seed" in the family which had created the amiable Johnny. On another occasion we took a bus to Penrice Castle and walked down the steep winding road leading down to Oxwich Marches where, my Mum recalled, in her youth, a holiday charabanc careering out of control and people being badly hurt, if not killed.

We walked as far as Oxwich Bay and I can remember the in-coming tide lapping at the bank of pebbles near the shore and, the green of its tree covered point curving away to the south. Out in the bay there was a wrecked merchant ship, resting on a sandbank, its hull split in half.

Quite soon after this, I spied the house proud Ethel sweeping dust under the carpet in the holy room. Totally lacking in discretion, I had the temerity to tell my Mum of the incident. I must have been over heard because our stay came to an abrupt end and the next morning we were boarding an army lorry on a one way trip to remote country area Carmarthenshire!

The plan was that we would cadge a lift to the market town of Ammanford and then take the local bus to the hamlet of Pumpsaint, where there was a cottage we could rent from some distant relative. I can remember being lifted up and clutching a rope hanging from the roof at the back of the lorry. There were a couple of soldiers who chatted to us, but sometimes it was difficult to hear what was said because of the roar of the engine. The ride was very bumpy and the pile of old sacks I sat on did little to cushion the shocks. My Mum and Granny perched on old hay bales clutching their suit cases. Granny sat bolt upright as she always did. She had a stoic look on her face -- her nose was purple with the cold, and her hair, as usual, was tightly curled. My Mum wore a red spotted head scarf and her cheeks were pink. She looked excited and I remember thinking how pretty she was. We were embarking on a new adventure, looking forward to being on our own.

We waited in the cold for what seemed an age for the bus to arrive. When it did it soon filled up with friendly passengers clutching baskets of shopping, returning to local villages. They all talked and joked in their lilting accents in a mixture of Welsh and English. Somehow or other, they found room for us and our bulky luggage. I had a seat close to the driver, with a good view of the countryside, as we wended our way through the hills and round the mountains, with much grinding of gears and frequent stops at remote farms and villages. When we finally arrived at Pumsaint it was almost dark. There were no street lights but the stars and crescent moon shone brightly through the clouds which drifted overhead in a strong breeze. The first thing I noticed, as we stood in the lane with the little bus turning to go over the bridge, was the noise of rushing water. The small pink cottage we had come to stood on the bank of a river. We left our cases outside the door and walked up the lane, past the bridge to the farmhouse where we were to collect the key. After a friendly exchange of greetings we were ushered into a large cosy room with a roaring fire in an inglenook fire place. We sat around the blaze gratefully warming our hands, drinking tea and eating welsh cakes. My eyes followed the flames as they danced upwards and then noticed to my astonishment huge hams, hanging on hooks being smoked in the chimney breast. Seeing my look of amazement the farmer said with a laugh "You can get your eggs and bacon from us – as much as you like!" After more lively banter we took the key and returned to "Rose Cottage" which was to be our home for the winter. I must have fallen asleep almost immediately because I can't remember unpacking or anything that evening.

I awoke the next morning in bed next to my Mum. I looked out of the window to discover that it was raining and the river was running fast in the meadow below. Rose Cottage was a one up and one down dwelling with a ladder connecting the two rooms. I don't remember a kitchen and I think we cooked on an oil stove in the downstairs room where my granny slept. There was no electricity and we relied on oil lamps and candles at night. A well stood in the garden and we had to pump water into buckets and carry them inside for cooking. We tended to eat what the countryside provided in abundance and I can remember consuming lots of off-ration eggs and bacon and fried bread and mushrooms dripping in fat.

Although I was allowed to do "wo wo" in a potty at night time "business", as my granny called it, was something else! I discovered that Pumpsaint's sanitary arrangements were even more primitive than Auntie Ethel's! Attached to one side of the bridge over the river was a precarious wooden walkway and halfway across there were benches with holes cut at intervals. We had to perch on these seats -- bear our bottoms, and dispatch our "big jobbies" into the raging torrent 20 feet below. This early morning ritual was very exhilarating and I would regularly join villagers and farm hands all chatting away engaging in this act of collective defecation!

Some of the local practices were positively medieval. The farm, that we rented the cottage from, killed and butchered its own pigs. Sometimes, we would hear blood curdling screams of terror as the porkers were dispatched by a knife to the throat. Once, three of them in a death defying bid, broke free and hurled themselves in to the fast flowing river and were swept pass our cottage to a very uncertain fate.

There were some evacuees from the East-end of London billeted in the hamlet, and I kicked a rolled up bag of rags, which passed for a football, around with them and flew home made kites made from a cross of sticks and cloth with long tails of string and twisted paper. Sometimes we played "Hee" and Hide and Seek. They were a tough lot. On one occasion a big girl, who seemed to be leader of the gang," lifted up her skirt and pulled off one of her stockings. She then put a stone in it, whirred it around her head and let go unexpectedly, allowing the missile to fly up and then crash down on any un-expecting kid that happened to be in the way.

What I remember most of the winter of 1942 in Pumpsaint was the rain. Almost every-day, the leaden clouds would roll down from the mountains unleashing their heavy load -- causing streams to flood and waterfalls to cascade down the hills. The locals would look up at the sky and shout "Bwrw Glaw!" (Welsh for rain). Our morning routine of doing our "business" became even more exciting as the river turned into a raging torrent and the water surged higher and higher under the arch of the bridge. Finally the river broke its banks and flooded into the ground floor of our little cottage bringing our stay in Wales abruptly to an end.

The Chubb family seemed well blessed in its variety of Uncles and Aunts. Mum claimed at least two uncles called Bert. After we had gathered up what remained of our sodden possessions, we made a tortuous trip by bus and train to Uncle Bert 1 who lived in Bigbury-on-sea with his wife Mable and daughter Mamie. I can remember Uncle being a jolly chap with a pleasant West Country accent. He ran an amusement arcade on the pier and I was thrilled when he gave me a bag of pennies to work the slot machines. I can recall a machine which whisked ball bearings around a maze and you got a prize if all the balls got home without being lost in various traps! Also, turning the handle of the "What the Butler Saw" machines and seeing

Edwardian ladies in their "scanties" thrilled me with wonder! One day we took a trip to Burgh Island (where Agatha Christie wrote "And Then There Were None") in a war-time Duck which had tracks like a tank but could float in deep water like a boat – driven by a propeller at the back. I think we spent all day on the island and walked to the far side skirting a big hotel that was fenced off. On the return trip the sea was much rougher and the duck lurched from side to side before clawing itself back up the beach at Bigbury. When we got back there was a rather formal tea neatly set out on a starched table cloth with napkins rolled in silver bands and I remember thinking that Aunt Mable was rather severe. She put a stop to my excited babbling at the table and had the kind of spinsterish deportment which implied that children should be seen but not heard. My Mum whispered later, that that Uncle Bert had said that he had "married a cold woman!" The Chubb's seemed an unlucky lot where love was considered. I stifled the thought that Uncle would have had a better time with the lady the butler saw!

I think we stayed about a week and then were off travelling again by train to Uncle Bert 2 in Wantage. I can remember him and his wife being very friendly. He was a Watchmaker by trade and I can recall looking at him in his workshop squinting through a spy-glass at the intricate workings of clocks and watches he was working on. Once he showed me how he used very delicate instruments to fit a tiny chain drive inside a pocket watch. In another room he had a beautiful collection of old musical boxes. He let me pull the lever of one, which worked the ratchet mechanism, backwards and forwards to wind it up. I was fascinated to see that as the brass roller, studded with little pins, slowly turned it plucked at the delicate keys which produced a haunting melody. Uncle showed me another lever, which when activated, shifted the roller a fraction and the wonderful box played another tune. Time pieces of all shapes and sizes were distributed around the house and there was a cacophony of bongs and chiming, as the ones he was testing, competed to sound out the passing hours.

Uncle had a lovely old Austin Twelve car and we made frequent trips to his garage where it lay in state! He would allow me to sink back into its richly padded seats and smell unforgettable tang of their leather upholstery. Sometimes, I would sit in the driving seat clutching the steering wheel and making deep-throated engine and gear changing noises. Uncle even indulged me when I squeezed the rubber bulb on the side of the bonnet and its horn rasped out a sharp warning to imaginary pedestrians. He showed me the engine, where he proudly pointed out that his treasured car had an advanced magneto and ignition system. Finally he said "How would you like to go for a spin?" Uncle repeated the suggestion at breakfast reinforced by my cries of – "I wanna go for a spin! I wanna go for a spin!" Uncle's suggestion seemed not to receive universal approval. My aunt looked worried and reminded him that he had not driven since the beginning of the war and that --embarrassed pause here-- he was a "bit past it for driving again!" My Granny made her trade mark "tut tut noise" with her tongue at the back of her teeth, while my Mum looked away. My Great Uncle was not to be over-ruled. "Fiddle-sticks!" He exclaimed "It's a beautiful day – the Boy would love a spin!" Later that day the garage doors were flung open and Uncle climbed into the driving seat, only to discover that the battery was flat. Undeterred, he took out the starting handle -- "a few swings should do it!" He announced. Five minutes later an exhausted Uncle was lifting the bonnet and peering at his "new fangled" magneto and the wires leading to the plugs "There must be a spark!" He opined. I was instructed to climb into the driver's seat and move an advance/retard lever on the steering column in accordance with his instructions. My Great-Aunt, Granny and Mum -- all attired in their going out clothes gathered around. Uncle gave the car another swing and there was a cough from the engine and a puff of blue smoke. Another swing, and the engine chattered uncertainly into life, this time with clouds of exhaust fumes. "Jump in everybody!" yelled my Uncle, seizing the steering wheel and thrusting me to one side. The car meandered down the drive and turned uncertainly into the lane. Uncle had taught himself to drive, and while he had digested the mechanical rudiments of changing gear and double-de-clutching, he seemed to have only a passing familiarity with the Highway Code. The Austin 12 was a heavy car that seemed, once going, to develop a momentum of its own. At the end of the lane we turned too quickly into a larger road, narrowly missing an on-coming car, by Uncle depressing the clutch and cutting the drive to the transmission. When Uncle deemed that the danger was over he let in the clutch too quickly and the car bucked in the air like a prancing mule! There were shrieks from the ladies in the back and entreaties to slow down. After another couple of near misses and a close shave with a farm cart, we turned into a lane which led back home. I think we were all relieved, Uncle included, when we finally returned. Nothing more was said and we eventually sat down to a great meal of tea, scones and jam tarts. It was notable that when our very pleasant stay came to an end we ordered a taxi to the station rather than put uncle to a further test! As it turned out, we would probably have been in safer hands in Uncle's car.

After we loaded our cases the journey started well enough. Although the frequent crashing of gears indicated the cabbie may also have been self-taught. Our route to the station required the navigation of a railway crossing. Halfway across the taxi stalled. We looked out of the window and were horrified to see a train steaming towards us. I can recall screaming in terror —"Let's get out! Let's get out!" The driver told us to stay where we were, and made desperate efforts to re-start the engine. I can remember the whine of the starter motor and the fear which engulfed us all as the train came towards us. As if by a miracle at the very last second the engine fired and we crawled off the track just in time!

It was a relief to climb into a railway carriage, put our cases on the racks above us, and know we were going home. I suspect that, at this time, the fear of invasion had receded, but in any event, we had run out of kind friends and loving family and our voluntary evacuation was coming to an end. Looking back our experiences had been probably more exciting than crouching in the dugout at home listening to enemy bombers droning overhead.

We returned home to find that Farmer Ford and his wife had done a good job of looking after things for us. The house was intact, although it smelt even more musty than usual. The back garden and orchard, where we had kept chickens, looked even more of a jungle than before. While Dad's beloved terraced lawns were knee high in grass. Mum got Ernie (who she nick named "Shut-eye"), from the farm, to scythe them flat and we made a small haystack at the bottom of the garden. Uncle Norm visited and we got Dad's old push mower out of the garage. He made some "reins" out of rope and tethered me to the front of the mower. With me hauling from the front, and him pushing from behind we laboured to cut off the remaining tusks of grass. When the rain came and the grass turned green again, Mum and I continued to mow in this way. Instead of cutting the grass in neat straight lines as Dad, had done, we started with a "V" for victory cut and gradually widened it out until the whole of the lawn was finished. We would then retire to the dining room where Dad kept his pipe and pouch of tobacco by the fire place. Mum would read and re-read his airmail letters, and we would toast the ends of his old cigar butts in the fire to remind ourselves of his existence and pray for his safe return. Mum would sometimes light up a Turkish cigarette. With her jet black hair and blue-green eyes and sometimes excitable gestures, I think she was regarded as something of a "Spanish beauty"--The Family joked that the Chubb's, with their black hair and sallow completions and West Country origin, were related to survivors of the Amada. She never inhaled and would let the smoke of the cigarette curl slowly upwards in a theatrical manner like a film star. In those days she would often wear simple knitted dresses which revealed the natural curves of her body. When lipstick was applied, and with a necklace of red beads about her neck, she was full of allure which at this time had little chance of being acknowledged – apart, of course, from the goggle-eyed four year old at her feet! Mum, with her puritan background would never have strayed from the "straight and narrow" as she put it. However, she always saw the best in everyone and welcomed all who came to the door.

Mr Marsh worked on his smallholding just up the road from us. He had experienced shell-shock in the First World War and was rumoured to have an uncontrollable temper. When he popped round to deliver vegetables Mum would ply him with cups of tea or "Camp Coffee" while he rambled on garrulously -- all the time eyeing my Mum with his little piggy eyes from behind the foliage of a large ginger beard. When the conversation faulted my Mum would be moved to offer him another drink while Granny hovered in the background on chaperone parade.

Despite the war, the formalities of country living carried on much as usual--the baker delivered the bread every other day. Periodically coal would be transported in dirty black sacks to be tipped into our shed opposite the back door. Every year, a big smelly tanker would call to pump out the contents of our septic tank at the bottom of our orchard. And once a week Grace, Carol's mother, who was married to Tom Smith who ran the Pound Green Stores, came to take the order. Although Mum and Grace were firm friends, and, had lots of laughs together the ritual of "taking the order" was regarded as a serious business. Grace would perch on the edge of her chair, notebook in hand and prompt Mum with grocery ideas. Such as "How are you off for bacon?" Or "Do you need another bag of flour for those Welsh Cakes of yours?" and "Has Mick -- (they called me Mick until I re-invented myself in late teens as Mike.)--had his full sweet ration?" Methodically lists would be compiled and "points" extracted from ration books and handed over and money would be exchanged. Mum now had to pay all the bills and make all the decisions and, I think, she relished the new won freedom which the war had afforded her. The session would always end in a gossip over tea and home-made cakes and I would ear-wig into the latest goings on in the village. Madeline Birch, whose husband worked at Barclays

Bank in Uckfield, I learned, had been seeing an awful lot of Mr Block, an amiable builder and odd job man! Alison Lyle who lived in Spotted Cow Lane, always wore her long blond plats wound around the top of her head. She was the attractive Mum of Camilla and Ian --who were my best friends. I heard was something called a "grass widow" because of the very infrequent appearances of her husband Gordon, who was always away on "business" of some ill-defined kind. Mr Hanson, a bachelor, who lived in a cottage at the end of the Twitten on the way to the Common was "bullied" by his spinster sister. Such was the minutia of village life that it was a big deal when someone painted their garden gate another colour!

As I grew up, I came to understand that there was a kind of rigid pecking order in the village that was almost medieval. At the top of the pile were rich land owners like the Hammerseys. Then there well healed retirees who gave themselves "airs and graces" like colonels and admirals. Next there were people regarded as "professional" like doctors and solicitors. Somewhere in the middle were small farmers like Mr Ford who rented their land, small business owners and shop keepers, and clerical workers like my Dad. Further down were the farm labourers like Ernie who counted them-selves lucky to live in tied cottages and doffed their caps to "gentry". At the bottom there were gypsies, who sold pegs and did odd jobs when they passed through, and "misfits" like poor Mr Marsh and sad tramps, like Mrs Farnes, who wended her way from workhouse to workhouse in all weathers talking gibberish and selling lucky charms. Looking back I think the implicit norms of this society ordered our existence. I would be allowed to go off and play with my friends for hours on end But Tom, the son of a local gardener, who I liked, would often excuse himself from coming back to tea with Ian, Camilla and Carol my more middle class friends. My guess is that even if my dyslexia and poor health hadn't jeopardised my early education, my parents would have still opted to send me to middle class dame schools rather than expose me to the vicissitudes of the local village school.

During the war Uncle Norm visited quite a good deal. Once, he brought a friend called Guy Mannering who had helped him get his job as a Factory Inspector. On another occasion he came with a suitcase full of his books on Marxism for safe keeping in our attic just in case the Civil Service pried too closely into his radical provenance! He helped improve our dug-out shelter and made brick walls and ledges on the inside to support candles and a hurricane lantern. He encouraged me to make more advanced Meccano models and, together, we set about mending holes in the wire netting of our chicken-run where the foxes had burrowed through. We found some planks of old wood Dad had stored in the garage next to his beloved Ford 8 and worked together repairing the old hen coup. We bought some "day old chicks" and Mum looked out a large stone hot water bottle and Granny made a little jacket to fit over it, so that the chicks would be able to nestle close to it to keep them warm without getting burnt. We kept them in a small cage in the scullery. I was amazed how quickly they developed – loudly chirping and pecking at the husks of barley we had gleaned and scratching in their straw bed. Within a few months our Road Island Reds, together with two noisy cocks, were running around in their re-furbished run happily clucking away and providing us with fresh eggs. We even had a barrow load of chicken poo to fertilise the tomato plants that Mum had planted in Dad's greenhouse.

An obsession with pooh, of course, features in the mind of most small boys. In my case my interest was fanned by my Granny's Victorian belief in the virtues of regularity. I already had some idea when productive visits had been made to the lavatory because Granny's poo usually smelt of liquorice, while my Mum's commanded a sweeter odour. But Granny was determined to leave nothing to chance in the pursuit of training me in "good habits," as she put it. It was arranged that I would "do my business" every morning in the outside lavatory. To encourage me Granny was prepared to climb up the large laurel tree which grew outside. Granny would ascend the lower branches first and call for progress reports. Negative bulletins would require that she climb further up the tree. Sometimes I would hold on as long as possible so that she was swinging in the highest branches before I let go! Granny's "training" did pay dividends and to this day my system methodically fires off its "sputnik" in the early hours of every morning!

Granny's views on child develop were sometimes more questionable. By 1943 fears of a German invasion were over and Mum rekindled her friendship with "Auntie Ethel" by asking her to come and stay. Her visit required that I be "good." Muddles had to be tidied away and areas and times of play restricted. I seem to recall hours of vicarage type tea parties and "Auntie" nattering on at length about her likes and dislikes. "Remember Vera", she would opine for the umpteenth time --"my tea must be served with hot water with just a dash poured from the pot." --"And remember I like my egg boiled just so ...!" Suddenly the little world which had focused on me had "Auntie" centre stage. In a desperate effort to regain the focus of attention, I climbed on the back of the sofa promptly fell off awkwardly breaking my arm in the process! My arm was in plaster for a few weeks and this encouraged me to start to write with my left hand. This frustrated Granny attempts to train me to write with my right as dictated by Victorian folk lore. When the cast was finally removed Granny tied a piece of wool around my arm to remind me of the virtues of dexterity. My mental processes were further confused, later in the war, when I was running around the garden with a group of friends playing at being "dooglebugs" with my arms out-stretched -- making blood curdling ram jet noises – when I tripped and nosedived down some steps breaking my other arm! My Mum was a terrible speller and I probably inherited my dyslexia from her side of the family, but breaking both arms during these formative years did nothing to enhance my mental development. To this day I am mildly ambidextrous, often doing mechanical things with my left hand but writing with my right.

Looking through a few family mementos of these years I discovered a faded photo of me in a battered old pedal car next to my mum and the path by our front door. I can remember it was painted red and as I grew older and more lanky, it became more difficult to work the pedals without knocking my chin with my knees. My Mum is standing next to me wearing a grey skirt etched with pattern of red squares. On one side of the fireplace we had a photo of my Uncle Les looking like Errol Flynn and a pastel sketch of my Dad wearing army uniform and a beret after the style of Field Marshall Montgomery. On top of the cupboard, next to Dad's pipe rack were posed Poly Photos of an angelic me clutching a fluffy toy rabbit and Mum and Dad getting married.

Later in the year of 1943 Uncle Norm bought me a second-hand bike. It was brown with solid tyres and a brake on the front wheel. Uncle taught me to ride, giving me confidence by running behind me clutching the saddle to maintain my equilibrium. One day when I was speeding along the road with Uncle puffing behind I suddenly sensed that he was not there. I craned my neck round to see him standing in the lane laughing. Whereupon, I promptly fell off! But eureka! I had covered fifty yards under my own steam -- I could ride. This was a rite of passage -- I could join the world of the bigger boys and girls. And what a time I had! The "gang" would call for me early in the morning and with a short break for lunch, we would play all day. Apart from the standard childhood pastimes of "Hide and Seek" and "Chain Hee," we would invent our own. One of these was named "Olympic Games" which we played in one of Farmer Ford's fields with our home made jumps and obstacle races. Sometimes, we would attempt to "fly" from one hayrick to another. Trips to the farm always meant that we return home scarred from our exploits -- our clothes scudded with grass stains and smeared from cow pats. On other occasions we would have pine cone fights out- side the "Posh" home of the Barratts (who owned a shoe factory in the Midlands) in Spotted Cow Lane on the way back to Ian and Camilla's house and Tom's cottage. Sometimes, the encounters were more intimate such as playing "Doctors and Nurses" with Carol Smith in the old pig sty at the bottom of the garden where mutual medical examinations provided an only child like me with much needed anatomical information.

We also played games of "Dare." One cold winter's day we all cycled over to Hunters Pond to slide on its frozen surface. A thaw had set in and when we ventured on the ice we could hear it groaning under our weight. There was a frozen tree stump in the middle of the pond and soon we were daring each other to climb on to it and jump on to the ice. We all took turns in performing this dangerous exercise – all frightened of being labelled "Chicken", if we did not take part in the Dare. I was last in line after Camilla. She was the heaviest of all of us and when she jumped the ice splintered to an alarming degree. Suddenly, it was my turn. I stood trembling on the tree stump to a chorus of "Jump Jump!" Finally I launched myself off. The ice gave way immediately and I was floundering out of my depth in freezing water! Fortunately, I surfaced inside the hole made by my entry, but when I tried to grab on to the surrounding ice it simply broke off in my hands. Somehow or other, by clutching on to other pieces of ice, which also broke away, I gradually steered a channel toward the shore and finally pulled myself out of the pond to be surrounded by a frightened and rather guilty group of friends. I can remember cycling back home wet through and blue with cold. I don't think the gravity of my "near death experience" really sunk in and I was scolded because the dye had run in my new green corduroy trousers. Granny resorted to disciplinary "tut tutting" and kettles were boiled to give me a hot bath to ward off me getting a "chill". Which I seem to remember I developed anyway!

In June 1944 the first of Hitler's "terror weapons"—the V1's and V2's started to cross the English Channel precipitating what became known as the "Baby Blitz". Although their main target was London, the V1's in particular, were notoriously inaccurate and could be diverted from their planned destination as a result of clever manoeuvre by our fighters, or shot down by defensive gun batteries - - in some cases they simply ran out of fuel and plunged to earth prematurely. Consequently, quite a number of them crashed in the rural parts of the Home Counties. We had become used to night time raids and assumed that they would always strike under cover of darkness. But because they were pilotless rockets, which could be fired at any time, part of their appeal to Hitler's High Command was the sheer terror created by their random attacks by day or night. Whereas V2's were supersonic and dropped from near space delivering their deadly payload without warning. The V1's were subsonic flying bombs powered by a ram-jet which droned overhead with a rhythmic throbbing beat. I can remember crouching in our outside shelter, as the "doodlebugs" flew over hoping and hoping that they would fly on – over Ford's Farm Yard -- over the next two fields --over Waste Wood! Because we all knew that once the engine cut it was a matter of seconds before the flying bomb would fall to earth with a loud explosion. On one occasion, after nights of heavy raids, and our dug out had been flooded by torrential rain, we were invited, along with some other villagers, to spend the night in the Barratt's large under-ground shelter. I think we accepted the offer with trepidation as Mum was rather reluctant to do obeisance to the rather superior Mrs Barratt. After the wail of the siren, I can remember descending some concrete steps. Inside the shelter we were all tightly crammed in together, like a posh game of "sardines", as the different social strata's of the Pound Green community competed for territory. From my position, sitting on the concrete floor with some other kids I had a worm's eye view of seamed stockings, trouser turn ups, and different types of foot-ware, and heard snippets of rather stilted conversation. There were a few attempts at bonhomie and rumbles of nervous laughter. Towards the early hours of the morning, I discovered that there appeared to be no lavatory facilities and let out a whispered whine of "I wanna go wo wo, I wanna go wo wo!" Only to be shushed into silence as the pee dribbled down my leg! In the early morning after the "all clear" had sounded we left as quickly as we could with the other villagers all, muttering our deferential appreciations to the lady of the house.

In the weeks that followed, we foreswore further offers to seek sanctuary in the Barratt's shelter, and, since the conditions in our dug-out were still rather grim, decided to crouch under the stairs in our own house when the dooglebugs flew over. Sometimes, Granny tired of camping under the stairs, would return to her bed upstairs saying -- "If Hitler is going to get me – he's going to get me!". One night I had a terrible nightmare. Mum and I are hiding in the dark recess under the stairs, when the back door is flung open and Hitler marches in followed by a group of storm-troopers. As I peeped out from the shadows I could see their shining jackboots and grey uniforms. They fail to see us and then Hitler barks out on order and they go upstairs. Suddenly, there are sounds of violence and screams of terror from my Granny and I wake up in a cold sweat yelling the house down! This nightmare was so vivid that it repeated as a recurring dream long after the mini-blitz had ended.

Not all dangers were imaginary, later the next day we heard that a doodlebug had crashed on a house in Buxted killing everyone inside. Later in the week I was playing on my own around Ford's Farm, when I see what I think is an aeroplane on fire in the sky. I climb up a ladder on to the top of a hayrick to get a better look, and to see if I could see a pilot bail out and a parachute float to earth. Suddenly, the fire went out. Seconds later there was blinding flash and the rush of the shockwave which blew me off the hayrick and – fortunately for me -- on to another one lower down. When I ran back to the house I found that half our greenhouse had been demolished and the back door leading to the kitchen had been staved in by the blast!

I think my Mum and Granny panicked, and within a week our house was shut up, and it was agreed that Farmer Ford and Ernie would keep an eye on things and look after our chicken. We would become part of a middle class group nick named the "Bomb Doggers" seeking voluntary evacuation at this time. Uncle Norm's girlfriend Gladys had a sister who had beach hut in Dunster in Somerset and it was agreed that we would stay there until the end of the "terror attacks". I can remember a long line of chalets on the edge of a very wide sandy beach. There was a castle at the top of a steep hill which we used to walk to and a small shop. The beach hut was quite cramped for three, with some bunks and simple cooking facilities, and an oil stove to keep us warm. The sea would go out for miles, and, on the turn, would flood in almost at walking speed, quickly flooding into the wave marks left in the sand. It was a very safe place to paddle and you could wade out to quite a distance before getting out of your depth.

As I became more confident in the water I gradually taught myself to swim by holding my breath and plunging in trying a few strokes before I let my feet touch the bottom. Mum would take me on long walks and entertain me with "make up" stories she invented about two dogs called Mupsie and Flopsie. Most of the other beach huts were unoccupied, and I don't remember having many other playmates, so I was left rather to my own devices. I made lots of castles and waterworks in the sand, and I sometimes flew a kite bought at the village stores. I spent some time on a nearby building plot collecting old bits of wire and electrical equipment and dreamed of making devices like those I had seen in Dad's radio collection. I helped Granny roll the wool she had just unpicked into new balls. I also played with a homemade tank made out of a cotton reel, and a matchstick set in a piece of old candle and a rubber band. There were notches cut into the rim of the cotton reel and when the rubber band was wound up the tank climbed quite well over small objects. By the end of 1944 the Mini- Blitz was over and I think we were all pleased to be going home.

We returned to a world which seemed familiar – but was already changing. Our lovely old Persian Tom Cat, called Kip, sauntered into the kitchen to roll over on his back as if nothing had changed. A phalanx of "farm cats" still clustered outside the back door in search of scraps. Ian and I discovered a "nest" of "wild kittens" in the hedge close to our shelter and set about "civilising them." Farmer Ford still kept three beautiful chestnut cart horses in the stable, but in the open shed behind, proudly displayed, was an American Ford Tractor, resplendent with great metal wheels at the back, and a vertical exhaust pipe which belched out black smoke when Percy (Farmer Ford's son-in-law) swung the starting handle and its engine burst into life.

German prisoners of War worked in the fields and Mum befriended one called Otto who came to tea on a number of occasions. I remember having boisterous games of darts with him, with my arrows mainly bouncing off and cascading on to the floor. We also played Rummy and a card game, Mum knew, called "Strip Jack Naked." Mum said he was a nice German -- it was his wife who was the Nazi!

There was a camp for American soldiers in the village and quite suddenly there appeared GI's everywhere, spending money at Grace Smith's shop and drinking at the Eight Bells Pub. They befriended us kids with wraps of gum and sticks of candy and we were soon swaggering about imitating their slang. There were jeeps and staff cars parked in parked in our lane and in the main road a huge convoy of army lorries and transporters carrying tanks droned by for hour after hour. One crashed down a steep bank into the garden of our friends who lived in Bridge House, opposite the little green outside our house. It was suspended perilously halfway down and held from falling further by the pine trees which grew there. The lines of military traffic never stopped and we had to wait for ages for an opportunity to dash across to the other side to inspect the damage.

Although no one knew it at the time this must have been the build-up for "D Day". There was a feeling of anticipation in the air. The camp at Buxted must have been a staging post for troops getting ready to embark for their perilous voyage to the Normandy beaches. Mum, Grace Smith, Alison Lyle and other villagers were anxious to "do their bit" and send off parties were arranged. Some old Christmas decorations were hung from our cherry tree by the front gate and welcome notices were scrawled on bits of card. Garden tables were carried on to the lawn in front of our house and Mum and Granny got to work making sandwiches and cooking jam tarts and Welsh cakes, jellies and trifles – as far as rationing, and our limited stocks, would allow. I can't remember whether Mum raided Dad's tiny supply of spirits or the big stone jar of cider brewed by Uncle Les and him before they left for war. My guess is that, with the reputation of the Yanks had for heavy drinking, these remained hidden. Instead, there were huge urns for tea, supplies by someone in the village, and lots of bottles of Lyle's fizzy lemonade manufactured by an outlet owned by Ian's Dad.

 Quite a crowd of GI's showed up and Camilla and Carol and the other girls did their best to entertain them posing as dancers and doing cart wheels all over the lawn. While us boys competed with headstands and walking on our hands. The adults turned out in their Sunday best -- my Mum sported a red ribbon in her hair. The Yanks were friendly, but Mum noticed a group of black soldiers who hung back from the rest and went out of her way to pay them special attention. As twilight descended Mum went into the lounge and started to play the piano. Soon hits from American musicals from the 1930's like "Anything goes." and "Porgy and Bess" and "Lady Behave" mixed with English songs like "Pollywollydoodle" and "Old Macdonald had a Farm" filtered through the open window. Sometimes, she would play Welsh favourites like "Men of Harlech" and carols such as "Silent Night". She was in her element and Granny put me to bed, as Mum was engaged in entertaining the troops! Later that night, when the party was in full swing, Mum popped up to kiss me goodnight. By this time Granny was in full chaperone mode "tell them to go Vera!" she entreated, but Mum played on and we could hear the strains of Vera Lynn's latest hit drifting up the stairs. What with the noise of laughter, the community singing, and Granny pacing to and fro on the landing, I couldn't sleep and took to peering through the banisters and ear-wigging on snatches of conversation. As midnight approached the party started to thin out and Granny, on the pre-text of washing up, sallied downstairs in an attempt to call time. Finally, there was one personable American Lieutenant left -- who pleaded –"It's a long way back to camp Ma'am!" The conversation went on for some-time longer but by this time I was fast asleep on a pillow half out of my bedroom door. Not much was said at breakfast the next morning but I suspect that Granny succeeded in defending my Mum's virtue.

A few weeks later news came through on the BBC of the successful Normandy Landings. Although I can't help wondering, even to this day, how many of the brave American soldiers who had come to our party perished on the Omaha and Utah beachheads in Vierville and Quineville.

A month later Mum received an air-mail from Dad saying he was coming back on Embarkation Leave. And in what seemed no time at all – there he was walking up the garden path with a huge kit bag on his back. As he hugged my Mum under the front porch, he looked just like the pastel drawing of him which stood by his tins of Three Nuns Tobacco, I had gazed at throughout the war. As he threw me in the air I saw how sunburnt he was – the conquering hero come to reclaim all that was his!

Mike's Mum and Dad

Chapter 2
Growing up in the 1940s

There was of course great rejoicing on Dad's return home. Although it turned out that "embarkation leave" meant that he would have to return to his regiment in three weeks time, and not be fully demobbed until he had served more time in Egypt. Dad railed against the stupid bureaucracy of it all, and said he had had enough of over-crowded troop ships, where three-quarters of the space was reserved for the officers, while other ranks were confined to the lower decks. This was one factor which caused him to join Mum, a lifelong socialist, in voting Labour in 1945.

I, of course, hero worshipped Dad and followed him everywhere during his brief spell of leave. We searched the garage together for old sheets of glass and lengths of wood to patch up the damaged greenhouse. And, I stood by dutifully for hours on end, handing him his hammer and nails and stirring sweet smelling linseed oil into an old tin of putty for him, as he attempted to fix the panes into position on the ramshackle structure we had repaired.

We pushed the Ford Eight out of the garage, but no amount of cursing --swinging with the starting handle, and fiddling with the points and carburettor produced any reaction apart from the sudden and dramatic departure of a nest of rats who had made their home under its seats! That evening, after milking, we all visited Farmer Ford and his family in their little farmhouse at the end of our lane to seek advice. After the usual formalities of cups of tea, admiring his collection of marble clocks, which he often bought at various auctions, and listening to Dot, his adopted daughter, who was a nurse in a London hospital, recount at length on the great size of various growths, she had seen removed in theatre! A plan of action was agreed.

The next day we were pushing the Ford 8 down the drive and the ploughman was waiting with a beautiful chestnut carthorse already harnessed up to tow our car along the road. I can remember it being a great effort with a number of false starts before the engine finally stuttered into life. Then Dad was driving down the steep hill at the end of Pound Green to the sound of cheers from a small crowd.

In the time remaining, before Dad's return to his regiment, I followed him everywhere. We walked together to collect the milk and I led him back through the farmyard, showing him the barn where new calves were being suckled and the shed which housed ancient machinery for mincing turnips. Finally, I led him to the lean-to where the new Ford tractor was proudly displayed. I jumped into its metal seat and clutched the steering wheel as if, in my ignorance, I was personally advocating the war-time " Lease Lend Deal" which was the beginning of a revolution which was to shortly see the demise of the three beautiful cart horses which stood in their stable. This was just the start, and the coming of combined harvesters, and artificial fertilizers, spelt and the end to the annual ritual of gleaning the fields and the flowering meadows of my childhood.

I showed Dad some of the places on the farm where us kids indulged our childhood imaginations as athletes in our own "Olympic Games," and the hayricks with "soft landings" where we attempted to fly – Ian, who was a year older than me, had told us that it was perfectly possible as he had read a book about a levitating monk! And, as we headed back, I showed him my secret shortcut home, where we crawled through the hedge and emerged on top of our dug-out shelter.

Mum of course, rejoiced at Dad's safe return. In his honour we opened a Red Cross parcel from Canada and sampled a tin of bacon which we all declared to be delicious. Not to be out done, Dad went out to dig up one of his own tins of bully beef which he had hidden under the garage before he left for war, and proceeded to devour the contents despite cries from Mum and Gran that he would be sure to die of botulism. "Fiddlesticks!" said Dad winking at me. Although he was smiling there was a hidden message here. He was back on the home front -- having faced god knows what terrors at Tobruk and Monte Cassino -- gently challenging the power of petticoat government which had grown up in his absence. I felt a warm glow of adoration welling inside me and smiled back at Dad to indicate that I was on his side. Later we pulled his old crystal radio out of the cupboard in the Drawing Room and played with it together all afternoon, but despite our best efforts, and a few sparks from a newly charged accumulator, it remained totally inert. After supper Dad read me the first chapter of "Treasure Island" and by the time Mum came up to kiss me goodnight and hear me say my prayers I was too drowsy to take in much of one of her dog stories.

During his period of embarkation leave my "love affair with Dad", which was really making up for lost time for his long absence, was sometimes interrupted by one of my recurring nightmares. Hitler and his henchmen were again inflicting terrible violence on my Granny -- and I woke up in cold sweat screaming the house down. Mum of course, would have to come and comfort me, but usually I failed to fall asleep again and my whimpers would persist until she finally gave in and reluctantly returned with me to the marital bed where I would defiantly straddle the mattress between my two frustrated parents! Sometimes, when Hitler failed to materialise, it would be a damp patch on the ceiling, or a branch tapping on the window in the wind, which my fertile imagination would then conjure into a ghostly apparition to produce the same chain of events. Dad was clearly not pleased and said that I had been mollycoddled in his absence. Mum vaguely defended me as being "highly strung"—whatever that meant -- while Uncle Norm, when called in to adjudicate, talked to me in his special psychological voice and later hinted at dark oedipal forces!

A week or so before Dad was due to return to his regiment to await his de-mob papers Mari Pew had her birthday party which was held at a big house with a rambling garden at the end of the Twitten close to Buxted Common. All my friends were there, together with a whole lot of kids I had never met before. There was a big table which was loaded with cakes, jellies, blancmanges, trifles and cakes of all kinds, flanked by a large brown teapot. For some reason, I decided to "show off" and, together with a group of other naughty boys, we thought it was more fun to crawl under the table rather than sitting dutifully for someone called Mrs Inkpen to serve us. At first we got the others to feed us in our den by passing buns and sticky cakes under the table. After a while, when they failed to oblige, we discovered that we could "fish" blindly for the party sweat-meats by cocking out arms around the side of the table and manoeuvre them to its edge until they fell into our grasp. Finally, we hit upon the idea of tugging the tablecloth so that an even greater hoard of goodies would cascade from above! Suddenly, there was a huge crash and the large teapot full of boiling water fell from the table. Its lid flew off and its scalding contents were disgorged over the legs of the leading miscreant which were sticking out from beneath the table. The pain was excruciating and I let out a piercing scream. As the other kids drew back in fear I was surrounded by a group of adults who seemed enraged and anxious at the same time. There was a hurried debate about the best treatment for burns and I think someone applied butter to my inflamed thighs and crotch. Suddenly Mum and Dad were kneeling besides me and I was wrapped in a blanket and carried out of the house, blubbing like a baby, to be deposited in the back of our Ford Eight cradled in my Mum's arms with Dad driving like a maniac. My recollection of my treatment in the Casualty Department of Uckfield hospital is somewhat blurred.

But I ended up with both legs being wrapped in bandages and then plaster casts being applied. I looked like a mummified boy-king from ancient Egypt. I was totally immobile and confined to bed -- unable to start my first term Greenfield School with Elwyn, Osragh, Carol Ian and Camilla and the rest of my friends.

Mum and Dad were as shocked as I was, and the family rallied around to lavish me with love and attention. However, the vulnerability and problematic nature of their only child was born home to them. In their mind's eye an image of my master-status was beginning to form which was not wholly positive. In addition, to my night attacks of insomnia and nightmares, was added the image of an over-impulsive accident prone kid. My self-image suffered a further set back when I developed a stammer – probably the result of the shock of the accident. Fortunately, my speech impediment, at this time, was short lived.

During my convalescence Dad had to return to his regiment to await his de-mob papers and Mum and Gran reasserted their authority. I drew pictures and did jigsaw puzzles in bed and Mum took over the task of reading me the rest of "Treasure Island", interspersed with the "Tales of Sam Pig" by Alison Uttley and her own make up stories. My friends came to visit me and wrote messages on my casts and I watched Swifts fly past my bedroom window and a new batch of fledging House Martins peep out of their mud nests under the eaves. Finally, the great day arrived when Dr Sadlier came to remove my leg plasters. I can remember him sawing away and finally splitting them open and the excruciating pain when the bandages were finally pulled away from my legs because the hairs of my legs had grown into them and the kindest way to perform the operation was to pull them away in one go. It was a relief to find that my legs had healed well with the exception of a scar high up on my left thigh frighteningly close to my privates. Had the trajectory of the falling teapot been an inch to the right I might have had no children or grandchildren to read my story!

My legs were weak from their enforced confinement and I was allowed a further week playing with my '0' gauge Hornby train set and our tom cat Kipp, before I was deemed strong enough to join my friends at Miss Pear's and Miss Brown' Dame School. Their kindergarten was housed in a wooden scout hut in Framfield Road in Buxted, which was basically one long room with little kids at the far end under the tutelage of Miss Brown, and the "big ones" at the other taught by Miss Pear. There was a coke stove in the middle – rather like the one described in the village school room by Laurie Lee in "Cider with Rosie." A piano stood in one corner, and there was a shelf on one wall which a money box shaped like a house for donations for Dr Barnardo's.

The middle class nature of the school was underlined by the fact that Miss Pear and Miss Brown would sometimes collect the little children furthest away, who had just started, in their own cars. The drive would lead to comical incidents. Miss Pear would often start the "pick up" from Pound Green and then drive up the steep hill past Smith's Grocery Stores, collecting Carol, before turning by the big conker tree flanked by spiked railings into Limes Lane. Here, she would attempt to eke out her petrol ration by cutting the engine and free-wheeling down the hill. When the car slowed, as we approached the bend leading up-hill to Framfield Road, near the school, she would suddenly let in the clutch causing the car to kangaroo violently -- pitching us kids off the seats and tangling us in a laughing heap at the back!

The classes, which were only held in the morning, always started in the same way with a roll call and the singing of either "Onward Christian "Soldiers or "There is a Green Hill Far Away", which seemed to be the limit of Miss Pear's piano repertoire. The teaching was very formal and we sat in serried ranks at small wooden desks with inkwells and pens with metal nibs. Often we would laboriously copy letters written in copper-plate on the blackboard, our pens scratching on the paper -- often disgorging blots and smudges as we struggled to form our letters. These were the days before Piaget's ideas of "learning by discovery", and there was no attempt to make our educational experience exciting or meaningful. Schooling was viewed as a gradgrind exercise almost completely devoid of pleasure, where the space between childhood and adolescence required the continuous acquisition of facts. There were times in summer, when the sun shone through the windows and the dust from the board rubber swam in an incandescent haze above our heads, when it seemed a crime against nature to confine us at our cramped desks. We waited and waited for the ringing of the bell when we could scramble to the rear door and escape into the playground for our quarter of an hour break, where we could indulge our fantasies, roll in the long grass and buttercups of the unkempt meadow, and gallop around playing endless games of "IT" and "Chain Hee".

Even today the supporters of the New Right view of Education, like Dyson and Cox, react against the child centred education of the Progressives. And I would grant that knowing your ABC and Maths tables has some merit, but at this time at Miss Pear and Miss Browns', almost everything was reduced to rote learning – like naming the Dominions and the Colonies in the British Empire against a big map of the world. Every week we collectively chanted an epic poem of some kind like -- "The boy stood on the burning deck" and at the end of the week each of us had to stand up in turn to recite it. For some reason I was quite good at this, parroting the narrative word, for word, and even harboured the belief that I might become a great actor one day. However, when I moved up to the big class with Miss Pear and we had to learn the poem by copying it off the board I singularly failed to pull off the same party trick. My mental processes simply ceased up – maybe I was exhibiting short-term memory loss characteristic of dyslexia – at any event I stood tongue-tied and cowed in front of the red faced and unsympathetic teacher. She later recorded in my end of term report that I was -- "self-conscious and lacking in confidence".

There were of course, lighter incidents at Greenfield School. In the lower class we discovered that Miss Brown was allergic to chalk dust. When she entered the large cupboard in search of teaching materials we would bang the board rubber on the desk and produce clouds of dust. On her return she would have a fit of sneezing. We would then crane forward in anticipation as she lifted her shirt to reveal her bright blue bloomers in order to retrieve a hankie from the elasticated bottoms of this exciting garment!

On another occasion my Mum gave me a bunch of raffle tickets in support of a local good cause. "Be sure Miss Pear and Miss Brown, buy some tickets", she said, as she kissed me goodbye. I badgered Miss Brown into buying some but at break time I couldn't find Miss Pear anywhere. Time was getting on and I decided to go "wo wo" before the bell rang. I went to the only privy at back of the school and banged the door open, only to discover Miss Pear sitting on the pan with her pink bloomers around her knees. Instead of backing off, as decorum demanded, conscious of my Mum's entreaty, I launched into my sales pitch -- "Please Miss, please Miss would you like to buy a raffle ticket?!" Her reaction was quite dramatic. Her face turned bright purple as she screamed "Don't be so impertinent!" and kicked the door shut.

Michael Steele was the school dare-devil. When I was older, and walked to school with my friends, he would speed past us on his bike and career down the hills in Limes Lane with both his hands high in the air. One break time he got into the store house at the side of the school, where the scouts kept all their equipment, and found some torches they had prepared for bomb-fire night. He also discovered a can of paraffin and, without a care for the consequences, poured some of the contents over the rags bound to the top of the torches. He produced a box of matches and set fire to them one by one -- handing them out to the awe struck groups of kids clustered outside. Where upon we went screaming like lunatics around the perimeter of the playground. Our defiant cries rang out for longer, than we dared hope, before retribution, as we knew it must, befell us. Miss Pear and Miss Brown emerged from the Scout Hut with looks of utter disbelief at the scene of mayhem unfolding before them. Suddenly, they were striding purposely towards us bellowing the most terrible threats of vengeance. Our five minute revolution was at an end! I can't remember if Michael Steele was identified as the main culprit, and I think the punishment didn't amount to much more than a terrible telling off, and being kept back to sit in sullen silence for half an hour after lessons finished.

I was a sickly kid and hardly a week went by without me being stricken by a feverish cold or some other ailment. Mum would always wrap me up in lots of woollies in an effort to avoid me catching "chills". Another precaution was to buy me a "sou'wester fishermen's hat" complete with ear muffs, which looked surprisingly like the hat worn by Christopher Robin in the A.A.Milne stories. I hated Christopher Robin, who I regarded as a "sissy"-- and this headpiece -- as I was teased unmercifully as soon as I put it on. It also made me instantly identifiable when we were attacked by the tougher children from the village school while we queued up for our two-penny ice creams outside Larkin's Shop on our way home. For the Buxted boys and girls, whose gladiatorial skills had been honed in the tar-macadam playground down the road, my sartorial wear symbolised all they hated about the pupils of Greenfield Dame School. "There he is!" they yelled, as my hiding place behind the ice-cream advertising board was revealed, and I ran for my life down Framfield Road and turned into the beginning of Limes Lane. I knew from previous encounters that there was a deep ditch shielded from the road by a thick tangle of brambles leading to a screen of tall bamboo and pampas grass. I ran for this high screen of undergrowth and crawled along the muddy water course tearing off the wretched sou'wester and keeping my head low. After combing the foliage on each side of the road, the toughs, mystified by my apparent disappearance, grew tired of the chase and the gang members started to disperse. I, however, was too scared to come out of the gulley and crawled most of the way home to be scolded by Mum for the terrible state of my mud soaked short trousers and crumpled hat.

I never remember being beaten at Greenfield School, but a rap across the knuckles with a heavy ruler was a not infrequent punishment for inattention or misbehaviour. Most of the time, the children methodically chanted their tables, or copied long, largely unexplained passages, off the blackboard. I can remember little art, or classes which inspired the spirit of enquiry or our creative energies. I think there were occasional "nature walks" and questions around the class afterwards with some kids pumping the air and intoning "Miss, Miss, Miss" in their eagerness to attract attention. I can only identify one moment of triumph when I was the only one to know that dew rose from the ground rather from dropping like rain. However, as time went on, and I continued to miss more and more schooling through childhood illness, such successes became less and less frequent. Miss Pear, in particular, was a stranger to child psychology and I can remember once, when I proudly produced a new fountain pen I had been given, being forced to copy lines with the inscription —"I must try and write better with my new pen". A succession of damming end of term reports eventually prompted a family visit from Uncle Norm.

Dad was finally de-mobbed in 1945 and resumed his job as Chief Clerk at Lloyds in Uckfield. Life began to fall back into a pre-war pattern of segregated gender roles with married women based in the home as house wives and men as primary bread winners. Dad took his income generating responsibilities very seriously, but his heart was never in banking. He was a bright boy who had won a scholarship to Skinner's Grammar School and after matriculation harboured ambitions either to teach or become a doctor. However, the early death of his father, who ran a post office and general stores in Tunbridge Wells, meant that, like Uncle Norm, Dad had to assume the major responsibility for the material wellbeing of his mother and two younger sisters, Gladys and Elsie. Against the background of the great depression banking was considered a safe occupation, and Dad left school earlier than planned to enter a grey Bob Cratchit world of dusty ledgers and monthly balances.

I saw far less of Grandma Strange than Grandma Chubb when I was growing up. She lived in the top half of a Victorian villa in Tunbridge Wells. The downstairs area of this house was occupied by a tenant and she also derived an income from some commercial property bequeathed to her by my Grandfather. She often wore black, and was far stricter than Grandma Chubb. She was almost blind, when I knew her, and was probably suffering from macular degeneration, which also afflicted my Dad in his later years, she also had asthma – a condition which later affected me. Visiting her was always something of an ordeal, as her flat appeared to be a play free area with walls lined with shelves and cabinets displaying delicate porcelain figurines which looked as if they would shatter if you raised your voice above a whisper. The main room always appeared dark and the bay window was flanked by thick curtains tied back by braided cord. Antimacassars were draped over the head rests of the chairs and a smell of stale violets seemed to hang in the air. There was a small kitchen at the rear of the flat, next to a bathroom. For some reason, never explained, the bath always appeared to be full of old junk. As Granny was at pains to distance herself from the class of people who might be tempted to keep coal in such a receptacle, the mystery of her daily ablutions, or lack of them, remained unsolved!

Granny was old school and subscribed to the view that generally "small children should be seen and not heard" the strain of being good and quiet for what seemed like hours became almost unbearable towards the end of our visits, which always ended in the same way with her announcing that she had a treat for me. Whereupon, she would make her way uncertainly across the room and reach into a low cupboard and retrieve a jar of Quince jam, which I knew from bitter experience had "gone off" and was topped by a thick layer of fungus. This dire preparation was then smeared on to buttered scones. The ritual of tea-time had begun. Failure to comply carried the penalty that the half-crown "for good behaviour" to be pressed into my itching palm the end of the afternoon might be withheld.

Granny's Methodist background meant that she had a very puritan view of life. Whereas the Chubb family, under the influence of Uncle Norm, liberally mixed the hope of the New Testament with the Socialism born of the Welsh Valleys, Grandma Strange read texts from the Old Testament and embraced the Calvinism of John Knox. Every Christmas I would receive some worthy self-improving text — such as "Foxe's book of Martyrs" or "Pilgrims Progress". Sometimes I would be sent the same up-lifting text two years running lest I slip from the "Straight and Narrow!"

Dad first met my Mum when he was canvassing for members of an amateur dramatics group he belonged to. The family story goes that he knocked on the door of the manse in Hawkenbury, when Norm was still presiding as Minister, and was so taken by the vivacious girl who let him in that he left his gloves behind, accidently on purpose, so that he could return, once he had summoned up enough courage, to ask Vera out. She remembered that on the first visit to Dad's home, one Sunday in Tunbridge Wells, she saw a piano in the corner of the front room, and sat down and went into her male voice choir routine -- touch playing a medley of favourite hymns and songs. Suddenly, a chill descended, and she looked up to see Dad's mother standing in the doorway with a face like thunder. She later complained to Frank, that her whole day had been ruined because merriment has taken place on the Sabbath!

As a child, Dad had been compelled to attend church three times on Sunday, and when he married Vera he totally reacted against his upbringing, and I never remember us going to Church as a family, on a regular basis. Visiting the House of the Lord was confined to weddings, funerals and carol services and the odd trip to a Congregational Chapel, when Uncle Norm was allowed to preach an occasional sermon. I was never sent to Sunday School, and, even the Scouts were considered too authoritarian an establishment.

Dad's side of the family were generally more conservative than the Chubb's. His younger sister Elsie married Bob who ran a printing business in Maidstone which did well in the post-war years, allowing the family to move from a semi to a beautiful Tudor house with its own swimming pool and tennis court. The family was more conventional than my own, with regular, but not obsessive, church attendance. Support for the Royal Family was much in evidence, and there was more emphasis on etiquette and formality than I was accustomed to. There was a great deal of dressing up for occasions, and I was amazed to see elaborately coutured ladies, self-consciously sitting around the dinner table, sipping tea from tiny cups wearing a variety silly hats.

 Uncle Bob was a member of the Maidstone Chamber of Commerce and the family bought into Harold Macmillian's Conservative dream of the 1950's. The pursuit of affluence was viewed as a measure of success. The move to the beautiful Tudor house provided a luxuriant backdrop against which the Baker family could experiment with their new middle class life style -- Holywood Bowl manqué had arrived in the Maidstone suburbs. I can remember Mum being somewhat embarrassed on a hot day by the swimming pool to see the lady guests suddenly stripped off, to reveal that they had already changed into their elaborately boned corselet type bathing costumes, leaving her to retreat behind a bush to climb into her woolly two piece.

Elsie had two children Pamela and Allen. In 1960 Pamela married Malcolm who worked for ICI. They were regular church goers and Malcolm became heavily involved in the Conservative Party. Although their view of the world is very different to my own, I have always been very fond of Pam and appreciate how successful Malcolm and she have been in raising a large and loving family together. These day's Lisbeth (my second wife) and I, often stop off to visit them in Budleigh Salterton on our way to Devon or Cornwall. Apart from a brief re-union in 2015 I haven't seen Alan since his wedding in Wigan in 1975. He is now retired from Coutts Bank and he and his wife live most of the year in America.

Dad's older sister Gladys emigrated to Australia with her husband Howard at the end of the war and toured around the continent on a motor bike. After some adventures, and a number of false starts, they managed a fruit farm and canning factory, and settled in Queensland. I can remember them coming on an extended visit to Britain in the middle 1950's and touring around the family accompanied by their daughter Diane. I think Mum felt a little in ore of Dad's elder sister who, she thought, seemed over concerned with material status symbols and appearances – feigning mock surprise at the absence many household gadgets -- "that we simply couldn't do without at home!" Howard played the role of the "Pom made good" – the successful entrepreneur who had "struck it rich down under". Phrases like "You still jogging along in the old Country Frank?" were thinly concealed put downs, which Mum resented more than my Dad. They had brought an early Kodak movie camera and projector with them and the message of colonial success was reinforced by flickering images of Howard and Gladys diving into their "very own swimming pool", or entertaining their friends with a large barbeque supper, or sunning themselves on the family yacht.

We did our best to give them a good time, and one Sunday we took them to Brighton beach. It was a hot day, and Dad and I started to strip off for a swim almost as soon as we sat on a mound of pebbles. Suddenly, there was a wail of concern from Gladys concerning the absence of bathing huts. "I'm not fussy!" said Dad, yanking on his red bathers with abandon. Suddenly, the sun bronzed amazons from "god's own country" were in a state panic, and poor Diane, who had started to disrobe, was almost smothered in a great tent of brightly coloured towels as her distraught parents sought to defend her modesty.

On the whole I got on very well with Diane and met her again in 1961 for a meal when I was working for the Electricity Generating Board in London and she came back to the "old country" as part of a lighting tour of Europe with some friends. She is married to Tim and has two daughters. I have never visited Australia and she has not returned to Britain, so that our communication is limited to occasional E-Mail and long phone calls at Christmas and birthdays.

After Uncle Howard died Aunty Gladys came on holiday, quite late in her life to stay with Dad, and his second wife Mary, at Plovers Barrow in Buxted, and with her sister in Maidstone. By all accounts, the visit proved fairly stressful for all involved. Dad had arranged for his favourite sister to meet a variety of friends they had both grown up with in Tunbridge Wells. As some of the characters involved were in their eighties, and Frank and Gladys' faculties not as sharp as they had been, it sometimes became difficult to keep to the arranged itinerary. Poor Dad found the heavy traffic in his old town difficult to handle and was perplexed by the fact that what, at first, seemed familiar streets had turned into busy one-way thoroughfares. Gladys, perhaps used to a more easy-going life style back in Surface Paradise, insisted in being decanted right outside the street dwellings of old friends, irrespective of traffic flow and double yellow lines. In some cases poor Dad was left in the illegally parked car besieged by irate motorists, while his sister meandered uncertainly along the road searching for an old acquaintance whose address, in some cases, was now the local cemetery. Not surprisingly tempers frayed. Aunty, in particular, had the most terrible temper tantrums and was given to stamping her foot if her slightest wish was denied!

We had a bit of a family get-together near the end of her stay. Both Dad and Uncle Norm were accomplished amateur artists, and Dad presented Aunty with a portrait he had painted of her as a leaving present. Norm had also brought some pictures of country landscapes to show her. Whereas, she casually accepted Dad's gift she ostentatiously insisted on paying Uncle for his work, implying that "real quality" had to carry a price tag. Dad never commented on this studied putdown, but it must have hurt.

Looking back, Dad and his sisters did well to escape the puritanical gloom of the house in Tunbridge Wells where they grew up. Elsie suffered a bout of amnesia regarding her true age and married good old dependable, brave Bob, who was tank commander during the war, and 13 years her junior -- just in time to start a happy family. Gladys must have shown real guts to emigrate with Howard and ride pinion around the outback in Australia, scratching a precarious living until they finally made it. And my shy diffident father, chancing everything on his bright eyed consumptive Vera -- his love, a steadfast challenge to the medical orthodoxy of the day – embracing a new world of excitable Welsh relatives.

Despite the tension, which existed between my Mum and Dad's side of the family, I do remember happy visits to the Baker family in Maidstone and playing great games of tennis with Uncle Bob, and going on a very interesting tour of his printing works. In the years before her death, I grew very fond of Auntie Elsie and admired her sharp sense of humour and dedication to family values. Lisbeth and I would collect her from Stoke Poges, where she lived with my Cousin

Pam, and invite her for a meal at our home in St Albans. She never complained about the absence of silver cutlery or the lack of napkins rolled tightly in their silver rings!

Returning to civil life after the war proved a testing time for many. Some men came back to unfaithful wives -- others pined for the beautiful Greek and Italian girls they had left behind. Divorce rates soared and moralists struggled to res-erect a pre-war world which had gone forever. Dad had had what some people described as a "good war". His mathematical skills had been put to use and he had spent much of the time behind the front-line working out firing trajectories for the gun crew he was attached to. Like many who returned, he made light of his experiences -- emphasising the tranquillizing effect of Ouzo, which he probably imbibed to excess -- and his ability to fall asleep under almost any circumstances. On one occasion, he claimed he was pulled inert from an ammo dump by his mates who feared for his safety!

 He deftly parried more searching questions about the more horrific aspects of the conflict by simply saying that in his theatre or the war "Jerry" was on the run most of the time. He did let slip, however, that when he was at Monte Cassino he was more frightened by "friendly fire" from American bombers than anything coming from the German gun en-placements dug in underneath the monastery. I think that in many ways the war was a liberating event for my Dad, and, for the first time in his life, he mixed with a variety of people from different classes and backgrounds outside his previous orbit of experience.

Extreme danger breeds strange bedfellows, and for years afterwards Dad would talk approvingly about his old mate Chalkie White, who supplemented his army pay with doggy deals selling off army stores in the cookhouse to local crooks. "But", he insisted, "Chalkie would stand by you in a crisis – brave as a Bull was Chalkie!" After Dad was demobbed, much to the dismay of my Mum, a series of characters from a similar mould as Chalkie turned up and carted Dad off to the local pub to engage in more reminiscing and "blood brother bonding".

Uncle Les didn't enjoy such a good war and was lucky to survive, when he had all the clothes blown off his back, when a supply truck he was driving suffered a direct hit. He was demobbed about the same time as my Dad, but unlike Frank, he lacked the security of a regular peace-time job to come back to. He returned to his job as a commercial traveller, trading in coffee for Cecil Joscelyne, who ran a successful bakery and cafes in Tonbridge and Tunbridge wells. However, Cecil Josceyln was Edith's father, and I am not sure how well this relationship fared after Uncle Norm separated from his daughter. Uncle Les was the baby of the Chubb family being 13 years younger than my Mum and was thoroughly indulged by his older sister. He sported a Clark Gable moustache and ran a sporty Morris Eight with blue leather seats, which had survived the war well in another of Farmer Ford's barns. He had a great sense of humour, was a good mimic, with quite a flamboyant personality. He had picked up a little Italian and was good at imitating their exaggerated hand gestures and singsong accent. In short he was a card – always prepared to perform his party tricks to entertain his impressionable nephew. Dad was very fond of Uncle Les and, to emphasise his closeness to the Chubb family, unconsciously imitated some of his brother in law's mannerisms. So, along with Uncle Norm, they all called my Mum "Sis" as a term of endearment.

Dad and Les enjoyed a heightened sense of camaraderie through their wartime experiences', and liked nothing more than a good chin wag about their various encounters with the "Jerries,""Ities"and

"Gypos". When they first returned home it took them some time to adjust to life on the home front. Not long after a marital spat, regarding Chalkie and his chums, Frank and Les received a similar dressing down from my Mum after meanderingly uncertainly back from the "Eight Bells" pub an hour and a half late for their Sunday roast! Later they both complained that the keg of homemade cider they had laid down before the war had run dry! The mystery persisted and no one mentioned the send-off party held for the American GI's on a balmy summer evening in 1944. A sense of family amnesia pervaded the whole incident, and, in later years, Dad was given to thinking that either Les, or he, had failed to properly close the tap on the stone keg before the war.

Uncle Les like to play the role of "jack the lad" and hinted that his job as a commercial traveller allowed him to indulge in a variety of romantic liaisons scattered across the breath of East Sussex. Although Mum disapproved of pre-marital "hanky panky", as she put it, she rather indulged his romantic fantasies. He certainly brought a variety of girlfriends to our home and even claimed on one occasion to have seduced Aunt Mable's daughter -- Amie. Grace Smith, Carol's Mum, certainly had a bit of a crush on him and I believe her swarthy Brummie husband, who meticulously sliced our bacon ration on a revolving guillotine, at the Pound Green Stores, was reputed to have warned Les off!

I was just beginning to enjoy Richmal Compton's William stories, which Dad would sometimes read to me at bed-time – and appreciated that the ritual of Les' girlfriends coming to afternoon tea was performed in a similar way to those described by her, although Uncle Les was more confident and talkative than William's shy, fawning brother Robert. The girls often calculated that the best way to get a good review from Les's elder sister was to be nice to me. And I was given a variety of gifts and unsolicited half-crowns! One pretty girl, who I think was called Marion, gave me a stuffed rabbit and a jig saw puzzle featuring an advert for Pear's Soap. She paid me a lot of attention and I can remember being reluctant to go to bed, when the formal proceeding of the tea drew to a close and the young couple wished to embark on a romantic tour of the garden.

Most of the time, however, there was no contest between us, and Uncle Les liked to initiate me into the secrets of the adult world of spooning. He would sometimes take me for trips in his Morris Eight to beauty spots in Sussex where he would reminisce about his loving experiences, the war, politics, and life in general. Sometimes, we would drive out to Beachy Head and walk to the old lighthouse on the edge of the crumbling headland and look out to sea from the top of the Severn Sisters cliffs. One of Uncle's favourite spots was Birling Gap where we would clamber down the steep cliff path and lay on a bank of pebbles, growing pink in the summer sun, with the water lapping at our feet. Eventually, we would retreat to the old tea rooms on top of the cliff where he would treat me to a glass of "fizzy lemonade" and ice-cream and, occasionally, a "Knicker-Bocker Glory".

The thing about Uncle Les was that he never talked down to you. Although he had attended Judds Grammar School in Tonbridge, he lacked the academic training of his older brother, or the seriousness of my father. What distinguished him was his kindly and winning sense of humour, and his ability to get on well with almost everyone he met. His natural acting ability meant that, even in casual conversation, he could take on many parts. He could easily affect Cockney, Welsh or foreign accents and often won arguments by the use of his quick-witted repartee. His showman's abilities contributed to him being a good commercial traveller. However, in everyday life, his ability to project his personality and attract others sometimes led him into difficulties with the opposite sex. Les attracted girls with an effortless charm but sometimes had difficulty with a long lasting single attachment. At least, this is how it appeared, to the mind of a seven year old boy in the spring of 1945.

My Uncle was very generous, and one day he promised he would give me his old wind-up gramophone together with a whole set of Rex 78 records he had got cheap when the firm who manufactured them went bust. The only problem, he said, was that it currently resided in the house of an old flame called Joan Benge and he would have to choose the right time to collect it. The "right time" meant summoning up enough courage to knock on her door. The weeks elapsed and each time Uncle called in at our home I reminded him of his promise. Finally, one afternoon there was a throaty tootle from Uncle's old car and I rushed down the garden path to find him lifting an exciting looking black box off the rear seat, together with a case of old 78 records. He looked rather emotionally frazzled by the act of retrieval and said he needed a stiff drink!

Mum's ability to touch play, and Dad's love of opera and the violin, seem somehow missing from my gene pool. I appear to be incapable of singing in tune and even Mum, forever anxious to give me the benefit of the doubt, labelled me "tone deaf". Apart from a swop at school which procured me a vinyl copy of Glenn Miller's "In the Mood" and a brief flirtation with Bill Haley and "Rock around the Clock", the music of the sixties seems to have passed me by. I never went to gigs (apart from a few jazz sessions) or music festivals. I like the sound of the Beatles, as a kind of nostalgic backdrop to my memories of that era – but at the time I never bought their records. And, I am afraid my attendance at Saturday night dances at University College owed more to my attraction to the opposite sex, than my love of music, or fleetness of foot on the dance floor! But in those far off days in the 1940's I fell in love with Uncle's old records and the whole experience of winding up the gramophone and fitting "His Master's Voice" needles, and the seductive hiss at the end of a song when the needle slid into the spinning centre of the record. Uncanny as it may seem, I can still sing along to ancient, long forgotten, pre-war hits like -- "I Wanna Woo!", "Mr and Mrs is the Name!", " Saddle your Blues to a Wild Mustang and Gallop Your Troubles Away!", "Polly Wally Doodle!", "Knock Knock Whose There?","Blue Moon!" .....

As my frequent feverish colds showed no sign of abating, and I missed more and more schooling, listening to Uncle's records, when I was confined to my sick bed, was a source of great pleasure. At this time, I Also made efforts to begin to decipher the technical English in the more advanced Meccano manuals so that I could harness my number two clockwork motor to power more complex models. And I started to listen on regular basis to the BBC Home Service. I enjoyed Children's Hour, especially plays and series like "Larry the Lamb" – laughing at the thick German accent given to Dennis the Dachshund. I liked the adventures that the children had at "Cowlease Farm" and "Norman and Henry Bones the Boy Detectives". I even bought into the idea of fictional Uncles and Aunts on the programme and Uncle Mac at the end saying "Good night children everywhere!" Although, I wondered where David fitted in the scheme of things, as he appeared to be nobodies relative. Mum and Dad enjoyed listening to Saturday Night Theatre, which often produced good radio plays, and sometimes I was allowed to come downstairs in my pyjamas to tune in with them. I also enjoyed the Valentine Dyall series "The Man in Black", which specialised in macabre and ghostly events, and I campaigned to regularly listen to this programme, to the horror of my parents, who had already lost quite enough sleep because of my fear of dark night time shadows!

The first General Election since the end of the 1930's was held on my birthday on 5th July 1945 with results declared on the 26th July. Mum and Dad had put up a big poster of Clement Attlee in the garden. And one of Hammersley's daughters was married to someone at the BBC, called Eckersley who stood as a Labour candidate. Change was certainly in the air. There was no formal results coverage, as there is today, but it was exciting to hear programmes interrupted on The Home Service, as one after another, the results flooded in. The outcome was truly stunning. Labour had won by a landslide, securing a swing of 12% against the Tories -- the biggest in electoral history. The country had overwhelmingly rejected Mr Churchill, in favour of a radical socialist programme to set up a comprehensive Welfare State, establish a National Health Service, free at the point of use, and nationalise the Grammar Schools. Not-to-mention -- a pledge to give Home Rule to India and a variety of other colonial territories. Some of the red bits on Miss Pear's' world map would now have a new colour!

Although, my illnesses appeared genuine enough, I was beginning to enjoy my periods of convalescence away from Greenfield School where I started to think that I might educate myself listening to good radio programmes, playing with my Meccano, and having my indulgent Mum and Dad, and my and attentive Uncles, read me bedtime stories! Sadly not everyone shared my utopian dream!

Time was passing, and my old pram, which Mr Block had refashioned into a kind of primitive dodgem car before the end of the war -- allowing us kids to career down the slopes of Dad's lawn, and brake at the last moment, before crashing into the hedge at the bottom, finally gave up the ghost. Ian and I took off the wheels to make a "Go-Cart" and then dragged the rotting carcass, along with other detritus we had collected, and hid it under the big laurel tree next to the outside lavatory in my garden. Our aim was to make our very own secret den. One of our games was to imagine that we were research scientists working on a secret project. In this context, quite ordinary objects like old light bulbs or radio valves -- seen as "scientific objects"-- assumed almost mystical properties. I had brought back some pieces of electrical wire, and a broken switch from a building site in Dunster, I had collected on my second wartime evacuation, and added these to our pile of sacred objects. We then took to wandering around Ford's Farm collecting old discarded spark plugs and bits of rusty iron from long discarded harrows and rotting carts. One day, after a trip to the milking parlour, I took my usual short cut back home, past familiar barns and sheds, and discovered a large oily gear wheel by the side of the muddy path. I was spell-bound by this find, and, in reality surrendered all reason. Part of me knew that this object was in a totally different category to the other relics Ian and I had amassed, and I knew it should be left well alone. Another part coveted it, and sought to reassure my young conscience that the gear wheel was just another piece of old junk! As if in a dream, I gathered it in my arms and struggled through the hedge and over the top of our old air-raid shelter and headed for the den. The very next day all hell broke loose next door and we heard Percy, Farmer Ford's son in law, and second in command, bellowing obscenities. Later when Mum returned from fetching our milk, she said that —"Poor Percy was in a right state because the main crown wheel had gone missing from the Ford tractor!" "Apparently", she continued, "Poor Percy was working on it only yesterday trying to get everything ready for the harvest and now he can't find the missing part!" She fixed me with a quizzical look "You don't know anything about it I suppose?" I suddenly felt numb with fear "Err no Mum" I mumbled indistinctly. The next day things were even worse, Percy was at our back door totally distraught and gesticulating violently. Mum called me out "Do you know anything about this Mick?" Head bowed low, I shuffled uneasily besides her "Err no Mum …" The following day there was even more gnashing of teeth from the farm yard. Finally, the sickness of my guilt overwhelmed me and I broke down in floods of tears! My punishment was that I had to take the gearwheel to Percy on my own, and to apologise. I think that he was so relieved to retrieve it, and get on with his repairs to the tractor, that he didn't waste too much time telling me off. And suddenly I felt a great wave of relief course through my whole being. Some might regard this as a seminal learning experience. Certainly, since this time, I have found it difficult to lie, but have a weakness to look guilty in situations where I am totally innocent.

In the late 1940's life started to settle back into more familiar patterns. Uncle Norm was promoted and moved to Brighton to inspect factories over a wide area in South East England. He lived with his future wife, Aunty Gladys in 14a Buckingham Road in the same city, and Granny Chubb moved into a flat opposite, although she still retained her room in our house in Buxted, and stayed with us on a regular basis. Mum became more of the conventional housewife -- no mean task for someone with breathing problems and anaemia, in a world without washing machines and refrigerators. I can remember my frail Mum adding something called "blue bag" to a great mound of washing in the bath upstairs, and stirring it with a stout stick before changing the water to rinse out the soap. Then sheets, blankets and other clothes were twisted in individual loads for transport outside. The heavy cast iron mangle would then have to be manhandled out of the garage, and the washing squeezed between its rollers, before finally being hung out to dry.

Dad settled into the routine of working at Lloyds Bank in Uckfield. He complained that younger staff had been promoted over those who had fought in the war, and he suffered a rather strained relationship with Mr Black, the Manager, who he found pedantic and rather two faced. He looked upon work as a kind of chore which took him away from his home and garden. He particularly hated working on Saturday mornings and would often suffer bad headaches the night before, at the thought of this invasion into his weekend.

By the standards of the day, Dad was no chauvinist, but he expected, what we would now call the "Full English breakfast". This would consist of two over cooked rashers of streaky bacon (ration permitting), home produced fried eggs and tomatoes, (when the hens weren't laying these would come a large crock full of a white liquid which was supposed to preserve them), and, out of season, the tomatoes came from "Kilner jars", designed to keep them through the winter. When we could pick mushrooms from Farmer Ford's fields these we added to the frying pan, together with fried bread cooked in "dripping" from left over fat. These would often be proceeded, by a big helping of porridge or Kellogg's Corn Flakes. The whole lot would be swilled down by a cup of tea, or Camp Coffee. On the days, when he didn't return for lunch, Mum would have a neatly wrapped a pack of sandwiches for him. At the beginning of the week these would be made from the left-overs from our Sunday lunch. After kisses and goodbyes, Dad who often feared being late, would charge out through the backdoor. Sometimes, he would return in a panic when the Ford Eight failed to start, and we had to push him out of the garage and down the drive, and even along the road and down the hill before the engine would fire.

Before Dad got married he used to ride a motorbike. When Vera came on the scene, I think he attached a side car, and later had a series of cars, including an early Morgan with inflatable seats. Mum recalled that these finally perished -- contributing to sore backsides on long journeys. Dad was rather shy with visiting neighbours he didn't know very well, and, in desperation as a party piece, he would fall back on reciting a litany of old car stories. When there was a lull in the conversation Mum and I always knew what was coming and could recite the episodes by heart.

Although many people supported the new reforming Labour Government, and were relieved that there was no return to the mass unemployment of the inter-war years -- this was still a period of shortages and austerity. In an effort to improve the performance of our old car, which belched out clouds of evil smelling blue smoke, and cut down on garage costs, Dad removed its crank shaft, with Uncle's Les' help and had it "Reground". They also took out the engine block and got the cylinders "Re-bored". I watched in awe from a dank corner of our garage as, somehow, with a super-human effort, and much cursing, they managed to fit the larger pistons they had purchased, and eventually reassembled the whole engine.

There were shortages of basic materials like paint, and Dad had less luck, when he purchased some dubious substance from a local spiv to repaint the walls of our dining room. Try as he might the "paint" coagulated in unseemly lumps which flaked off as soon as they dried. He had no better luck with the white "Paint" he applied to our stairs, in an attempt to brighten up our dark passageway. The stuff simply crumbled off over-night and had to be swept up the next morning.

Dad was much more successful at gardening, although it was a huge and never ending task, to keep its wilder parts from encroaching on the more civilised areas. He was very proud of his roses, and well-kept lawns, but we also has big areas of kitchen garden where he grew potatoes, leeks, celery, brussels sprouts, runner beans and a great variety of other vegetables. In the wilder parts we regularly harvested walnuts and almonds as well as a variety of plums and apples, gooseberries, currants and raspberries. The whole family, including Aunty Elsie and Uncle Bob and Pam and Alan, as well as the

Chubb contingent, and later my new cousin Linda, would regularly descend on us during the jam making and bottling season and return home with car loads of fruit. Despite his urban childhood in Tunbridge Wells, Dad fully embraced the rural life and would often turn out in the middle of the night to help farmer Ford deliver new calves or baby lambs.

Pound Green was little more than a hamlet, about a mile from Buxted to the south, and the small village of Hadlow Down to the north. There were few facilities like children's play grounds close at hand. So we had to use our own imagination as kids and create our own games. In the school holidays I would usually meet up with Ian Lyle and we would discuss how we would spend the day. We invented our own special whistle, as a call sign, and would stand outside each other's homes furiously blowing through pursed lips until our Mum's were driven to open the door to us. Ian lived across the main road from me in Spotted Cow Lane. His home was called Applegath, and had once been a pub. It was very old, and the front wall was almost hidden by thick winding branches of wisteria, which burst into purple flowering tails in the spring. It had small lead latticed windows, and inside the ceilings hung low with oak beams. Upstairs there was a long twisting passage which gave access to the bedrooms and bathroom, and where you could look over the back garden which sloped steeply away from the rear of the house. On a good day, you could see Buxted Common in the valley below and beyond, rising from a blue-green mist, the RADA towers of Kings Standing. Stan lived in a small cottage down a steep track to the left of Ian's house and "Goggles", who was older than us, and did swops for Hotspur and Wizard Comics, lived somewhere near the Inkpens who were in a house off the "twitten", which Spotted Cow Lane eventually turned into.

I can honestly say that, in the holidays, I was hardly ever bored as a young boy. My opening greeting to Ian was almost always the same – "What are we going to do today?" And we would start to trade various options. On wet days or cold winter afternoons inside in each other's homes we would sometimes play Monopoly. Ian had two sets and, occasionally, we would combine the two, so that there was virtually no limit to the number of hotels that we could acquire in our struggle to become property moguls. Other times we would race our toy cars the full length of the upstairs corridor at Applegarth. Ian preferred Dinky toys whereas I liked Minic cars best, as they had real clockwork motors, which, when fully wound, would easily run the full length of the passageway. Sometimes, when we varied the game and had competitions for the slowest vehicle, I would modify the clockwork mechanism of my Minic cars by adding a second governor to the escapement to slow their passage to the finishing line.

Looking back to those far off days, we do seem to have been quite a competitive lot! There was the "Flying off" the Hayricks at Ford's Farm, I have already described. And "Olympic Games," competitions, where we all came back battered and bruised from jumping on the hard earth in the big meadow next to the farm yard. Apart from the incident on the ice at Hunters Pond, there were other games of "dare" -- almost as dangerous. Like climbing the straw elevators -- which were propped against the stacks at an acute angle -- which required that we crawl up the spike studded chain belt designed to convey the bales of straw to the top. Once Carol, Camilla, Ian and I collected jig saw puzzles of an equal size and completed against the clock in my house to see who could finish first. Sometimes, we would trudge up the hill towards Hadlow Down, and walk up the long drive to the Hammersely's imposing mansion, and ask very politely if we could play tennis on their private courts. Most of the time the family agreed, and we then had a riotous time serving and volleying our balding balls. Occasionally, Ian and I would sky one of the balls over the wire fence which cordoned the court off from the rhododendron bushes which surrounded it. In our gauche way, we thought that searching for balls in the dense undergrowth, would lead to romantic encounters with one of the girls! We were not always disappointed.

The County town of Lewes is still regarded as the "Bonfire Capital of the World" and the whole of East Sussex is still home to a big variety of Bomb Fire Societies, November 5th is taken very seriously. In Lewes they still roll tar barrels down the street, in memory of the Gun Powder Plot of 1605, and Guy Fawkes' attempt to blow up the House of Lords.

 In the sleepy world of Pound Green in the late 1940's the prospect of building a large bonfire and saving up for fireworks griped the imaginations of most young children. We would set about making our guys out of a skeleton of sticks bound together with binder twine with a mangel-wurzel for a head. An old tattered suit, begged from our parents, would then be draped around this contraption and stuffed with newspaper and handfuls of dried grass. Finishing touches would include old gloves for the hands and a hat of some sort to crown its head. In addition, we would sometimes hollow out large turnips, and make lanterns out these in the way that today's kids celebrate Halloween with pumpkins. There were no street lights where we lived, and one year I made a particularly scary one with a gruesome face and a piece of red glass mounted behind it's hollowed out eye sockets. It was illuminated by a large night light and hung from a long pole. One dark night I hid behind our thick hedge and waited for some poor unsuspecting person to pass by with their can of milk from the farm. On hearing footsteps in the road I suddenly raised the whole contraption skyward, at the same uttering a blood curdling scream. The result was quite dramatic, and to this day I am very relieved the poor old lady involved didn't suffer heart failure!

Procuring money to buy fireworks was always a problem. I earned a shilling a week for mowing the lawns but this didn't go very far to raising the minimum of five shillings considered sufficient to buy a good stash of Rockets, Catherine Wheels, Bangers and Jumping Jacks. To get more money us kids mounted our guys in old prams and paraded outside the entrance to Ford's Farm at milking time. Shouting out "Penny for the Guy" and rattling our collecting tins loudly under the noses of the passers-by. Sometimes, if this didn't raise enough money, we would resort to badgering our Mums and Dads for bits of old bric-a-brac, and set up a shop out- side Ian and Camilla's garage in Spotted Cow Lane to realise more funds.

Lots of local people contributed rubbish for the building of a huge bomb-fire in one of Farmer Ford's fields, well away from his cluster of hay and straw ricks. Our guys would be hoisted to the top to lay alongside the official one of Guy Fawkes made by the local bomb-fire society. Memory may play tricks, but the fireworks you could buy in local shops, especially the bangers, seemed to have more firepower than today – especially "Jumping Jacks" and "Fliers" which are now banned. In a pre-television age, the Fifth of November was a significant event in rural communities to brighten up the night sky as the chill of winter descended. Big parades, however, could easily get out of hand and we never went to Lewes, where hooligans were reputed throw fireworks and casualties occurred. Even local bomb-fires could attract a kind of bucolic thuggery with local Teddyboys, in the early 1950's, chanting ancient prejudices against Catholics and the Pope. Torch light possessions sometimes assumed the threat of Black-Shirt Rallies, and we usually avoided these and often just burnt our guys on home-made bomb-fires, and set off our fireworks with a few friends.

Generally speaking, life moved quite slowly in our little hamlet. It was a big deal if someone new moved in or others left. It was an event when our landlord tore up some of the bramble bushes near our house, which hung heavy with black fruit in late summer, to make room for five flowering cherry trees to mark the birth of his five Daughters. I can remember crying uncontrollably when a retired Colonel moved in at the far side of our green, to start a market garden, and cut down the beautiful pine trees, which had framed the view I had had of the world, since I was old enough to remember. But, rail as I might, against a change I had no control over -- life was moving forward. After three years at Greenfield school, marked by poor health and long absences, and a set of discouraging reports, the score card for Mum and Dad's "son and heir" was looking decidedly bleak! Thinking that the very damp condition of our house might be a contributory cause of my feverish colds, Dad asked Mr Hammerseley to undertake to improve the drainage system to remove the stagnant water which resided permanently under our floor boards. The answer came, that this was a very expensive undertaking and that we should either pay for the work ourselves, or face a big increase in our rent -- conditions, which were not possible, for our family to meet.

Furthermore, my score card was not wholly negative. I had a good vocabulary, a good (perhaps too good an imagination!), I could read, after a fashion, but my spelling was almost undecipherable. I was an adventurous boy, but clumsy to the point of self-destruction. I appeared good with ideas, but poor at retaining facts. I was good at doing puzzles and persisted well with projects which interested me, (like making Meccano models) but was often dreamy and inattentive. The focus of the debate was changing from altering the unhealthy physical environment of our house, to that of exploring my inner psyche. It was time to bring in Dr Freud in the shape of Uncle Norm!

Granny Chubb

Granny Strange

From left to right; Uncle Norm and Uncle Les

Chapter 3
A.S. Neill and all that

Family get-togethers were always an excuse for Mum to put on a great feast which seemed to go on for most of the day, starting with a roast lunch and finishing with a never ending high tea of jellies, jam tarts, trifle and welsh Cakes. Norm brought his new wife Gladys and Uncle Les came with a different girl friend called Doris who seemed a little more worldly wise than his usual sweethearts. For some reason, I was the centre of attention, even more than usual. Aunty Gladys and Doris helped me do a jigsaw puzzle and *marvelled* at my ability to quickly find the missing pieces to fill the vacant spaces! I was even allowed to read out a short story I had written in my indecipherable "Sanscript". It was a bit of a crib on a character called Myrtle, an air-head society girl, satirised in an anti-fascist magazine called "Lilliput" which my Dad subscribed to, along with the "New Statesman and

Nation" and "The Artist". It was a leftwing version of Punch with beautiful colour illustrations on the front cover by a German graphic artist called Walter Trier. The publication specialised in political comment, humorous short stories, and photography. For some reason, when you picked up the periodical, it often fell open at a nude centre-spread, or a raunchy picture of film stars like Jane Russell in come-hither poses!

The main character in my story was called Mirabelle. She was what my Mum would have called a "Good time Charlie" forever, painting her face and plucking her eyebrows in the pursuit of "Mr Right" who was probably some brylcreemed creep in "Accounts" or an "About Town Playboy". My narrative would follow a very predictable plot with Mirabelle going on car trips or cycle rides with some adoring beau, only to discover that bits of her under-ware seemed to have a life of their own. I had ear-wigged on enough conversations between Mum and Grace Smith, to gain some familiarity with the secret world of lingerie. My Mirabelle adventures often featured failed elastic, popped suspenders, and broken bra straps as my femme fatal gaily led a series of suitors into a variety of romantic encounters!

For some reason -- my sometimes deadpan readings of my stories -- seemed to cause much merriment and hysterical laughter amongst the assembled relatives. I was emboldened by this, and felt that maybe I was following in the footsteps of Uncle Les as a great raconteur and entertainer. Indeed, I may of course, unconsciously drawn material for my stories by listening to his accounts of his experiences with the likes of Joan Benge and Marion. The family meeting, however, had a hidden agenda, and, as the day wore on Uncle Norm drew me aside and introduced me to a series of tests. "Just a bit of fun Boy!" He reassured me. Initially I was encouraged to play with poster paints and draw pictures. Then Uncle produced what looked like a big ink blot of a butterfly. "What does that remind you of?" He quizzed. Later I was encouraged to draw a picture of a house and then add other things to the picture I thought to be important. "Hum, hum" murmured Uncle encouragingly, using his psychological voice. I was then given a series of cards to put in sequence. One was of a burglar in a striped pullover climbing through an open window and then escaping with a bag conveniently marked "swag", another was a series of triangles with one upside down, that had to be identified as the odd one out, in a test for spatial awareness -- which I now recognise as being part of an IQ test. Finally, Uncle asked me to describe the nightmares, I still sometimes had, which disrupted the peaceful slumbers of my parents.

I realised that something was up. And, after I had been put to bed, I crawled out onto the corridor outside my room in the hope of catching snatches of adult conversation floating up from below, as my concerned parents gathered in conference with Uncle Norm. The outcome of Uncle's voodoo like interpretation of Rorchach Tests and other psychological paraphernalia soon became apparent as key phrases drifted up the stairs, like bulletins on my psychic condition. The Boy was "Repressed" suffered from a "Mother Fixation" – "Morbid Obsessions ….." This analysis, plus scrutiny of my appalling spelling, in an age before an understanding of the symptoms of dyslexia, coupled with a series of damming reports and absences from Greenfield School, was enough to seal my fate. A new school for problem children had recently opened at Forest Row near East Grinstead. The school was run on the same principles as those pioneered by A.S. Neill at Summerhill in the 1920's, and I was to start as a weekly boarder at the beginning of the next term.

As the countdown to the beginning of the new term reached its final hours I was suffused with a feeling of utter dread at being separated from Mum and Dad and my friends our house, Fords Farm, our beloved tom cat Kipp and my lovely toys, for my weekly dose of "Modern Education". Finally, the terrible day arrived and I was carried kicking and screaming to the front seat of our Ford Eight yelling that I didn't want freedom!

Tilehurst School was a large, rather tumbledown house, standing in its own grounds. It, had been requisitioned by the Canadian forces during the war, and messages from home- sick soldiers and graffiti were still scrawled on some of the walls. The contents of my small suit case were quickly transferred to a tiny bedside locker in a mixed dormitory and Dad, looking rather upset, said his perfunctory goodbyes and hurried away, as he was anxious to back to his work at Lloyds Bank. The lady who first greeted me, enthusiastically advanced the cause of the "Freedom School". "We are all friends here" she enthused. "We all call each other by our Christian names. Call me Pansy -- you don't have to go to classes if you don't want!" She continued. "In fact most of your class are playing in our beautiful woods – You can join them if you like." She pointed down the garden to a gap in the hedge and I dutifully sauntered off to join the other children. I found some of them lazing in the long-grass.

Some were swinging from ropes suspended from tall trees. Others were playing at being couples and were kissing and cuddling, a few had stripped off and were in the nude. Some of them seemed quite lethargic and didn't seem to be making the best use of the woods in the way Ian and myself would have done back home on our own turf. I introduced myself, and they immediately wanted to know what my problem was. I said I didn't know that I had a problem. "We all have problems" they chorused, and one by one they proceeded to outline their reasons for being at Tylehurst. Their knowledge of psychological terms and abnormal behaviour would have put Uncle Norm to shame. It slowly began to dawn on me that this school, hidden away the lush countryside of Forest Row, was a kind of concentration camp for the wayward kids --- A depository for precocious middle class sons and daughters, whose parents had failed to control in a normal family setting.

I also discovered that "freedom" at the school was qualified in a variety of ways. Vegetarianism was compulsory, despite the fact that, in the immediate post-war period there was a great shortage of fresh fruit from aboard like oranges. Real bananas were substituted by dried ones -- the colour of stale turds! The school operated a small market garden and our "Freedom" was periodically interrupted by being press ganged into periods of supervised digging, weeding and picking. The fruits of our efforts were supposed to supplement our meagre diet. However, the food at meal times seemed immensely boring and I missed the fried eggs and bacon regularly served up at home. On one occasion, having failed to masticate a revolting mixture of beetroot and turnip, my teeth sunk into something I initially thought to be more succulent, only to discover that I had bitten into a slug!

I felt miserable and homesick for most of the short period I spent at Tylehurst. The freedom regime was certainly a contrast to the Dame School run by Miss Pear and Miss Brown. But most of the time, I felt that the people running the institution, concentrated on expositing their own radical philosophy, irrespective, of whether it was helpful, or appropriate, to the children in their charge. They assumed that our "Behavioural Problems" were the result of deep repressions, which had to be exorcised. Sometimes, this took bizarre forms. On one occasion Sandra asked the class where rain came from. As, I was quite good at natural science, and had experienced a good deal of rain, or, "bwrw glaw", when I was evacuated to the Welsh mountains, I started to reply. But, before I could finish my answer, Sandra interrupted to say that – "Rain was God's piss!" – a piece of total scientific nonsense designed , I imagine , to liberate the dark libidinal forces within me. Attitudes towards the free expression of bodily functions were monitored and we were encouraged to defecate publically on a toilet in a communal bathroom. I missed my Granny climbing up the laurel tree by our outside lavatory at home to encourage my daily "business", and refused to participate in this particular piece of performance art, preferring to slink away, when, I thought no one was looking -- to shit in the thick undergrowth outside. No doubt, my failure to comply marked me out as suffering from some anal complex -- condemning me to a lower level of personality development. Some of the naturism we were encouraged to practice, possibly, had its liberating aspects and, I can remember the nude pillow fights we had in the mixed dormitories being something of a revelation for me as an only child.

A key tenet of the "Free School Philosophy" was that children should never be compelled to learn. But, that they should come to the class-room of their own accord, when they were ready. I am sure this is a good idea, in theory -- however, it assumed that children were purely self- motivated and not influenced by their own peer group. After a few weeks of "freedom", running around in the woods with the other children, I grew rather bored with playing at the Noble Savage. I was also aware that Mum and Dad were making sacrifices at home to invest in the transformation of my educational progress. I looked at the time-table and decided to present myself at Dierdre's English lesson. There were no other children in the class-room and she looked rather put out when I entered. "I'd like you to teach me some English" I said. She rather grudgingly obliged, and I spent quite a happy hour with her. When I came out, however, there was a posse of other kids waiting for me. My absence from the woods had been noticed and I was accused of being a Black-Leg. I was then given a black-eye for defying the norms of the group.

After seven weeks, I developed badly infected leg from an untreated cut, sustained in the woods at Forest Row, and Mum and Dad, no doubt worn down by the weekly trauma of escorting their unwilling son for his dose of "Freedom", decided that the experiment was at an end and I was withdrawn from Tilehurst at half term.

There could be no going back to Greenfield School, and Mum and Dad enrolled me at a smaller Dame School, which provided more personal tuition to small groups of children at an institution near Maresfield. It was run by a jolly rather portly lady called Miss Punt. She had a very nice sense of humour and her style was much gentler and understanding than the hectoring approach of Miss Pear or the laid back, laissez-faire regime at Tylehurst. On one occasion I took along a model boat, Ian and I had been playing with which worked on jet propulsion. The mechanism was very simple comprising of a screwed top container connected by two pipes leading to the rear of the boat. To achieve thrust you put in a tea spoon of "Eno Salts" (a well-known laxative of the day) fill the canister up with water, give it a good shake, and place the boat in the water. Whereupon, the agitated salts would perform their purgative task forcing a rapid surge of water out of the rear pipes and forcing the craft forward at high speed. When I solemnly explained this to Miss Punt, she had an uncontrollable laughing fit ending in her gasping for breath! Fortunately, an incident, like my earnest attempt to sell a raffle ticket to Miss Pear on the privy, never occurred at her academy, but I feel, that if it had, she would have contrived to see the funny side.

Over the next couple of years she painstakingly set about trying to fill in the alarming gaps in my early education. There was more emphasis on art and the creative side of education -- like writing imaginative stories than I had experienced before and, although my spelling remained a problem, she was sensitive enough not to cover my efforts with too much discouraging red ink.

While I was at Miss Punt's I suffered the first pangs of true love. There was a beautiful little girl with fair hair and blue eyes called Kim

Martens. During break times we spent most of the time inside a large wooden beer barrel attempting to roll it along from inside -- the uncertain motion of this large keg, and our close confinement in a small dark space, no doubt contributing to our passions. Miss Punt believed in the importance of deportment and co-ordination and, each week, the children attended dancing classes. After a couple of heavy footed performances on the dance floor, myself and another boy called Michael were singled out as suffering from symptoms of dyspraxia. We were then dispatched to another room for what seemed like endless sessions of skipping in an attempt to correct our condition. Eventually, we were then allowed to return the main hall for the last dance. Our partners were chosen for us, and each time I prayed that I would be paired off with Kim. Most of the time the dancing mistress took pity on me and I blissfully cavorted around the room with my sweetheart to the strains of "Now is the Hour that we must say Goodbye!" My infatuation was so great that I even danced around my bedroom at home clutching a cushion and humming the tune of that lilting refrain.

It was good to be a Day Boy again after my hated experience of boarding at Tylehurst and I appreciated my home comforts and my friends in Pound Green even more. Ian had begun building balsa wood model aeroplanes and I was anxious to follow in his footsteps. Dad helped me make a simple workbench in my room comprising of a wooden top mounted on two old packing cases. We bought a construction kit from a toy shop in Uckfield and I set about pinning out plans for the fuselage on my Ajax rubber powered monoplane designed by Mick Smee. Dad also procured copies of old 11+ test papers to reinforce Miss Punt's caring approach to education with his own home tuition. In an attempt to deal with my spelling problems, he suggested that I spend most of my post office savings on an Oliver portable typewriter, in the hope that typing out my short stories might improve my understanding of how combinations of letters related to the words I wished to write. The typewriter was great fun and Ian, Camilla and I started our own magazine which we called "The Red Lion" and set about writing our own stories of "daring do" loosely based on hero figures we had read about in comics like the "Rover" and "Hotspur".

At the same time Ian and I competed to finish our aeroplanes for our test flights. Our earlier vision of being lone inventers in small backrooms struggling against the odds now started to seem achievable. Poor Ian suffered a set-back when Camilla accidently sat on a delicate part of his construction, while I discovered that the application of too much dope caused the wings of my model to warp out of true. Finally, after numerous setbacks and trips to Cysters Model Shop at Ringles Cross to procure more spare parts, the great day dawned and we were climbing over the old air-raid shelter with Dad and heading towards Farmer Ford's biggest meadow. We were highly excited, making engine noises and "wizard prang!" exclamations to one another as we twisted the propellers of our frail craft to wind up their rubber motors. Finally, we reached the centre of the field, faced the wind, and one by one launched our planes skywards. The results were not what we anticipated and instead of climbing into the blue yonder our planes either stalled, and then crashed back to earth, or, nose-dived into the ground. At the end of our maiden flights we were left with sad the task of gathering up shattered wings and broken nose cones. In quick order we were heading back home determined to undertake our repairs and consult our " Aeromodeller" and "Boys Own" Magazines for clues on trimming and launching technique. We were stoic in the face of defeat and, although the flying of model aeroplanes was always a bitter-sweet experience, successful flights just about outnumbered crashes.

Over the years we progressed to making quite advanced models. These included jet planes powered by solid fuel "Jetex" engines, one of which reached a great height and then suddenly nose-dived straight on to a hayrick to the great alarm of farmer Ford. We both made frequent trips to Cysters model shop and dreamed of building bigger and bigger models. Radio control was in its infancy, but older kids like Goggles had started to make control line aeroplanes which circled at high speed controlled by two wires. Cysters undertook to supply advanced ram- jet engines to power some of these which sounded just like miniature V1 terror weapons. No amount of badgering would make our cautious parents fork out for such terrifying kit but we did eventually get given little diesel engines for our birthdays. Ian used his to power a propeller driven control line plane, while I specialised in free flight. The problem with this, of course, was that you had no control over the craft after it was launched, apart from what was called a "de-thermaliser". This was a very problematic piece of kit designed to prevent the plane gliding miles away after the engine had run out of fuel. A slow burning fuse was supposed to allow the tail of the plane to tip up as a "spoiler" bringing the craft gently to earth. I never mastered the complexities of this device and relied on putting only a little diesel in the fuel-tank of my model to limit the duration of its flight.

One evening Dad accompanied me to the biggest field we could find for the test flight of a lovely monoplane I had made powered by my new Mills 0.75cc diesel engine. The flight exceeded my wildest expectations and the little plane spiralled round and round climbing higher and higher. Then elation turned to horror as the engine failed to cut out and my model became a tiny dot in the sky. When the fuel finally ran out the torque from the propeller was removed it glided straight over Waste Wood. Although we started to run after it we knew that further pursuit was impossible. The darkness of trees in the growing dusk seemed as impenetrable as the Amazon jungle, and we sadly headed home. Further searches, over the next few days revealed no clues, and we asked Ernie from the farm, who frequently visited the wood to lay traps, to keep an eye out. Seven months later, in the middle of winter when all the leaves had fallen he spied it high up in a tree and knocked it down. The plane was a sodden wreck of twisted spars and wet paper but the engine was fine and I used it to power a beautiful scale model I made of a Tiger Moth by-plane. In order to make my model as realistic as possible I used coloured dope to decorate it. The effect of this was to make it too heavy to fly far so I was never in fear of losing it, indeed, I was lucky to get it to climb much above head height.

Model making may seem nerdy to those children growing up in the 21st Century reared on a diet of "Game-boy" and "Wee" machines. But to my eyes, such devices appear essentially reactive since the players are simple responding to a pre-determined programme rather than initiating the course of events. I marvel at the passivity of modern games where children seriously claim that they gain as much fun from a simulated game of tennis or bowels as the real thing. Rightly or wrongly, in the early 1950's Ian and myself felt that struggling, against the odds, to make things work was character building and practical. Although Ian became a successful chartered accountant, the building skills he honed as a child, never deserted him and, after he married, he went on to construct, virtually single handed, a huge extension made out of reclaimed oak beams and bricks to his Tudor cottage in the Weald. This masterpiece took him five years to complete -- working part time in the evening and weekends. In my case the knowledge that I could make exciting cranes, model cars and tractors out of Meccano and construct aeroplanes which sometimes flew, helped sustain me during the dark days when illness and dyslexia combined to label me as Educationally Sub-normal.

Although, I was happy at Miss Punt's my feverish colds still persisted causing me to miss school. Operations to remove the Tonsils and adenoids of young children were popular at this time and I was booked in for surgery in the hope that this would cure my problem. Uckfield Cottage Hospital was a small institution and there was no children's ward. I was assigned to a large male ward dealing with respiratory problems. Some of the men seemed very old to me and I am sure that many of them were acutely ill -- their loud moans and hacking coughs rattled long into the night. In those days, there was no simple "pre-med" prick with a hypodermic to knock you out before the operation, and I was wheeled fully conscious into the operating theatre. I remember looking up at the powerful arc lights, which almost blinded me, and glimpsing druid like figures bending over me before a disgusting ether soaked pad was thrust in my face and I was retching and gagging for air. When I woke up back in the ward I was violently sick and suffered from a terrible sore throat. I felt hot and feverish. In the early 1950's matrons ruled the wards with an iron discipline and visits from friends and relatives were considered disruptive to routine. I honestly can't remember how long I stayed only that I never saw my Mum or Dad for what seemed like weeks. I know that my stay was prolonged because the operation was botched and my wound went septic. I think I must have been delirious some of the time because the screams of the sick echoing out of the darkness at night time seemed to exceed my worst war-time nightmares. I was eventually allowed home only for my infection to flare up again. I ran a high temperature and suffered fits of delirium which caused vivid hallucinations. I was prescribed "M and B", regarded as a wonder pill at the time. This kill or cure technique caused me to sweat like a pig and I woke up after a long and troubled sleep entwined in sodden sheets, but with my fever much reduced. Dr Sadlier prescribed a period of rest and recuperation. The consequence of all this was that I missed sitting the 11+ test-- which I probably would have failed anyway -- and my worried parents were looking at the prospect of continuing to fund my private education. With the memory of my bizarre experience at Tylehurst fresh in their minds, they opted for the conventional middle class route, and it was arranged for me to attend Duds House Preparatory School in Crowborough as a dayboy.

The school was situated in a suburban road next to a rival establishment called Prior's Park. The school uniform code was vigorously adhered to and I had to wear a cap with bright blue stripes and a matching blazer, with its lapels stitched with blue braid, and short grey trousers. My legs were engulfed in grey stockings gartered below the knee and my feet were encased in sensible black leather shoes that I was ordered never to "scuff". The Prior's Parkites were attired in purple caps and blazers suitably embellished with lashings of braid garnishing. This exotic uniform was designed, of course, to advertise the exclusivity of these two competing establishments, and to distinguish us from the common herd attending state schools. When the day boys from each school poured out of their school gates at the end of the afternoon we looked like swarms of brightly coloured insects. Indeed we nicknamed the kids from Prior's Park the Colorado Beetles – a potato pest so feared that the government gave money for dead specimens. We were constantly reminded by masters that we should each act as a talisman for our rival schools -- a command which many of us resented since our colourful uniform meant we could be easily identified when any misdemeanours occurred.

The majority of boys at Duds House were boarders, and I was surprised at the morning assembly when in addition to taking a roll call Mr Canning the Headmaster asked the resident boys personal questions such as whether they had had a bowel movement that day and commenting publically on those who had missed a day. He also read out lists of boys who had to see him in his study and it appeared that some were going to be beaten for poor work as well as misbehaviour. I remember him as being a large rather un-gamely man with a florid complexion and receding chin. I fell foul of him almost immediately. At break time we were all given small milk bottles each sealed by a cardboard washer at its top and a straw. I was unfamiliar with this procedure and had difficulty puncturing the centre of the seal.

"In trouble boy?" boomed the masterful Mr Canning

"I can't seem to get the straw in, Sir" I said.

"Put your thumb in boy" Mr Canning loomed threateningly over me. I tried but without success.

"Push harder Boy! Don't pussy-foot-about" He leaned lower and I caught sight of the red veins which flecked his cheeks. I pushed with all my might. Suddenly, there was and a huge explosion. Under pressure the seal suddenly gave way and a shower of milk shot in the air and enveloped the whole of Mr Canning's face and cascaded down the front of his shirt and trousers.

"You stupid boy!" he exclaimed. He raised his hand to hit me -- but thought better of it at the last moment and retreated to change his clothes before the beginning of the next class.

The early 1950s was, of course, another age and it must be difficult for those growing up at the end of the twentieth century to imagine a world of casual sexism. Where teachers and even older boys had the power to cane young boys, and although homosexuality was still illegal, and those who practiced same sex relationships went in fear of discovery, a blind eye was often turned to acts of paedophilia in closed institutions. When I arrived at Duds House in the mornings Mr Canning would often be playing a piano organ in the main entrance hall. He used the occasion to summarily talk to Parents and to harangue small boys. His Wife could often be seen hovering at a discreet distance talking to the Matrons and Kitchen Staff.

Sometimes, without warning, he would sound off homilies about his views on life in general. Augustus John we learned was a complete "Pillock". Modern Art would lead to the ruin of civilisation. Platonic love was of a higher order than love between a man and a woman. Men were born to lead. A good beating could make a man of you....

I had the misfortune to attend his classes in Latin and English Grammar. His teaching method was positively Victorian and purely rhetorical. He would bark out a question such as "What is the ablative absolute of Possum?" The questioning would start at the top of the class and then be passed along the front row of desks, moving on to the middle row and finally the back row. The first boy to answer the question correctly would literally have to leave his desk and move up to the top of the form while everyone else moved down. The questioning was highly repetitive and very occasionally I got the right answer by chance, or the law of averages -- whereupon, I would spend the rest of the class laboriously moving down to the bottom. The system was pernicious, reinforcing feelings of superiority amongst an able elite, while negatively labelling the rest of the class.

Mr Canning regularly ladled our punishment for poor performance. Without warning, he would appear behind the desk of some unfortunate boy, roughly pinching his cheek with one hand and smacking the other. Boys would be regularly beaten at the front of the class for what were deemed minor infractions of the rules or the failure to parrot recitations of Latin verbs. Even at the age of eleven I appreciated that Mr Canning derived pleasure from these random acts of sadism. There was a pretty boy at the front of the class with red hair called Evans. He was good at Latin and almost always got the answers right. This frustrated the Headmaster who clearly harboured an urge to assault the boy in some way. On one occasion when his class pet had correctly conjugated some obscure Latin verb he called him out to the front and forced him to lie face down over his knees saying "This time Evans I am going to beat you, not as a punishment boy, but as a reward!" He then proceeded to spank him in front of the whole class.

English classes with Mr Canning were no better. There was no attempt to explore English Literature or Creative Writing. The same question and answer technique was applied to the mechanical parsing of sentences. I found the whole process meaningless and boring and consequently performed almost as badly at English as I did at Latin. Before long this was recorded at the Friday Afternoon School Assembly where the marks of every boy were read out and I had to later join the queue of miscreants outside the Headmasters study for my dose of corporal punishment. Regular beatings were, of course, were no cure for stupidity or dyslexia, and eventually I was transferred to Mr Jones's English class.

He was a new teacher who had just joined the school and appeared almost as bemused by the strange institutional mores of Duds House as I was. He was a kind and sympathetic Master who regularly read stories to the class and encouraged the boys to write interesting essays and stories. I had recently heard a radio dramatisation of H.G.Wells' "War of the Worlds" which had so impressed me that I had written my own science fiction story called "Moon Base" which imagined that advanced creatures from outer space had established a secret colony on the moon, and were using flying saucers to kidnap earthlings to learn more about their behaviour prior to an invasion of our planet. Dad had helped me translate my appalling spelling into understandable English and we had typed it up on my portable typewriter. I can remember that it ran into quite a number of foolscap pages and thinking that it was quite a good effort for a boy of eleven. Mr Jones was also impressed and I can remember feeling an overwhelming sense of relief that my writing was one area where some ability of mine was recognised by the adult world. Such recognition and encouragement from Mr Jones just about sustained my existence at my Preparatory School. I showed little aptitude for games, although in response to the terrifying screams of Mr Canning, I heavily tackled some unsuspecting full-back and was rewarded by roars of "Up-school, up-school, up-school" by a class of new boys, frog marched in for the occasion, as the ball trickled over the goal line.

The whole institution seemed to encourage a blind obedience to all kinds of authority. Meal times and Assemblies were pieces of supporting theatre where the masters all wore black gowns with senior staff sitting in elevated positions above the rest. Women were confined to minor roles -- suitably costumed as Matrons or Serving Staff. While the Headmaster orchestrated proceedings from a raised dais. Conversations with adults were often limited to "yes sir" "no sir" deferential responses. "Day-bugs" were frowned upon, but I was grateful that I was spared the full twenty-four hour exposure to a total institution which seemed dedicated to grinding down every last ounce of childhood individuality. The strain was so great that when the day boys were released at the end of classes we soon forgot about all about our mission to advertise the good manners of the school, and promptly sparred with the Prior Parkites who had to wait at the same bus stop as us. Once inside the bus we made for the top deck where we were less likely to be supervised by the conductor. Sometimes we would encourage Bannister to do his party piece. He was a German boy who somehow had been granted special dispensation regarding school uniform. He was decked out in leather lederhosen and even sported an early crew cut. His trick was to bury his head in the seat exposing his vast bum to the ceiling, and, by a supreme act of contortion, he would produce a box of red matches and endeavour to ignite an enormous fart he has saved up for the purpose! We all gazed in awe expecting at least a massive bang or flash of blue light. But most of the time Banister simply produced a big stink.

Halfway back to Ringles Cross the bus picked up pupils from a girls school. They seemed older and more mature than us boys and we felt they were rather "stuck up". One in particular was called Jane, and as she lived in a caravan just down the lane from my home. The job of picking us up was shared between her Mum and my Dad. For some reason, I found her rather superior, and, in a moment of weakness, hit upon the idea of pulling the back of her skirt through the gap of the seat in front of me. When the bell rang for our stop and she got up to leave, but then discovered that she was routed to the spot. She panicked, of course, fearing that greater effort would disrobe her bottom half completely. As the bus slowed I released my grip and she shot forward into the back of the seat in front of her. As soon as we dismounted from the tail board of the bus she launched a ferocious attack on me and we rolled over and over on the patch of green in front of her horror struck Mother who had just come to collect us in her Austin Seven.

At Duds House the boarders seemed a different breed to the day boys. They had their own slang and cliques of friends. They regarded us as an inferior species and took every opportunity to tease and humiliate us. On one occasion I took a little Minic clockwork bus into school to show the few friends I had. I left it in my satchel during games practice and discovered it was missing on my return. A few days later I entered the cloakroom just in time to see Crab secreting what looked like my bus in his tuck box.

"It's not yours" he said guiltily.

"Then whose is it?" I replied

Whereupon, he pulled out a white penknife and opened the blade and laid it in the palm of his hand.

"See my lily-white knife?" his voice was cool as ice.

"I could cut your throat with my lily-white knife!"

I never saw my lovely bus again.

In an effort to ingratiate myself with some of the nicer boarders I agreed to supply them with conkers in the Autumn Term. There was a large horse chestnut tree surrounded by spiked railings at the entrance to limes lane in our hamlet. I was in the habit of borrowing my Dad's bike and riding to the top of the lane. I would then prop the bike up against the railings and stand on the crossbar the reach up to pick the conkers off the higher branches. It was a stupid, foolhardy procedure thwart with danger. One day the inevitable happened. The bike fell from under me and I was impaled -- left hanging on the spikes. There was no one around. I had frightening images of being found the next day -- stiff as a crucifix. Somehow, I managed to find the strength to grab the metal fence supporting the spikes and hauled myself up and over them. I was extremely lucky not to have severed a major artery and there was less blood than might have been expected. The bike was still intact and with a super effort I struggled to cycle past the Pound Green Stores and up the hill to the Hollies. I threw the bike down outside our coal shed and staggered to the back door. Mum thought I had simply fallen over until I pulled up my shirt revealing the blood dripping from the wound in my side.

I was rushed by ambulance to Tunbridge Wells Hospital and was given anaesthetic to explore the extent of my injuries. They discovered that I had punctured my lung. The wound was cleaned up and dressed and I was put on a course of penicillin injection to counter any infection I might have ingested from the rusty spikes. The surgeon implied that I had been very lucky and the outcome could have been much worse. I took his words to heart and I remember thinking to myself that if I was a cat I would have used up quite a few of my lives already. I made a resolution with myself to try to be less accident prone in the future. Time had moved on since my terrifying experiences in Uckfield Hospital. The dreaded ether pad was no longer in use and when I had my operation and I was given a modern pre-med injection. I was also kept on a children's ward which was quite good fun. We had trays mounted on wheels which stretched over our beds. One trick we used to play was to wait until one of the cleaners crawled under the bed and then push the tray backwards and forwards at high speed trapping them underneath. There was a happy atmosphere on the ward and most of them saw the funny side. However, the old rule that visiting children in hospital would upset them, and disrupt the running of the ward was still enforced, and I spent over a week in hospital with no visits from my Mum and Dad. For some reason, never explained, even letters and parcels were intercepted and not passed on.

The use of penicillin was in its infancy and no one checked whether I was allergic to it. Shortly after I returned home I suffered a massive reaction and the whole of my body became very swollen, and, for a time my face was so puffed up I could hardly see out of my eyes. Great wealds appeared on my bottom, where they had applied the injections so that for a time I had to crawl about on all fours to avoid sitting down. I was too ill to return to school for some time. As on previous periods of convalescence I fell back on to playing Uncle Les's 78 records, and listening to the BBC Home service and Light Programme. I would be transfixed by the adventures of Dick Barton Special Agent and radio plays of all kinds. I even listened to Henry Hall Guest night and Workers Playtime. I also read Donald Keyhoe's "Flying Saucers are Real" to give me material for my "Moon Base" story.

During the war fashions tended to be simple and in the case of younger women largely followed the natural contours of their bodies. Wartime shortages encouraged unfussy dresses with short hemlines. In 1947 Christian Dior launched a reaction against utility clothing. Haute Couture promoted the hour glass figure demanding a tiny waist, ample bosom and full hips. Skirts dropped to mid-calf and instead of wartime head scarves and berets, women were expected to wear a ridiculous array of matching gloves, shoes and purses. A wartime diet of bully beef, suet pudding, whale meat sausages and stockpot had not promoted natural hour glass figures and magazines like Women's Own published more and more adverts for corsets and girdles. In the village Madeleine Birch (Nick named Mad Birch) set herself up as a representative for Ambrose Wilson who specialised in manufacturing such instruments of torture, designed to sweep away the wonderful freedom of 1940's garters and suspender-belts. One day Mad Birch came calling, we could hear her cooing like a Midwich cuckoo as she came up the garden path. "The Devil take the woman!", hissed my Granny. I was surprised at her reaction as she was always tightly laced in some iron Victorian contraption which sometimes creaked as she mounted the stairs. But I believe that she was trying to protect my Mum, who she knew was soft hearted and anxious never to offend. Her entreaties were ignored, Mad Birch's foot was over the door step and she was already into her sales patter. I briefly glimpsed her elaborate hat and gloves through the serving hatch in the wall separating the kitchen from the dining room. "Just a trial offer" she wheedled, "Money back guarantee .... Marvellous for posture and good heath!"

My poor Mum did, of course, submit, and every morning she would sneak into my room to avoid the male gaze of my Dad in order to pull the strings and tighten the buckles of the fearful contraption she had purchased from Mad Birch. It has always amazed me that any woman, or man, for that matter, would wish to mortify their body in such a way. I suppose that in the early 1950's popular culture wished to re-establish more rigid male and female roles which had been disrupted during the war. The New Look and Women's magazines of the period reinforced the cult of the housewife. The helpless woman at home prettified for the return of the great breadwinner. Even my Dad, who prided himself on his progressive views, and readily undertook a good deal of house chores himself, played to this stereotype, sometimes commenting on my Mum's looks and grooming which would now seem odd in the 21st Century.

In the 1950s the average of marriage was 21. Girls at 25 were considered in danger of 'being left on the shelf. In our village, girls would have a brief and beautiful flowering. On marrying, many appeared to submit to a kind of calculated dowdiness associated with the role of the dutiful wife. It seemed to me that within months of taking their vows their beautiful long hair would be frizzed into a tight perm or tied into a prim bun. And their brightly coloured dresses discarded for sensible attire of a more sombre hue. In a few years, I mused, Mad Birch would come a-knocking at their door.

For all its excesses today's generation has a lot to thank the sexual revolution of the 1960's for. The pill, the mini-skirt Mary Quant's tights and the first Labour Government for thirteen years which started the Open University, abolished hanging and implemented the Wolfenden Report in 1967 -- which decriminalised homosexuality between consenting adults over 21, swept the stuffy world of the 1950's away forever. Today, the rigid demarcations between generations and genders have been put aside and we now enjoy a freer existence as a consequence.

In 1951 my period at Duds House School was drawing to a close and my educational future, was at a turning point. My failure to sit the 11+ exam meant that my poor parents were committed to spending more money in the private sector to further my secondary schooling. From conversations with Mr Jones, my sympathetic, English teacher, they were aware of the severe shortcoming of Duds House and toyed with sending me to St Christopher's, a co-educational School in Letchworth. Like the ill-fated Tylehurst, this school was also run on A.S. Neill principles -- although I am sure it was much better managed. We even went so far as to attend an open day. Although the staff and children appeared friendly and welcoming -- the sight of open-toed sandals, casual attire, and their informal behaviour, somehow, only served to awaken within me irrational fears of my Forest Row experience. Mum and Dad also had second thoughts after they discovered how high the fees were.

In the end they opted for a more conventional boys Public School in Wiltshire called Harper's College The school had grown out of a Farming Academy for the sons of wealthy local farmers. Its main claim to be progressive was the wearing of short trousers throughout the school. With the help of my Dad and encouragement of Mr Jones, I scrapped through the Common Entrance exam at my second attempt and set about trying to mentally prepare myself for life at boarding school. I was conscious of the huge financial effort my parents were making and was determined to make a success out of my long periods of incarceration away from home. My Mum, I think, embraced a rather romantic view of Public Schools and used to read me stories by Frank Richards which originally appeared in publications like the Magnet and Gem dating back to 1908. Unlike more realistic accounts of Public School bullying like "Tom Brown's School Days", Frank Richard's wrote a bowdlerised account of such institutions for a popular audience. The main character was a fat boy called Billy Bunter, nick named the "Fat Owl of the Remove" who attended a Public School called Greyfriars and spent all his money on vast amounts of food and tuck. He was always broke, but seemed to be readily supplied with postal orders from indulgent Aunts or loans he tricked out of his friends. He was the frequent victim of play fights with other boys and would often emerge from a tangled heap of bodies, with exclamations like -- "Yarooo, I say do get off you chaps!" He was regularly given "Six of the best" by Mr Squelch the Headmaster, but always contrived to come up trumps, aided by his chum, and defender, Bob Cherry. In preparation for my first term at Harper's College I read more of the Frank Richard stories which appeared in comics like "Wizard" and "Knockout" at this time in an effort to convince myself that I would soon be departing for a jolly adventure of my own.

In the second week of August 1952 we went on a family holiday to a boarding house in Ilfracombe in North Devon. We very rarely stayed at such places, preferring to lodge with my Mum's Uncle Bert's family in Bigbury on Sea or with a friend of Ethel Pentrechwyth on the Gower Peninsular in Wales, and I was intrigued by the formality of the place and the rather stilted conversations my Mum and Dad had with the other residents at meal times. Nevertheless, I enjoyed swimming at lovely places like Woolacombe Bay and Woody Bay.

There was a young boy about my age called Peter who I shared a bedroom with and we soon palled up. We found some bamboo bushes and cut lengths from the stem to make peashooters. We then filled our mouths with green elderberries and contrived to blow them with great ferocity through the hollow tubes we had made. There were two rather attractive girls, a little older than us, staying at the boarding house and we chased them around the garden and peppered them with our green buck shot! As the week went on we endeavoured to catch the eye of these girls at meal times and enjoyed more spirited chases following them into the shrubbery outside.

On the last day I went on a car trip to Lynton and the edge of edge of Dartmoor with my Mum and Dad. When we visited the Valley of the Rocks in the afternoon the sky when very black and my Mum said that she found the place very creepy and feared that something awful was going to happen. Suddenly, the sky opened and there was torrential rain. It was so heavy that water poured though the sunshine roof and the windscreen wipers of our Ford Eight were completely overwhelmed. We had the greatest difficulty finding our way back to Combe Martin. The storm increased in intensity, there were vivid flashes of forked lightening, and torrents of water surged down the road where we were staying. One by one bedraggled boarders struggled in with dire tales of floods and traffic chaos. Friday was the last day of our holiday and, after the evening meal it was agreed that, because the atrocious conditions, we should all have to make an early start. Peter and I were packed off to bed early and told not to read too late. On the way up to our bedroom we passed the two girls on the stairs giggling and looking secretive. We undressed and got into bed and listened to the rain drumming on the roof and cascading over the end of the guttering outside. We were too excited to go to sleep. Suddenly the door flew open and the two girls bounded into our room wearing black macs. They ran wildly around our room and jumped on to our beds. "Look" they screamed madly "We haven't got anything on under our pac-a-macs!" Peter and I were totally devastated we had no idea how to cope with the raw sensual energy of these lovely girls. Completely flummoxed we reached for our blow pipes and sprayed them with a grapeshot of green elderberries!

This, of course, was the year of the terrible Lynmouth flood where the river Lyn burst its banks and a great wall of water crashed through the little village, wrecking the harbour and sweeping, trees, cattle, cars, rocks and people into the raging sea. We had no car radio and were ignorant of the facts until we got home. The journey back was a nightmare and we had to make numerous detours to avoid blocked roads on our way out of Devon. On the long journey I had plenty of time to speculate about life in general, and what the next five years might hold for a rather gauche adolescent like me in a single sex boarding school.

Mike at school with his Mum, 1953

Chapter 4
A free spirit in a totalitarian institution

On our return from our eventful holiday in North Devon we found a
large brown envelop on the mat containing a prospectus from
Harpers College, together with information about school uniform,
and a long list of do's and don'ts for new boys starting their first
term. One feature, which supported the claim by the school to be
"Progressive," was the compulsory wearing of short trousers and

open necked shirts through to the age of 18. Daniel Neill's, the school outfitter, was based in London, and this required a visit for me to be fitted out in sombre beige uniform, including a cap and long woolly socks. The list also embraced expensive games kit for rugby and hockey – I seem to remember the shirts were green with black lateral stripes, making one look rather like an exotic bee. The kit for cricket was long white flannels and shirts – the open display of knobbly knees apparently deemed unsuitable for the posh cricket grounds of the other private schools in the West of England, where boys might be called upon to play. The long list of expensive items also included things like PT kit, a hockey stick and cricket bat, as well as a wooden tuck box and a large trunk reinforced by banded hoops. Small sundry items like vest and pants and even handkerchiefs (an inadequate supply in my case) were listed. The cost, on top of the first term's fees, must have come as quite a shock to my Mum and Dad, as was the required expensive train trip from Buxted to London to visit the outfitters, coming on top of a coach trip to the Festival of Britain and Battersea Funfair, we had taken a year earlier. Each item of clothing had to bear my name so that Matron could identify them for the school laundry and Granny Chubb was collected from her new flat in Brighton, opposite my Uncle Norm Auntie Gladys, to sew on the Cash's Name Tapes we were obliged to purchase.

Finally, the day of departure arrived. The Ford 8 was backed out of our garage and the luggage rack at the back was lowered before Dad and I carried out the new trunk -- heavy with the contents of what was to become the trappings of my new life. It was strapped in place and the wooden tuck box was somehow wedged in on the back seat together with a thermos flask of hot coffee, a box of sandwiches and welsh cakes, a primus stove, a can of paraffin, a bottle of methylated spirits (for priming the stove) together with a canister of tea, packet of sugar, and a screw top Lyle's pop bottle full of milk for picnics on the journey.

As I said good bye to our two domesticated cats, Kipp and Twinkle, and took a final wander of my favourite haunts in the house and garden, I felt the same cold stone of fear lodged deep in my chest, as I had experienced before, during my trips to the "Freedom School" in Forest Row. But this time, conscious of the great financial and emotional sacrifice my parents were making, I sought to hold back my tears and bit my lip. As I squeezed into the back seat of the car I tried to convince myself that that the new world I was about to enter would be devoid of the terrors outlined in Tom Brown's School Days. Instead of being roasted alive by bullies in front of a hot fire, I would welcomed by a Bob Cherry like character. There would be jolly dorm feasts, jovial pranks and hot buttered toast ……

The car started at the third attempt and with clouds of blue smoke belching from the heavily choked engine in the cold morning air. We meandered down the drive and joined the A272 heading past Pound Green Stores and the Conker tree surrounded by spiked railings at the top of Limes Lane and through Buxted towards Piltdown and Scaynes Hill. As we drove into Haywards Heath I caught a brief glimpse of Dinnages, a lovely toyshop which I sometimes visited before birthdays and Christmas. It was one of the few places in Sussex, apart from the Lanes in Brighton, to stock second hand supplies of Hornby trains and Meccano, in the period of austerity after the war, when much of the production of the Binns Road

Factory in Liverpool was concentrating on supplying overseas markets.

It was a bright day and the sun was just beginning to shine through the morning mist as we journeyed on through Cuckfield, Bolney, Cowfold and the lovely old village of Petworth, before making a diversion at Midhurst so that we could have our breakfast at Cowdray Park. The Park was surrounded by stables and stud farms and had a reputation for attracting the rich and the famous for Polo matches. But on this occasion it played humble host to Mum and Dad, and me, and one or two other family groups, as we sat on our wooden bench quaffing bacon sandwiches and sipping our milky tea. As I gazed at the swans gliding over the still lake, and the moorhens dipping in and out of the reeds, I had a feeling of time stopping, as if I was poised between one life and another. I knew that this was an illusion and that every mile we travelled through towns and villages, which were now growing increasingly unfamiliar, would bring me nearer and nearer to my destination. By lunch time, I calculated, we would be halfway there -- the tipping point would have been passed. Even if I feigned some mystery illness there would be less and less a case for turning back. The lump in my throat now froze my guts but I recognised that this was a rite of passage that I had to pass through and that, for good or ill, the next five years of incarceration in a boys' boarding school would determine my fate.

As we drove through Petersfield and Winchester I began to notice that the rolling down land, and small fields and intimate woods and streams of my childhood, were gradually being replaced by more open countryside with larger fields and moorland stretching as far as the horizon. By one o'clock we reached Salisbury and parked close to the cathedral for our lunch time picnic. While we sat in a walled garden eating our cheese and marmite sandwiches, and polishing off the last of Dad's home grown tomato's Mum, seeing my hangdog look, sought to reassure me. "It'll be half-term soon" she whispered "And then it will be Christmas. We'll dig your Christmas tree up as usual and have a big fire in the lounge..." As I turned towards her I could see she was on the point of tears and I realised that we were all making sacrifices of a kind. "You'll feed all the cats, not just Kipp and Twinkle" I said, thinking vaguely that they could act as surrogates for my enforced absence. Dad cleared his throat and drew me aside. "Look up" he said "The spire of Salisbury Cathedral – it's the tallest in England".

The last stage of our journey across Salisbury Plain seemed a very bleak contrast to the lush countryside of the Sussex Weald we had motored through in the morning. Acres and acres of grass seemed to stretch in all directions, and what few trees there were grew in small clumps, or were spaced at intervals along the roadside. Some areas were fenced off with barbed-wire with large KEEP OUT notices warning of firing ranges and MOD tank manoeuvres. We passed lots of military vehicles and slow moving tractors and carts and occasionally Neolithic burial mounds loomed out of the rising mist. Finally we saw a sign for Lavingham and the road turned downhill following the line of the Ridgeway towards the valley below. "We are almost there" announced my Dad "Let's stop for a last brew up" We drew into a lay-by and unloaded the primus stove and metal camping kettle and unrolled a plaid blanket. "Do you think it's worth it?" I questioned. "Of course it is!" exclaimed Dad." The thermos is dry and I'm not wasting money in some old tea shop". He squatted on all fours and poured paraffin through a hole into the base of the stove and, after applying the screw cap, he added methylated sprits to a metal tray under the burner at the top. He then struck a match but it was immediately blown out by the breeze. "Dam and blast it" he yelled "Pass me the windshield" I handed over a metal box which he turned on end. "This'll do it!" Finally a yellow flame licked itself around the base of burner and Dad pumped furiously to compress the paraffin so that it formed a gas which would be ignited by the flame at the head of the burner. Suddenly there was a bang and a hiss and the flame went out. "Quick!" yelled Dad "Hand me the Pricker" -- This was a patent metal handle with a pin at the end which he proceeded to use to unblock the burner. More meths, more furious pumping, and at last a blue flame like a gas jet was licking the underside of our metal kettle. "Halleluiah" said Dad.

Five minutes later we were sitting on the running board of the old Ford sipping our tea, eating Welsh cakes, and warming our fingers over the stove. Suddenly, there was the sound of tyres on the tarmac and a large Bentley drove past. The windows were down and I caught a glimpse of chequered scarves and Harpers College caps. The driver had a rubicund face and sported a check cap and his wife wore a fur coat. The boys in the back jeered and offered a two fingers salute. I discovered later that well to do parents would often arrive early so that they could book into the Bear Hotel in Devizes for an overnight stay and meal before decanting their sons at the school. Over the next five years it became a pattern that Mum and Dad would only book in for bed and breakfast at half-term, when boys were allowed out for two consecutive days, and that when they were simply delivering or collecting me they would economise by endeavouring to drive home the same day. This would not be the first time that we would be jeered at having our roadside picnic by the sons of rich Wiltshire Farmers or City Speculators, and the like, en route to the school. I admired my parents' stoic approach. The material sacrifices they were making made me determined somehow to succeed.

After saying our tearful goodbyes in the lay-by, we drove through , past the main school, and then turned right down a drive to the Junior House where I was to board for my first year. We were met by a reception party of Matrons and Masters suitably clothed in blue and white uniforms and black gowns for the occasion. Dad helped me carry my trunk upstairs to a large laundry room where all my clothes were sorted into piles by backstairs servants, and later we took my tuck box, containing more personal items, into a ground floor lobby. Looking rather sheepish and out of place, we joined a small group of parents and new boys hovering in the court yard waiting to be paired off with members of staff. The end, when it came, was quick and ruthless. Blubbing was deemed bad for morale. I noticed that some boys, who knew the drill from Prep School, formally shaking hands with their parents and even calling their fathers "Sir" as they bid their stilted farewells. Dad took his cue as we were introduced to an Assistant Housemaster called Mr Simon. "Goodbye old Chap." He said "Best of luck". Mum did her best to break the rules and gave my cheek a quick peck. The silly hat, she had bought for the occasion, partly obscured her face but I could see her shoulders shaking with emotion. Mr Simon quickly right-wheeled me to one side and marched me off to find my locker and receive instructions for the rest of the evening. I was glad we had said our real goodbyes earlier on the Ridgeway.

The evening meal in the Refectory reflected the hierarchical nature of the institution where ordinary residents like Under-Matrons and Staff Wives sat at the head of each table. While a high table was reserved for the Head of House and Senior Masters. By this time my "mufti" (the formal name for clothes worn at home in the holidays) had been removed and I was sitting on a wooden bench in my open neck shirt with a cold draught blowing up my short trousers. The minced meat was gristly, and reminded me of the thin gruel served up at Duds House, and I took some time to clear my plate. A boy on my left suddenly took objection to my eating style. "I say you chaps", he opined. "Strange holds his knife and fork all wrong! Looks like an ape." He proceeded to do an elaborate mime routine coupled with guttural or-rang-u-tang noises. Most of my immediate neighbours, anxious to appease the bully joined in: "Onk Onk they parroted, how strange, how strange!"

At the end of the meal the Housemaster J.M. Crough who I later learned had a Football Cap for playing for some important team, and had once appeared on Children's Hour, got up and formally welcomed us to the school. We were part of ancient tradition, he enthused, which went all the way back to Alderman Frederick Harper who founded a school for poor children in 1542. He then delivered grace in Latin "Bene Dictus Bene Di Cat", in a North Country accent. And we all trouped off to queue up for the next initiation ceremony, some of which was supervised by Prefects from the big school. As we progressed along the line we discovered that the mundane was mixed up with the intimate for everyone to hear. Pocket money had to be handed in to the school bank, C of E Confirmation classes had to be signed up to (a No in my case as a non-conformist) Medical information meant that you had to recall childhood illnesses and vaccinations, plus an "on the spot test" where you had to drop your trousers and a doctor held your balls and asked you to cough while matron recorded the results. We were then allocated a bed in one of the dormitories. At the end J.M. Crouch, who I discovered was nicknamed Cotch for some unaccountable reason, shook hands with each new boy in turn and outlined the schedule for the following day which was a Sunday. We would rise at 7.00 am and after breakfast walk in crocodile to the village church to attend a school service. We would then return to the Junior House to write our supervised letter home. After lunch we would go on a compulsory walk in threes. There then followed a period of free time (which would turn into a supervised study session as soon as we started classes). After this we would have an evening meal followed by a second church service held in the Junior House before bedtime.

Soon after I was dispatched, the bell rang and I learned that it was time to go to my dormitory. It dawned upon me that from now on my life in this institution would be increasingly be governed by bells, sets of complex rules, and lists of various kinds. It would also become more impersonal. I noticed that no one was referred to by their christen name. The cavernous dormitories, classrooms and common rooms meant that all personal space had become public space. As I mounted the stairs in search of my dormitory I was brutally reminded of this fact as the bully called after me: "There he goes Strange by name Strange by nature!" And a heap of yelling bodies descended upon me dragging me to the ground in the dark passage beyond.

After I found my bed and changed in to my pyjamas I discovered that we were allowed to read for a quarter of an hour before lights out. I quickly ran down stairs to retrieve an Eagle comic from my locker. As I lay in bed I hoped to shield my anonymity behind its large pages and eavesdropped in on the various conversations taking place. I was immediately shocked by the aggressive swearing which seemed to be the norm for the scorn reserved for any kind of deviant behaviour. The just of the overheard conversation went something like this:

"I say, Smithson, what are you looking at me like that for? Want me to be your bum-chum? You Montague!" (The name of a Lord in the 1950s cited by the News of the World for supposed homosexual behaviour) .

"Shut your trap Hawkings you Beaulieu" (The surname of the Lord accused of gross indecency at this time) Chorus from other boys "Beaulieu!" Beaulieu!", Beaulieu!"

"I say Sanderson where did you get them shag spots from?" Been knocking off some village tart? You filthy beast!" ......

Five minutes later Mr Simon popped his head around the corner to say goodnight and the lights were extinguished. As his footsteps receded down the corridor a lone voice rang out from the gloom: "Stop wanking Redgrave you fucking pervert!" Guilty giggles all round....

Next morning I was wakened from a fitful sleep by the bell and followed the other boys into an adjacent bathroom. The water in the showers was freezing cold and I succeeded in avoiding the preying eye of a Prefect, standing sentinel, and dunked my head briefly under a basin tap and quickly made for the door. I got dressed and put on a tie which I discovered we were required to wear on a Sunday. As I made my way towards the Refectory for breakfast I heard the bully calling my nick name again -- except that he had corrupted it to "Strangle!" "There he goes Strangle, Strangle!" The label stuck and helped blight my time at Harper's College.

After the meal, and a roll call, we assembled outside in the courtyard for our walk to the village church. It was a sunny day. The Junior House was a fine Tudor building with tall ornamental chimneys silhouetted against a blue sky. It stood on high ground fronted by ornamental gardens, and a coquet lawn, reserved for important members of staff and visiting dignitaries, behind a formal balustrade. Beyond this, the land sloped sharply away into a valley where a stream fed into an open air swimming pool. The ground then rose steeply and a well-trodden path led into the trees. At the end of the wood we joined the main road leading through the village of Lavingham and joined a flock of older boys from the main school. At this point it was near impossible for members of staff to control the flow of uniformed bodies. And I noticed that older boys from the First Fifteen Rugby Team draped their chequered scarves across each others' shoulders and, linking arms, walked assertively down the centre of the road. When they encountered local boys from the village they roared out a chant of "Oiks Oiks Oiks!" and elbowed them out of the way. I shuddered inwardly at this open display of arrogance and wondered how such boys would treat the likes of Tom or Carol Smith back home.

The Church service was reserved exclusively for the school. It was, of course Anglican and I noticed that there was much more emphasis on ritual than I had previously experienced from my infrequent visits to Congregational Chapels. It provided a good opportunity to display the ability of the school choir which, I had to admit, was quite impressive, although I couldn't help thinking that amongst the array of angelic cherubs singing treble, lurked my bully, and some of the wankers from my dormitory. The sermon, one of the many I was to experience over the next five years, lacked the reformist zeal and passion of the ones given by my Uncle Norm. At Harper's College the preacher usually stuck to well-worn themes designed to bolster the hierarchal, and patriotic traditions of the school, as a backdrop to hymns exhorting us to "fight the good fight with all our might".

After the service we walked back to the Junior House to have our lunch. When this was over we were dispatched to what was called the Prep Room to write our compulsory letter home. "COTCH" claimed that they were not censured, which I doubted. However, I am sure that over the years the ones I wrote were self-censured. Conscious of what my Mum and Dad had invested in my future I left out references to contentious issues like bullying and homosexuality. I concentrated, instead on complaining about the dreadful food – which had the unintended consequence of my Mum increasing the size of the tuck parcels she regularly sent me. I also complained about the rigours of compulsory games, at which I was a complete duffer, and the horrors of changing into PT kit in an unheated Gym on a frosty morning. I also played into Mum's interest in the Greyfriars Stories, featured in her old editions of Gem and Magnet, by inventing largely fictitious characters with a passing resemblance to Jones Minor and Billy Bunter.

There were exceptions to this rule. Near the end of one summer term, when I was in the Lower Sixth Form, I contracted a nasty bout of Whooping Cough. I was ill for quite a long time with chronic sickness and a retching cough which was very debilitating. I was confined to the sanatorium and isolated with a couple of other patients for fear that the infection would spread. When I passed the usual incubation period, and as I had already sat my end of year exams, I had nothing to keep me, and I was bored and depressed. I was told that I would be allowed home early if my parents agreed to collect me. I immediately wrote a rather sad letter home demanding that I be fetched, as soon as possible, and another even more desperate request a few days later. It was, of course, impossible for Dad to get time off from the Bank to collect me and I had to bide my time for a week or so. When they did eventually arrive to pick me up Dad, in particular, was rather cool with me, implying that I should have displayed rather more Public School grit.

On another occasion I wrote to Kim Martens, my first love, who I had last embraced inside a barrel and at dancing classes at Miss Punt's Dame School. Risking any punishment which might come from censorship, I threw caution to the winds, and instead of asking her to become my Pen Pal or join the Eagle Comic Club, I declared my undying love for her, suggesting that we might meet up in the holidays. Her letter must have been forwarded by her mother to her boarding school and ten day later I received a very prissy reply which must have been dictated by her headmistress, or a mother superior figure. The letter read: "Please don't write to me again. I found what you said very upsetting…."

After I had dispatched my first letter home I was paired off with two other boys for my first compulsory walk. I hadn't talked to them before but they seemed pleasant enough. We walked around the grounds of the Junior House and then explored the stream which flowed into the swimming pool before walking through the woods and around the village. I asked them why we had to walk in threes. They looked rather pityingly at me. "It's about buggery" said one. I still looked vacant. "You know" said the other "Montague Beaulieu, Bum Chums all that …." I must have still looked rather blank, and, even today, I wonder about the state of mind of those who compiled the complex rules which ordered our 1950's world designed to defend us against the sin of sodomy.

The next day, us new boys, had our first experience of lessons in the big school. And after breakfast, and a roll call, to check that nobody had absconded, we walked again through the valley and wood, which flanked the Junior House, to the village of Lavingham (nick-named Bogs by the boys) and then down a tree-lined drive, past the Headmaster's house to the main school. The entrance opened out into a large hall topped by a bell tower with a rope hanging down. One wall carried imposing looking teak frames bearing the names of famous old boys embellished in gold lettering. While another bore a large notice board displaying time-tables for various classes and numerous notices about games matches and practices. A flight of stairs curved upwards and connected to balcony leading to the upstairs, dormitories while, on the ground floor, various passages led off to the classrooms. On the right hand side, near the entrance, was a smaller room, which I later discovered was the Prefects Common Room.

My first impression was one of austerity. The walls of the passages were lined with brown tiles and the stone floor under my feet felt hard and unforgiving. The bell tower focused and amplified the sound of innumerable teenage boys as they jostled each other and hurried about their business. The ancient desks and wood panelling in the classrooms were heavily scarred with what looked like graffiti and ink stains which pock marked their surface and disfigured the walls. It was later explained to us, during a tour designed to initiate us into the mores of the school, that this was all part of tradition dating back to goodness knows when, which would, in some mysterious way, mould our character and instil the qualities of leadership for which Public School Boys were renowned.

We were then paired off into form groups, and I learnt that my indifferent performance in the Common Entrance Exam meant that I was consigned to the 'C 'Stream, which was mainly reserved for the non-academic sons of Wiltshire farmers. They were destined to inherit their fathers' estates and their period spent at the school, milking cows, castrating pigs, driving tractors, while learning the rudiments of numeracy and literacy was part of a rite of passage enabling them to join the country gentry. They might be shovelling shit now but they would graduate at the end of the Fifth Form as muck spreaders extraordinaire. The intangible laws of the public school spirit would enter their souls. A process of social osmosis would ensure that they left at 16 with a languid drawl, which replaced their rural accent --- and a deportment, honed by the school's Combined Cadet Force and extra periods of PT, defining them as leaders of men -- at least in the eyes the peasants back home. It was noticeable that this group of boys were among those most loyal to the Old Boy's Association; returning to speech days and sports days in their fathers' expensive cars. They would cheer in unison at the touchlines of rugby matches and in the front row of school plays with their chequered scarves ostentatiously draped over their tweed mufti suits.

During the five years I was at Harper's College I sensed that a transition was taking place. Although the school liked to trumpet its ancient connections, it was in fact a grant aided school, and accepted a number day boys on scholarships from the local community. Also, although it had developed as an agricultural college at the end of the 19th Century, and the Headmaster in 1952 was Mr R. M. Preston who had previously worked as a scientist at Rothhamsted Agricultural Institute, there were moves to distance the school from this tradition. This was reinforced in 1955 when Raymond Bassett, from Western College, took over as the Head and emphasised the Public School ethos by encouraging even more House competition by segregating pupils into different buildings. Under his leadership the links with local agriculture were down-played and he went out of his way to forge connections with other more prestigious public schools through membership of the private schools Headmasters Conference.

Although I took part in a tour of the farm buildings on the first teaching day I discovered that I formed another section of the 'C' Stream intake also considered to be non-academic. Such boys would be excluded from agricultural duties. Instead we would attend fewer Latin classes in favour of double periods of Woodwork. As the dreaded Mr Canning at Dud's Academy had destroyed any interest I might have in the classics, I enjoyed this arrangement. The Latin teacher for the third form, a Miss Trant, was almost the only female member of the teaching staff. She was a wiry grey haired spinster with a reputation for strict discipline. For some unaccountable reason, she was nick- named "Fanny T". In contrast Mr Fox, who lived in the village and spoke with a broad Wiltshire accent, was a good and patient teacher. Under his tutelage I learnt how to make dovetail joints, mix up disgusting smelling fish glue, and use a wood plane. He helped give me the confidence, in later life, to build a garage and pottery studio. He also ran the tuck shop which sold buns at break time. Unlike other members of staff, who were enveloped in their flapping black gowns, he always wore a brown overall. Some boys, conscious of his humble status within the institution, treated him with great disrespect yelling commands like "Gimme the glue Fox!" or grabbing their buns before being served. But he never lost his temper, quietly insisting that he should always be addressed as "Mr Fox".

The streaming system was pretty rigid and I don't recall being put in a higher set for subjects like English and History in which I had some potential to succeed. The boys accepted their C grade label with aplomb and were generally undisciplined and poorly behaved -- unless subject to rigid discipline. One poor maths teacher, nick named "Stinky", and reputed to have once been something of an egg-head in his own field, suffered terrible treatment. Paper pellets fired from elastic bands released from clenched teeth would fly in all directions, and bullies would flick ink over their victims without fear of retribution. Stinky was short-sighted, and under the pretence of taking their books to the front, to be marked, some of the bolder boys would use the opportunity to secure his gown to the desk with drawing pins. When he rose to complete a sum on the blackboard they would collapse in raucous mirth as he sought to tear himself free.

During my first year at Harper's College's life gradually settled into a routine. My existence completely orchestrated, with little free-time. Even the completion of home-work was supervised as "prep". Although I continued to get feverish colds, I discovered that admission to the sanatorium was strictly controlled, and you had to be almost at death's door with a high temperature to qualify. As a consequence, I often attended classes, and even played games, with a very thick head, clutching a bag of sodden bits of lavatory roll I had used in a vain attempt to stem the flow of snot streaming from my nose. On one occasion, I contracted sinusitis which gave me a terrible headache. Despite desperate entreaties to Nurse Prudence at the big school she refused to sign me off classes. The infection persisted for weeks and eventually the inside lining of my sinuses came out in long strips! In one way, forcing me to have a more stoic attitude towards illness did pay dividends, and I began to make some progress in my school work as my physical health improved. My emotional state was another matter. Like many new boys I was home- sick and I missed my Mum and Dad terribly. However, I hated the way that many of the boys conformed and kowtowed to bullies. People formed alliances and often picked on weaker kids for fear that if they didn't, they, in turn, would become the scapegoat. I don't know what possessed me, whether it was my congregational background, or the influence of my Mum's simple sense of fair play or Uncle Norm's Christian Socialism. But I refused to play the game. Maybe, in a naïve way, I was playing the role of Bob Cherry defending Jones Minor. The consequence, of course, was that the bullies turned on me. I had no defender. The ridiculous "no sneaking rule" meant that no one would split on the bullies, and masters, who should have done something, walked by on the other side. The isolation and victimisation eventually got to me and towards the end of my first year the stammer I had first experienced after I scalded my legs at the age of six, returned.

Not all was gloom and doom. In the second term I took a balsa aeroplane kit back to school. There was some space in some old stables, which lay at the back of the Junior House, and boys were allowed to make models and pursue hobbies in the short periods of free time afforded us. I made friends with Crisp (I never knew his Christian name but he was nick named "Cutie" because of his rather diminutive stature and slightly effeminate appearance). His real life outside the school defied this soubriquet. He lived on the Isle of White and regularly sailed his dingy across the Sound to the mainland. He was a strong swimmer and was crafting a fearsome looking spear gun out of aluminium. The shot was propelled by a thick rubber thong which had to be winched back under great pressure before being released by the trigger. I always gave Cutie a wide birth when he carried out his practice firings.

One evening some of the other boys dragged a big ladder across the stable floor and raised it to extend into a pigeon loft in the roof. The barn was opposite the Matron's quarters and it was rumoured that at bed time it was possible to witness extraordinary secrets as the portly lady shuffled out of her starchy uniform and donned a frilly negligee. One by one we climbed the ladder and excitedly groped in the gloom above until we could peer through a small grill across the court-yard to a window set in the eaves of the Junior House. A light flickered through the curtains and dim shadows could vaguely be discerned on the other side. It was like looking through a shaken kaleidoscope – except that the images projected upon our minds were mainly the products of our own fertile imaginations. Eventually one of the boys slipped in the dark and let out a cry as he struggled to hold on to the top of the ladder, and the light was immediately extinguished.

Later that night when we were assembled for the usual roll call Cotch suddenly appeared. The bonhomie, which he sometimes displayed on such occasions, and the jolly stories about how he won his football caps was cast aside. He was no longer an "Uncle Mac" figure of Children's Hour. He mounted the dais at the front of the classroom and leaned menacingly over the lectern. "I'll come straight to the point." He growled, "Matron's privacy has been violated by a band of evil minded dirty guttersnipes" His beady eyes glinted with venom and seemed to seek out every boy individually. Even boys who were not guilty flushed bright red and shuffled their feet.

He continued: "This is a very serious matter, so serious that the culprits may be RUSTICATED!" Somehow his hard vowelled Lancashire accent made expulsion sound like a capital offence. "We know who the wrongdoers are and your only hope of mitigating your punishment is to confess to me now! I shall be waiting in my study" At that he dramatically wheeled on his heel and left the room.

Later that evening, on the way to our dormitories, us guilty ones warily eyed each other up. We said nothing but we knew what we had to do. We did precisely nothing. We saw no point in turning Queen's Evidence against ourselves. This was the one occasion when the no sneaking rule worked in our favour. The matter of Matron's violation was never mentioned again.

The claustrophobic atmosphere of such a single sex institution invaded almost every aspect of our lives. Mr Simon, who was Cotch's second in command at the Junior House, on occasions would tour the dormitories at night. Sometime he would linger, and sit on one of the beds. Encouraged by some of the boys, who wished to defer the time for "Lights Out", and others who wanted to ingratiate themselves, he could be easily tempted into personal reminiscences. These were mainly about the war and his heroic role in various campaigns. The story lines had been well rehearsed and some boys instinctively waited for the punch line before admitting an awestruck intake of breath, or a guffaw of staged laughter. Something about the shared intimacy of these moments disturbed me. I think unconsciously I had him marked out as a Montague. I also questioned the veracity of some of his accounts.

One evening he caught me smiling in a rather detached way. Something snapped and his affable mood quickly evaporated. He suddenly pulled me out of bed and led me out of the room. "What's the matter with you Strange!" He yelled. He was shaking with rage "You're not one of us are you? Why don't you join in and play the game?"

When Mum and Dad took me out at half-term and in the holidays, life mainly returned to normal. However, it was almost as if my existence outside school was part of an alternative universe. I did my best to conceal my stammer by avoiding difficult words which began with a "B". And I abstained from talking about the dark side of the school's sub-culture -- consciously manufacturing a Bowdlerised account of Greyfriars type incidents to satisfy my Mum. Life went on much as before in Pound Green, and I continued to see a good deal of Ian, Camilla and Carol, and we played tennis together, as before, in the grounds of the landlord's estate, when the opportunity occurred. I still saw Tom but I was conscious of the fact that our lives were beginning to diverge. Nothing was said, but I became aware of the fact that certain Public School unconscious mannerisms were beginning to mark me out from some of my friends in the village.

Ian had been packed off to board at Tonbridge School, but we never discussed our school experiences in the holidays. We continued to fly our model aeroplanes together, and we had great fun with a large yellow ex-RAF box kite, a Christmas present from Uncle Norm -- which airmen, downed in the Channel, had used to attract the attention of rescuers. But time was moving on we were entering the uncertain world of adolescence. Ian was a year older than me and was attempting to coax the fluff on his chin into yellow stubble by shaving early. Camilla was a year older than Ian and her puppy fat was beginning to morph into attractive womanly curves. She had squeezed herself into some impossibly tight blue jeans and was mortified when I playfully smacked her bum to reveal the ghastly secret of the latex foundation beneath. Our games were becoming more dangerous. Ian had acquired an airgun and we fired it out of the upstairs window of his house in Spotted Cow Lane at some tin cans we had arranged on the top of the concrete air-raid shelter in his garden. One day Ian aimed too high and the stray pellet elicited a scream of righteous anger and threats of retribution from Sam the Gardener. Our archery became more refined -- with arrows enhanced with metal tips and chicken feathers used for flights. Customers walking to Ford's Farm to collect their milk must have been somewhat disconcerted to see our quivers reigning down at the end of my garden.

On one occasion Ian produced a spent 303 brass cartridge case and we proceeded to carry out an "experiment" which involved scraping the phosphorous off a box of matches and stuffing it into the hollow tube. We then mounted the cartridge in a hole bored in a piece of wood projecting upwards with a pencil stuffed in the end. Finally we applied a lighted candle to the other end and retired behind a bush to witness the historic launching of our "moon rocket". We waited for what seemed like ages and had almost given up hope when there was a loud bang and the deadly pencil whizzed dangerously close to our hiding place.

We loved lighting fires and cooking outside. On one occasion we discovered a wasp nest in the clay bank between my house and Ford's farm. We convinced ourselves that it would be our public duty to destroy the nest. Ian, also, against all the biological evidence, believed that somewhere deep in the nest we would discover honey combs dripping with nectar. We decided to smoke the wasps out and tied strips of cloth dipped in paraffin to the end of our arrows. We then ignited our missiles in a bomb-fire before firing them in the direction of the nest. At first all went well and we were surprised that there was no reaction. "The smoke must have drugged them". Ian shouted excitedly as he rushed forward to claim his 'honey'. Suddenly, as if to a preordained command a great crowd of wasps flew out of the nest and swarmed all over us. We both ran in panic to the back door of my house frantically tearing at our clothes in an effort to beat them away. We were stung all over and my Mum, who must have got used to dramas over the years, ran a cold bath for us and put in a "blue bag," she used for washing clothes, which, she confidently informed us, would neutralise the "acid" of the stings. Our bodies felt as if they were on fire and the cold water and the calamine lotion, which she later applied, did little to relieve our pain. "You are very silly boys" Mum scolded. "I hope this time you will learn your lesson!" In our agony we would have promised almost anything. "We will!" "We will!" we chorused.

In September 1953 I moved to live at the big school. The Harper's College prospectus made much of the "caring atmosphere" provided at the Junior House but I had few regrets at leaving Cotch's tender care until I discovered that I was one of the boys to be billeted at the Headmaster's house. The roof area had been converted into a large dormitory which housed thirty or so boys. The floors were bare and there was no heating of any kind. Requests for more blankets were mostly declined by the Headmaster's wife and we spent most of the winter months sleeping in extra games clothes and, even over-coats, we had smuggled in, in an effort to fight off the cold. In the morning the queue of shivering bodies waiting to use the rudimentary washing facilities wouldn't have looked out of place in Stalag 3.

I was determined to do as well as I could in Form 4C, and despite my terrible spelling I did start to make progress in science subjects and the humanities. I enjoyed the physics classes held by the Deputy Head Mr Redmain who made the sessions interesting with dramatic experiments to demonstrate atmospheric pressure and the effect of light waves passing through prisms. He was a very humanitarian man and gave civics lessons where he tried to question the predominately conservative view of the world held by many of the boys. I can remember standing as the Labour Candidate in a Mock Election and receiving 4 votes out of 300. This further confirmed my status as an outsider. I was not only a demented ape. "Strangle" was a Commie to-boot!

Apart from its commitment to short trousers and open neck shirts, the school boosted its "progressive image" by outlawing fagging – the demeaning system which many Public Schools deployed at this time -- to require younger pupils to undertake regular chores for senior boys -- which created a pecking order, reinforcing attitudes of patronage and deference. However, at Harper's College, prefects could still exact favours from younger boys, by way of a punishment for minor transgressions, like running in the corridor, or talking after lights out -- requiring them to polish their shoes or buy a bun for them from the Tuck Shop. Senior prefects were still allowed to beat younger boys for more serious offences, as I soon discovered.

During an evening prep session Stoneman, a large boy, who had a reputation as a bit of a bully, pleasured himself by jabbing the sharp point of a compass into my bottom from the desk behind. After numerous violations of my person I turned round and snarled "Do that again and I'll bash you!" Stoneman rose to the challenge and sunk the point even further into my buttocks just as the bell, marking the end of the homework session sounded. I hit him, as promised, and he responded. Suddenly the desks were pulled apart and the rest of the boys -- excited by the prospect of blood being drawn-- encircled us yelling "Fight, Fight, Fight!" In the first round Stoneman flailed his arms like a prize fighter and -- spurred on by the frenetic cries of his supporters -- landed some good punches. But in the second, blind panic took over and I felt I was fighting for my life. In the ensuing melee his specs fell off and suddenly my punches started to find their mark and I felt him reel back under the sheer volume of my blows. No one thought of calling time and the fight continued for a considerable time until a master, walking past in the corridor, screamed at us to desist. The next morning Stoneman was nowhere to be found and rumours spread that he was hospitalised in the Sanatorium. Retribution soon followed and I was summoned to the Head Prefect's room where he read me the riot act and administered "six of the best". Poor Stoneman emerged from the San a couple of days later his face was puffed up and one eye was surrounded by a greenish yellow bruise. I was mortified at seeing the evidence of my own brutality but I also realised that in this hostile environment, I wasn't going to survive by always following Queensberry Rules. Some of Stoneman's gang deserted him and started to follow me around hoping to curry favour with the new victor. But I, rather pompously, rejected their advances claiming, as I believed Bob Cherry would have done, that I didn't want "fair-weather friends". My hero's status was short lived and by the end of the week "Strangle" was being chased down dark corridors and de- bagged in the latrines. Stoneman, however, kept his compass folded and never laid a finger on me again.

As time went on I began to realise the school operated on two levels. There was the "ideal view" of the institution as represented in the prospectus and when the school was "on parade" at parents' Days and Speech Day's – a happy band of brothers in short trousers watched over by benevolent Masters -- boys competing at games and scholarly pursuits, serving God, the Queen – destined to be the future leaders of the Nation. And then there was the "behind the stage" version of events: Petty bullying, lonely outsiders, conformity, class prejudice and snobbery, ignorance of sex and an ever present fear of homosexuality and paedophilia. Inside the "Total Institution" we often felt we were in a cultural bubble. Like prisoners in jail we had to serve our time, but we were conscious that there was a world outside – a personal world of family and friends; that was moving on and from which we felt increasingly alienated. Love for many of us was reduced to an academic exercise – points to be remembered for an analysis of Romeo and Juliet or a romantic sonnet by Keats. In some cases boys, starved of female love and affection, would produce pictures of their younger sisters and pass them off as their girlfriends. Or invent tall stories about passionate liaisons with "Tarts" they picked up in the holidays.

During free periods I spent as much time in the Library and the adjoining Boys' Common Room as possible. This second room was fitted out with a large snooker table and also provided a wide choice of newspapers and periodicals providing us with a window on the outside world. It was also a good place to observe the behaviour of other boys in a place that was more relaxed than the rest of the institution. In my first term at big school, I was surprised to see younger boys with nick names like "Jackie" ("Cutie" was not involved) with freshly combed hair, sitting on the benches close to the snooker table openly ogling the older boys as they leaned over to strike the balls. These boys would respond in kind by giving the juniors long lingering glances as they elaborately chalked up the end of their cues and acknowledged the cries of support from their favoured boy, if they made a telling shot. Such behaviour was referred to as having a "pash" on another boy. It must have occurred in all Public Schools at this time, as indeed, it still pervades the Catholic Church today, and must be rife in the alienating environment of Prisons and all Single Sex Institutions. The teaching staff must have been aware of the problem and recruited Dr Matthews, a Consultant Psychiatrist, to give a whole day of sex lectures to forth formers. The initiative was well meant and the classes were very popular. However, although he criticised Baden Powell's dismissal of masturbation as "beastliness," he still talked vaguely of "wasted seed" and urged abstinence. His graphic slides of the vagina and details of intercourse were presented in a rather matter of fact way, but in general we learned nothing that we didn't already know-- to which the well-thumbed edition of Grays Anatomy in the Library, gave testimony. In such a closed environment, it was hoped that the excess of such adolescent cravings could be channelled into competitive games. However, it was rumoured that Matron, no doubt alerted by high laundry bill for stained sheets, had initiated more direct action, and ordered that bromide be applied to the late night drinks served at the evening meal.

The school timetable was fairly rigid -- with classes in the morning, and sport in the afternoon, followed by evening preparation. Soccer was thought to be too common for the Public School curriculum, and I soon discovered that I had no natural facility for Rugby which I considered to be a barbarous game. I fared little better at Hockey in the Spring Term, and in the Summer my facility for Cricket was such that I was often reluctantly drafted in as "Twelfth Man," which meant that I had to undertake all the boring chores of fielding, while having to run between wickets in support of an injured opening batsman -- thus being denied the chance to bat myself! Interest in sport was all embracing, and I was dismayed to discover that, even over the weekends, we were expected to turn out to cheer the school teams, along with some Masters and Matrons, whatever the weather.

PT sessions were conducted by Major Bigmore. I think he must have been an ex-NCO recruited from the regular army, but the pecking order of the school meant that he was given an honorary title, to distinguish him from the likes of Mr Fox. I quite enjoyed PT and liked doing upward circles and exercises on the parallel bars in the gym. My early experience competing in the "Olympic Games" sessions at Ford's Farm, with my friends at home, held me in good stead and I liked running and jumping. On one occasion I can remember practicing for a cross country race for an Inter House competition. The route was long and tough and took us over some rough terrain on the Ridgeway. On the way back a group of us decided to take a short cut and we were some of the first runners over the finishing line. As a consequence, we were picked for our house teams. On the day of the real race we discovered the route was to be closely policed by members of staff and boys in the Signals Division of the School Corps, monitoring our progress on Walkie-Talkies. We had under taken little training and the extra miles drained our energy away. I dimly remember us "favourites to win" struggling down the home straight coughing and wheezing – the last stragglers to stagger across the line.

Success at school was often measured in terms of prowess on the games field, leadership in the Combined Cadet Force (CCF), and academic ability leading to entry to ancient universities. Those who felt short of these goals -- myself included, were more likely to become outsiders in the institution. The same fate befell those who shunned the informal norms of the school. Pelham, for example was very good at art, but even worse at games than me, was labelled a "poofter"-- even by some of the boys who indulged in the daily romantic rituals in the Common Room. State Scholars, who attended as day boys from the local community, and gave the school its grant aided status, were often viewed as "persona non-grata" ,despite the fact that the school made much of its ancient heritage as a charitable institution founded for poor boys in the 19th Century. Other rather sad deviants --included "Hogo" Hunt, from Australia, who, I discovered when I visited Devizes with him, was a serial kleptomaniac. I was shocked to see that that he had stitched extra large pockets into his grey mac and specialised in looting a large number of books from W.H.Smith's for which he appeared to have no use at all. And a rather sad boy, nick named Psycho who spent a good deal of his time researching the various mental maladies he assumed he suffered from -- some of which were probably induced by the oppression of the institution itself.

There were, of course, exceptions to the rule, and Buja from Africa -- and as far as I can remember, the only black boy in the whole school -- was seen as an "official untouchable" and treated as a mascot by the boys and the teaching establishment alike.

Although there was some good teaching in subjects like History, English and General Science, I failed to make any progress in the chaotic Maths classes, conducted by Stinker and fared no better in Fanny T's Latin class. Although I struggled to make sense of the exercises in the Kennedy Latin primer I failed to see how laboured sentences like – "Having raped the Sabine Women, the Roman soldiers returned for tea." -- was supposed to improve my English expression. Some teaching was quite bizarre -- Cotch taught geography and conducted weekly tests which depended entirely on rote learning. Generations of boys knew that he kept two books in his desk which was never locked. One would include the questions written in blue and the other would record the answers written in red. He knew full well that as soon as the class finished we would crib the questions and learn the answers for the test to be given at the next class. "What are the main spinning towns in the North of England?" He would ask. And we would all parrot -- "Bingley Batley, Clackheaton, Leaton " I can never remember any explanations or lessons in social geography – just a recitation of facts and more facts... My 'C' Stream association with the farming group entailed occasional encounters with raw reality of nature. On a biological field trip to the piggery, the class was confronted by a dead piglet which was still warm. The teacher suddenly handed me a scalpel. "Reveal the rib cage for us Strange!" He commanded --whereupon, I felt sick, and fell down in a dead faint.

Other teaching was more enlightened and I enjoyed the English classes conducted by a very liberal teacher called Mr Platt. Although my work regularly came back to me covered all over with red ink correcting my abominable spelling, he recognised that I had some talent for free writing and included some of my pieces in the School Magazine which he edited. He also encouraged me to enter for the annual school Essay Writing Competition in which I did well. In addition, he conducted classes in Public Speaking. I chose to talk about Astronomy and I can remember him looking kindly upon me as he asked me to speak, fearing that he would have to come to my aid because of my debilitating stutter. I found however, to my surprise that in a set piece performance where I felt in control I could speak fluently and talked at length about the Solar System, Inter-stellar gas, Galaxies and Fred Hoyle and theories of the expanding universe. The articles in Dad's old Children's Magazines read to me as a child had served me well. I fared less well in French where I found the teaching more authoritarian. My progress was also inhibited because my poor short-term memory meant that I had great difficulty building up a reasonable vocabulary.

Even in the big school the weekends remained tightly scheduled with organised support for school teams competing in matches on Saturday afternoons, long religious services in the village church on Sunday morning, with a second service in the Founders Hall in school in the evening -- sometimes followed by a formal concert. Letters home, and compulsory walks in threes, remained a set part of the routine. Saturday evenings, however, were designed to be rather more relaxed where a film would normally be projected by one of the senior boys. Some classic movies like "Kind hearts and Coronets" were shown, but most featured tales of war-time heroism like "The Cruel Sea", "Cockle Shell Heroes" "The Dam Busters" and "The Douglas Bader Story". The films were generally popular and exciting eliciting cheers from the boys. But, taken together with patriotic sermons delivered on Sunday -- exhorting us make sacrifices and fight the good fight, and the marching of the School Corps on Friday afternoons, the "hidden curriculum" mysteriously known as the "Public School Sprit" was quietly reinforced. On the edge of the main playing field stood the Garden of Remembrance recording the names of old boys who had fallen in both world wars -- some barely out of their short trousers.

It was assumed that all boys would join the CCF. A tiny number of exemptions were granted on religious grounds but Mum and Dad, who disliked militarism, nevertheless felt that the family's allegiance to the Congregational Church and Uncle Norm's support of Christian Socialism, and the Kellogg Peace Pact, provided insufficient evidence for my exclusion. The brave war-time service of my Dad and Uncle Les also counted against me being regarded as a conscientious objector. In my second year at the big school I, therefore, found myself being measured for kaki uniform and fitted out with army boots, belt and gaiters, and given a rifle. Every Thursday evening we had to assemble in the Corps Hut to laboriously polish our brasses, clean our guns, shine our boots, and blanco our belts and gaiters. Some boys would be terrified of being "balled out" for dirty uniform at the parade held on Friday afternoons and would feverishly rub their brasses and spit and polish their boots until they gleamed. Despite humiliating punishments -- like having to scrub the corps floor with a toothbrush-- administered by masters dresses up as officers and older boys with sergeant's stripes on their tunics -- the best kit often went missing, leaving some boys desperately hunting for leftovers minutes before we lined up for inspection.

The School Corps was divided into two sections – the Army Cadets and the Air force Cadets. The latter regarded themselves as superior to the rest of us. They appeared to do less "Square Bashing" and did more interesting things like training in navigation, servicing old aeroplanes and going on occasional flights. The Army Cadets, to which I was assigned, spent almost all the time marching and drilling in preparation for the first year "Cert 'A'Part One" qualification, which seemed to be judged almost entirely on our ability to march in step, manoeuvring our rifles by "sloping arms" and coming to attention on parade. We also undertook some rudimentary fire arms training using live ammunition. Most memorable, was an attempt to re-in-act the horrors of an infantry attack -- requiring us to charge, screaming like lunatics, with fixed baronets at a sack full of saw-dust suspended from a post -- representing the dreaded Hun.

Although I was naturally clumsy, with two left feet, I managed eventually to march in a straight line with my shoulders squared back. Gaining a certificate was all about deference and blind obedience, and, in my first year of school soldiering, I duly obliged and passed the exam.

A year later it was a different story. Studying for Cert 'A' Part Two assumed that candidates were "officer material" We were encouraged to give orders to younger recruits and master map reading, and, using army jargon, work out plans for attack such as: "Three O'clock, Bushy Tops, Rapid Fire!" We had to undertake manoeuvres on army land bordering the Ridgeway pulling firing pins from imitation grenades -- shooting dummy rounds and charging through smoke screens. It all began to seem very realistic and I hated giving pretend orders to other boys knowing that in real life I might be sending them off to their certain death. Finally, the day of the examination arrived and we were quizzed by regular army colonel from the local Wiltshire Regiment. The test required that we had read Queens Regulations for Officers which had seemed not to have changed from the First World War. Like Cotch's geography classes we were expected to rote learn the questions and parrot out the answers. When I entered the room the Colonel gave me a mirthless stare, fingered his ginger moustache, and began:

"You are in no-man's land leading your men in "V" Formation. You come under enemy fire. What do you do?"

"Jump in a shell hole Sir!"

"Good, Good. You want to where the enemy fire is coming from. What do you do?"

I knew the standard answer was that I would ask Private Snooks to stand up. He would get shot through the head and I would know the direction of the fire. I could not in all conscience give such an appalling answer and needlessly sacrifice the life of one of my men. Instead I said:

"I would ask private Snooks to put his helmet on top of his rifle and raise it in the air. In this way I would determine the line of fire." The rotund face of Colonel suddenly flushed pink with rage.

"But it's not in Queen's Regulations!" he blurted out. He scribbled a big cross on the pad, in front of him, and regained his composure.

"You lead your men forward" He continued, "And you reach barbed wire entanglements near the enemy lines. What do you do?"

The answer he expected me to parrot out was that I would command private Snooks to lie on the barbed wire. He would get shot to smithereens I would then use his body as a vaulting horse to get over wire to baronet the enemy in their trenches. Instead I said:

"I would have had the foresight to carry over old pillows which I would lay on the barbed wire before crossing the defences and attacking the enemy".

The stout party in front of me let out a strangulated cry before screaming that my answer was not in Queens Regulations. I was failed on the spot and the interview came to an abrupt end.

News of my stubborn defiance soon got around. The two French Master who headed up the School Corps and assumed the aliases of Captain McMaster and Captain Grove on Friday afternoons ruled that I was "Not officer material" and I was doomed to spend the rest of my time in the CCF marching around and obeying the orders of younger boys who had risen through the ranks despite the fact that I had just scraped into the Sixth Form with four basic 'O' Levels and was studying 'A' Levels in History, Economics and Public Affairs and English Literature. The School Corps had a habit of promoting rather dull conformists and a very large boy called Chester, who was good at Rugby, became Sergeant Major. He marched around with a large red sash across his middle bellowing orders. On occasions he even attempted the crude repartee he had observed form the regular NCO's from the Wiltshire Regiment who visited the School to undertake training sessions. He would pick on some unfortunate marching out of step. "You are an imbecile Perkins!" What are you?" "An imbecile Sergeant Major!" He was eventually promoted to the position of Head Boy and was allowed to deliver little pompous homilies at the end of term extolling the virtues of Public School grit.

One day a rather inexperienced Corporal came to give us a tutorial on the Bren Gun. It was a very hot sunny day and we sat around in a circle on the grass outside the Memorial Garden listening to him drone on. When he got on to talking about the "return spring rod" I was reminded of the famous poem by Henry Reed called "Naming of Parts" about war-time Bren Gun instruction in a beautiful garden full of bees and Japonica trees set against the cruelty of war. I must have drifted off for a second and when I came to I was staring into the face of the Corporal who was angry at my inattention.

"This 'err Bren" He shouted, in an effort to get attention, "Can hit a fly at a thousand yards!"

For some un-accountable reason, I started laughing, and some of the other boys joined me. To this day I feel guilty at my bad behaviour since the Corporal was on alien territory and uneasy about being confronted by such an arrogant bunch of gauche teenagers.

"The point is" I persisted "Is that the Bren is a machine gun. It scatters bullets all over the place! It's not a precision weapon!"

As luck would have it, Captain Grove (who liked to be known as Jock Grove and spoke with a fake American accent) was passing by and over-heard the encounter. He waded into our midst and pointed his swagger stick directly at me.

"Right!" he yelled "You are all on a charge! You will run around the whole of the games area with your rifles above your heads!"

We did as commanded, but when we got half way round the complex of pitches that comprised the playing fields, we found our rifles felt extremely heavy. We were running in full kit with packs on our backs and the sweat was pouring off us. When we finally reached the starting point we were exhausted and dropped our rifles to one side and sank to the ground. Captain Grove now joined by Captain McMaster witnessed the incident and ordered us to run round the whole course again. Whereupon, I refused saying that the order was unreasonable. Astounded by such insubordination Captain Grove retorted that we were now on going to be "Court Martialled" and that the Commanding Officer would decide our fate. We were told to start running on the spot and then frog marched to the Corps Hut to be met by a grim faced Captain McMaster. I can't remember what punishment befell the others. But I held my ground saying that I wanted to resign from the School Corps. I was harangued and threatened for the rest of the afternoon. But I refused to budge. I rang up my Mum and Dad in the evening and explained the situation to them. They supported me and Mum said she never wanted me to be "in the silly old Corps anyway."

Eventually the mood of the authorities switched to one of moral persuasion. I had a special interview with the Headmaster who appealed to my conscience. "Surely" He said "You must feel guilty at the bad example you are setting to younger boys?" I still held my ground and eventually it was agreed that I was to spend the Friday afternoons, usually reserved for CCF activities, in the School Library. Instead of being tongue-lashed by Sergeant Major Chester, I would study for Scholarship level History and also sit a General Paper and 'S' Level Use of English Paper. My joy knew no bounds.

In my third year at Harper's College I moved into a dormitory in the big school. The boy in the next bed to me, called John Bussell, was initially quite friendly. However, my "Strangle" label and reputation for being a bit of an outsider preceded me, and he launched into a bulling routine -- starting with low level teasing like making me an "apple pie bed" and putting itching powder between the sheets. Emboldened by his initial success, and the support of others, he started to compose little ditties about me such as --"Strangle is a clumsy ape! ... Strangle is a commie! --Strangle is a pansy!" His derogatory cat calls would sometimes continue long into the night after lights out, often with the chorus of "Strangle, Strangle Strangle!" sung by his mates. One evening he produced a gigantic water pistol, he must have procured over the half-term weekend. The gun was designed to allow the attachment of separate water canisters to allow a continuous supply of ammunition. He then proceeded to squirt me for most of the night. His final act of juvenile sadism was to remove most of my bed springs so that the whole mattress crashed through to the floor as soon as I sat on it. The "no sneaking rule" allowed him to escape Scott Free while I was punished for the poor state of my bed and the sopping sheets. I tried to develop a kind of Buddha mind set, in an attempt cut off from this nightly assault. But the truth was that my mental carapace was wearing quite thin by the end of term, and I was very glad when the holidays arrived. Imagine my surprise, when on the second day at home the phone rang. Dad took the call and then called me to his side. "It's Colonel Bussell on the phone." He said. "Apparently you're great friends with his boy and they have invited you to stay for the weekend." I started to protest but to no avail. Dad continued -- he seemed to have a weakness for old colonels honed over the years in the Bank dealing with their investments --"That's very kind of you Colonel Bussell I'll bring him over in time for Saturday lunch". Mum also approved -- "Isn't it nice you have a special friend at school". She murmured

During my stay John Bussell put on a good act of being my "best friend", even inventing a purely fictional narrative of jolly japes at school with him playing the role of "Bob Cherry". He actually seemed pleased to see me and I felt he must have missed his term time role as my "Tormentor in Chief". He was careful not to lay a finger on me at bed-time. But the next day he revealed more of his true colours and produced a 0.22 rifle, which I assume had been given to him by his father. "Let's go hunting ". He announced. We wandered around his family's estate looking for prey. Suddenly we saw a beautiful Robin perched on a tree. Without a word my Tormentor bent down on one knee and took aim. There was a bang and the robin fell lifeless to the ground.

When I returned home I found Mum and Dad looking very worried. They had just had an official letter from Mr Hammersley's solicitors giving us notice to quit. Farmer Ford was retiring and our landlord wanted to give our house to the new Farm Manager who would take over. This was a big deal for all of us. Despite the problem with rising damp, Mum and Dad loved our house and ramshackle garden and the close friendships they had built up in Pound Green. Mum was adamant that she would never move to a town. And Dad hated change and had even regarded a temporary secondment to the Haywards Heath Branch of Lloyds Bank, seen at the time by Mum as a career enhancing experience, as a step too far. I felt also that the whole of my childhood -- from the laurel tree next to the outside lavatory, which my Granny used to climb -- to the pig sty where Carol Smith and I had played our secret games -- to the nut trees in the bottom corned of the orchard where Ian and I had first cut wood for our bows and arrows – was dematerialising before my eyes.

Although Dad was in his late 50's and felt he might be able to commute part of his Bank pension in order to take out a mortgage late in life, I felt guilty that the expensive school fees my parents had to pay for my education, made things even more difficult for them. At the end of the holiday I returned to school with a heavy heart, conscious of the fact that I had no control whatsoever over events which happened outside the institution.

I was now a member of the Sixth Form, and was given a room, which I shared with five other boys, where I could store my books and use for private study. I got on reasonably well with my companions but, like most dyslexics, I found it difficult to concentrate on my studies when they chatted or tuned into Radio Caroline on their portable radios. As a consequence I spent most of my free time in the Library and, when that was closed, even retreated to a lavatory cubical to get a bit of peace and quiet for reading or revision.

I found studying 'A' Level much more rewarding than 'O' Level, and I particularly enjoyed writing essays and arguing different view-points. I was pleased with my choice of subjects, but looking back I appreciate that my 'A' Level selection was partly determined by my inability in other academic areas. I was no good at foreign languages, and my poor showing in maths, limited my ability to study the sciences at an advanced level. I was lucky that the "straight jacket" of School Matriculation had been phased out and that the 'O' Level and 'A' Level exams allowed me to be judged on my performance in individual subjects. I was also fortunate that the School had recently introduced the Economics and Public Affairs 'A' Level which Mr Hay, who also taught English History, was teaching for the first time. He was a very encouraging and hardworking teacher, who only thinly disguised his support for the Labour party. His teaching style contrasted well with his colleague, nick named "Bogs Brush," because of a fulsome moustache matching that description, who often came late, and proceeded to dictate notes straight from a book on Edward's History Notes -- often without any following explanation. I really enjoyed Mr Platt's classes in English Literature and got stuck in to reading Chaucer, Spencer and Milton (Granny Strange would have been pleased that I had finally succumbed to reading Paradise Lost!), Five Shakespeare Plays, I think Mr Platt squeezed in two more than the syllabus required, and a variety of "Romantic Revival" poets like Wordsworth, Keats and Byron. Mr Platt made me one of the Editors of the School Magazine and I continued to win prizes in the School Essay Competition, after enlisting the help of a friend to straighten out my spelling.

Boys in the Sixth Form were assigned to a tutorial group which met periodically in different masters' houses. I was lucky enough to be in Mr Gates' group. He was a caring teacher who taught maths and I enjoyed visiting him and his wife in their house in the village outside the school. I believe she had also been a teacher before starting a young family, and enjoyed the warm maternal atmosphere of their home which starkly contrasted with the routine of school life. The couple showed great empathy for me as a rather troubled sprit and I sensed that they quietly agreed with some of my anti-establishment views.

The role of the tutorial sessions was partly to get boys to consider options for their futures. When I said that I might be interested in studying English Literature at University they suggested that entry to such a course would not be possible without at least 'O' Level Latin. Although, privately, I considered this a hurdle too high for me to climb; I talked this proposal over with Mum and Dad when I saw them at the end of term. I am sure they also had reservations, as Dad had already spent frustrating hours in the holidays trying to prepare me for a re-take in 'O' Level French using notes from an old Pelman correspondence course he had studied in his younger days. However, they said they would talk it over with teachers at the forthcoming Parents' Day.

Most boys found these occasions rather painful, since we expected to "market" good aspects of the school, and parade them around various exhibitions arranged to highlight the school's progress. We were also urged to clap dutifully in support the Old Boy's cricket match. And some boys would be worried in case their parents would over play their part as they clustered near the pavilion loudly braying out encouragements like "Jolly well played sir!" Even boys of parents with impeccable middle class qualifications feared that their Mums and Dads would commit some fearful violation of school etiquette, like eating an apple in public or showing a slip! Incredible as it may seem, we were fearful of the bullies, always on parade --like the Stazi – ready to use the slightest indiscretions of our parents as future labels to humiliate us. I usually worried that my Mum and Dad would be ostracised by some of the well healed gentry assembled. But they generally gave a good account of themselves – Dad well turned out with his plumb coloured waistcoat and Mum with a floral hat and lilting Welsh accent.

The climax of the day was the prizes and speeches held in a large marquee. Mum and Dad were pleased that I received a prize for my hard-work in the 'C' stream and, against the odds, ascending to the Lower Sixth. It was indeed a miracle, and they must have been relieved that all the sacrifices they had made were finally bearing fruit. After the main address given by an Old Boy who had risen to the rank of General, extolling us to work hard "to survive the battlefield of life!" Followed by a pep talk by the Headmaster and a "Ra Ra" homily from Chester, Dad talked to my Housemaster and, it was agreed, that I would be given extra Latin tuition by Mr Morrison.

At the beginning of the following term I went to his room, as arranged, to find a note pinned to the door asking me to wait for him. Five minutes later he entered in full games kit, fresh from refereeing a rugby match. We went through some exercises together and finished with a friendly chat about my interests. He knew I was studying English and kindly lent me a copy of Aldous Huxley's Brave New World which he said I would find interesting. At my second tutorial he corrected my homework, we had a short discussion about Aldous Huxley and we continued with some more Latin exercises. Mr Morrison was wearing his games kit, as before, and halfway through the lesson I became aware of his leg rubbing up against mine. I moved it out way but a minute later Mr Morrison's knee was rubbing the inside of my groin. I sat it out for the rest of the tutorial but there could be no mistake. An inner voice was whispering to me "Montague"! I liked Mr Morrison but I was worried where further recitation of "Amo, amass, amant …" might lead.

That evening I rang my Mum and Dad to say that the Latin tuition wasn't working out. The "no sneaking rule" forbade me for giving the reason why. A few weeks later Mr Morrison must tried it on with another boy who did squeal and a huge moral panic ensued. There was an emergency assembly in the Franklin Hall with the Headmaster Mr R.M Preston glaring over the lectern-- "Mr Morrison has left the school under cover of darkness never to darken the portals of the school again!" You could have heard a pin drop. No explanation was forthcoming. No one mentioned the word paedophile. I felt sorry for Mr Morrison, apart from the "footsie" incident, he had treated me in a civil way. I had a vision of him bundling a few personal belongings into a suitcase in the dead of night and leaving his miserable attic room at the top of the school and driving away in his Austin Seven— a lonely man facing a very uncertain future.

In 1955 Raymond Basset took over as Headmaster. He made much of his background at Western College and immediately set about trying to import similar traditions to Harper's College House spirit was to be encouraged by separating boys from different Houses into distinct areas of the school to encourage group loyalty and competition. The school was to isolate itself even more from the surrounding community and instead of being able to wander into the village in our free time all pupils, had to be signed out on exeats. This edict even included Sixth Formers, although, as a concession we were allowed to wear long trousers. Most of us resented our loss of freedom. We Had previously been allowed to travel anywhere on

"Benefactor's Day" (a school holiday in honour of the school's founder). Many of us had hitch hiked as far as Salisbury; some even visited Bristol. We would wear long macs to hide our short trousers, as best we could, and queue up to see 'A' certificated films like "High Society". The previous year a group of us had been granted permission to cycle out to Stonehenge in the middle of the night to see the Druid ceremony of the Summer Solstice.

 Mr and Mrs Basset (inevitably nick named "Tarty") took up residence in the old Headmaster's house and at the end of the Michaelmas Term (Christmas outside the Organisation) attempted to curry favour by appearing in an end of term concert dressed as boys in short trousers with the older boys dressed in gowns and mortar boards masquerading as masters. The sight of Tarty's bum squeezed into a pair of beige shorts brought the house down but I am not sure if this act of "role reversal" earned them the respect they craved.

Sometime towards the end of the next term I received a letter from Mum saying that they had found a nice house on Ashdown Forest not far from High Hurstwood. It was two old cottages knocked into one and had no electricity. The water had to be pumped upstairs. There was a big garden with a track leading straight on to the Forest and a two acre field where Dad cold grow soft fruit when he retired. There was a lot of work to be done and Dad was looking forward to my help in the holidays. I wrote back to say I was excited to see the new house and that I would help Dad in any way I could when I came home. I also included a long list of my prize possessions like my Meccano, Hornby train layout and model aeroplanes I wanted kept safe in the move.

When I returned to my new home in the spring I was shocked at how isolated it was simply one of few houses strung out on the A26 in an area called Five Ashdown between Uckfield and Crowborough. It was far from the shops and the bus only ran every two hours and stopped early in the evening. The previous occupants – two elderly spinsters, had been very religious and statutes of the Madonna and other religious icons were still displayed in the garden. There was a gravity feed of water from a spring at the far end of the field and there was an inside hand pump used to supply water for the feeder tank in the roof. A large Calor gas canister supplied power for the cooker and fed a gas light in the kitchen and another in the front room. The only other source of light was from oil lights and candles.

The lack of electricity meant that our valve radio was useless and Mum and Dad had to rely on a basic set run off an accumulator which had to be charged every week. There was a copper water tank in an airing cupboard heated by a coke stove in the kitchen, but apart from this there was no central heating of any kind, and they had resorted to using an old oil stove. I felt sorry for my Mum, with her bad chest and delicate constitution, marooned in this isolated place separated from all her friends in Pound Green with Dad out at work all day and me away at school. She, however, brushed my solicitations to one side. "It was a lovely house" she said "Full of potential". They had applied for mains electricity to be connected and Dad was paying for central heating to be installed – something, she reminded me, "We never had in the old house". Dad admitted to finding the up keep of the large formal garden --"A bit of a challenge"-- but said he was looking forward to growing raspberries and black currants in the field. We would put up a greenhouse and keep chickens and there was room for me to dig a pond at the bottom of the garden for goldfish. I found most of my toys and books had been safely transported from the Hollies and there was a box room in the new house where I could make my model aeroplanes. I discovered, however, that Mum had forgotten one request in my letter home and my complete set of Eagle Comics, I had kept since the first issue, had been given to a children's hospital. I felt a stab of acute sadness but said nothing. My exile at school had meant that a piece of my childhood had been taken from me without my consent. I tried to rationalise my loss and told myself that I had to grow up sometime.

I got stuck to helping Dad. Part of the condition of sale meant that we had to move a garage from the other side of the road to the end of our garden, and I helped take down the wooden structure and re-assemble it on our land on the concrete standing we had laid down. We now had no access to the garage which was perched on top of a high bank fifteen yards back from the road. We had no money to pay for a bulldozer, so it was my task to dig out a drive way with pick and shovel from the heavy clay and sandstone which characterised this part of Ashdown Forest. It was heavy back breaking work and Uncle Les sometimes came at weekends, with a navvy friend of his called Doug, to help. The driveway was just about finished by the time I went back to school and in the next holiday I dug the drains and enjoyed using the sandstones, we had collected from the Forest, to lay dry stone walls to line the sloping sides of the drive.

Back at School I started to work hard for my 'A' levels and made the best of the extra study time gained after my resignation from the school corps. The new Basset regime was in full flood and I got moved to a new dormitory catering solely for members of Franklin House of which I was a member. This had its positive aspect as I was separated from the predatory clutches of John Bussell. More Inter-House rivalry was promoted and I was unlucky enough to get picked to fight in a boxing competition. "But I can't fight" I protested "I've never been in a ring". The House Captain intervened and moral pressure was brought to bear --"Look Strange you're the only man we have of the right weight. You'll jolly well have to do the decent thing!" Thus my protests were overruled in a new wave of House chauvinism.

The competition was two weeks away and I had plenty of time to look out of the Library window across to the gym where my I could see, on a daily basis, my swarthy rival pounding the punch bag and doing press-ups. I did no training, convincing myself that my devotion to 'S' Level History was part of a higher calling. The great day was upon me all too soon, and as if in a daydream, I found myself stepping into the ring surrounded by spectators from different teams. There were a few cries of "Strangle, Strangle" but most were cheering my rival. Major Bigmore was the referee and the match started. I went out of my corner flailing punches and landed some lucky hits which unsettled my opponent. When he struck back I decided that my best defence was to jump out of the way. And the fight had to be halted, by Major Bigmore, who said this was against the rules. "Keep your feet on the canvas boy!" He ordered. Towards the end of the first round I landed a lucky punch and knocked my rival to the floor just as the bell sounded. There was a gasp of disbelief from the other corner and renewed cries of "Strangle! Strangle...!" louder this time.

In the second round, my lack of training became apparent, and I found the effort of simply holding my arms up, let alone landing punches, quite tiring, as a consequence, my opponent started to land more hits. In the third round I was staggering like a zombie. He started to overpower me and Major Bigmore threw in the towel. The fight was over. My Captain congratulated me on "Putting up a jolly good show" and the Franklin boys cheered as I crawled out of the ring. For a few days after, a small group of younger boys paid me homage, but my fame was short lived. I don't recall Stoneman being at the fight.

I liked playing tennis and played as often as I could at school. One day I was in the village spending my pocket money at the village shop buying extra rations of scones and butter to supplement the boring school diet when I got talking to a rather pretty girl. She "gave me the eye" but I was shy and my "chat up technique" was woefully inadequate. In the end, I fell back on the routine, deployed by Ian and myself, back in Pound Green. "Would you like to have a game of tennis?" I asked. To my surprise she agreed and we arranged to meet at one of the village courts. A couple of days later I sneaked off school in the afternoon with my tennis kit concealed in a big paper bag and made my way to the recreation ground in Lavingham

To my surprise she was waiting for me already dressed in a frilly white tennis skirt. She smiled at me indulgently as I, rather embarrassingly, disrobed and struggled into my sweatshirt and shorts at the side of the court. It was a hot summer's day and we played until the first evening shadows started to close in. When I looked at my watch I was surprised how late it was. When I said I had to go she gave me a long lingering look with her large hazel eyes. We fixed a date for another game and she squeezed my hand as we said our goodbyes. Nothing more was said, but my heart was singing as I made my way back to school.

The next day, more swiftly than I might have imagined, I received my comeuppance. At the end of the Morning Assembly the Headmaster railed angrily against anyone breaking bounds and fraternising with young people in the village. I was summoned up on the stage for a public dressing down.

"Strange has been seen playing tennis with a village girl and will receive the very severest punishment! Woe betide any other boy who might be tempted to follow such a bad example from a Sixth Former who ought to know better!"

I was led away to be ruthlessly beaten in his study. Each blow which rained down was punctuated by an angry rebuke:

"That's for breaking bounds!"
"That's for going out with a village girl!"
"They've all got the pox!....."

I later learned who had reported me – Mr. McMaster alias Captain McMaster had exacted his revenge.

My last year at school coincided with the Suez crisis and I spent long hours in the Common Room pouring over Eden's denial of collusion with the French and the Israeli's, and Aneurin Bevan's brilliant public attack on the Prime Minister. Although most boys followed their parents' line supporting the invasion of the Suez, a few favoured the Labour view and we had good discussions in our History and Politics classes about the issue. Mum wrote to me to say that my Cousin Pam's fiancée Malcolm who had been a part-time soldier in the Territorial Army had been called up. This, together with my experience of the CCF spurred me on to even greater academic effort in the hope that good 'A' Levels would help secure me a place at university so that I could defer my National Service.

In the holidays I continued to help Mum and Dad with their new home and garden. I dug out a big pond on a plot, near the bridleway which led up the forest, and cemented its base, adding rockery stones around its perimeter. I dug a small channel across the lawn and used some old curtain rods as pipes, sealed together in concrete, to provide water. I even fashioned a water wheel which turned when the water flowed. One day when I was thinning out some of the pond weed I had planted. I put my hand out to pluck what I thought was a large piece in the middle, only to be confronted by the open fangs of an adder which had slithered in from the Forest to eat the goldfish. I recoiled in horror. Somehow or other the image of this viper seemed symbolic of my situation. I resented the humiliating punishment, meted out to me at school, for something as simple as seeking friendship with a girl.

I was also worried about my mother's failing health. I had helped Dad dispose of the religious icons in the garden but I still found the house rather creepy. At night the wind would blow and whine through the eaves and the flickering oil lamps would cast weird shadows in the corners of the rooms. Above all I felt lonely. I missed seeing my friends in Pound Green and I needed the companionship of people of my own age. For all her brave talk about making a nice house, and her love for wild countryside, I felt that Mum felt isolated as well. Dad was out at work all day and then spent hours, in the evening and at weekends, battling to keep the garden under control. Mum always perked up when the family came to stay and we had a good sing song around the piano. But Uncle Norm had moved to inspect factories in Southeast London, and had a longer journey to make -- while Uncle Les and Aunty Doris, who still lived in Rottingdean, were very busy running a restaurant in the West End, and could make fewer visits.

Dad had taken pity on Mum and swallowed his dislike of organised religion. He now took her to Sunday Services at a Church in High Hurstwood in the hope of making friends. He also struck up a relationship with Farmer Curd and his wife half a mile up the road, and did his best to get on with a peppery old Rear Admiral who lived in the house opposite. But somehow, nothing made up for the absence of her old friends like Grace Smith, Alison Lyle, and Farmer Ford.

Then one afternoon, out of the blue, when I was home for the Easter holidays in my last year at school, there was a knock at the door and who should be there but Grace Smith and Carol. It had taken two bus trips and a long wait at Ringles Cross to reach us but they had finally made it. We were all overjoyed to see them. Mum busied herself making tea and serving up cakes. Carol was immaculately turned out in a tight fitting pencil skirt. Her beautiful chestnut hair seemed to radiate light as she confidently negotiated the room in her high heels and seemed stockings. When she sat down – or rather perched on the arm of the settee -- she revealed half an inch of darkened stocking top with the hint of a suspender beneath. I was absolutely gobsmacked. I was wearing tattered bits of my school uniform, as Mum said I had to wear it out in my final year. Fortunately, my attire included long trousers, but I still felt as if I inhabited another planet. "How nice to see you!" I faltered. "What are you doing these days?" "Look!" she said by way of an answer, and held up her left hand to reveal a ring sparkling in the afternoon light. "I'm engaged!" I felt a pang of sadness pass through me. Here was this beautiful creature -- that it seemed only yesterday had been tumbling down hayricks, and doing the high jump in our Olympic Games at Ford's Farm – now she was spoken for -- and me literally hardly out of short trousers.

I returned to Harper's College to revise as hard as I could and sit my exams. The world of the school seemed more claustrophobic than ever and I couldn't wait to leave. On the other hand I felt ignorant of the world and fearful of the future. The institution had emphasised leadership, but I felt diffident and unsure of my ability. Back at home in the holidays I started to have a recurring dream which persisted for a year or so. I dreamed that while I was the age I was now, no one recognised it and I was stuck in my first year in the Junior House in short trousers with five more years to serve. As during the war, I would wake from this nightmare in a cold sweat full of fear.

My exam results arrived in early August. I had done well in my 'A' Levels and 'S' Levels but I had failed my retake in French 'O' level. This was a Faculty requirement for entry to Manchester University to Study Economics and Political Studies and, therefore my provisional acceptance would be withdrawn. It was time to call in Uncle Norm again!

Chapter Five
First love

After a phone call to Uncle Norm telling him about my 'A' Level results and failure in 'O' Level French I was on the London train the next morning. He met me at Paddington Station and we took a bus to his favourite Joe Lyons Corner House close to his offices near the Inns of Court. "Look Boy" he said at the end of our snack lunch. "There must be a way – The National Portrait Gallery is on the way back to the Factory Inspectorate. I'll drop you off there and you can have a look round -- it's a great experience. I'll go on to my office to make a few phone calls, and check my post. I'll pick you up at 3 O' Clock OK?" Coming as a scholarship boy from the Welsh valleys, Uncle had adapted well to the rigours of city life. He sported a trilby hat and was every inch a "city slicker," as he jumped on to the tailboard of retreating busses or weaved his way through congested traffic. I was running to keep up – conscious of being the country bumpkin that I was.

I enjoyed wandering around the Gallery and he later met me in the entrance lobby as arranged. He laid his arm on my shoulder." Do you want to hear the good news or the bad news?" he questioned. Without waiting for an answer he continued: "The LSE offers a degree in Economics and Social Science which doesn't require a language qualification!" He continued without stopping: "The bad news is that they are full up for this year!" My heart sank, I had just escaped from Harper's College and the barking orders of Sergeant Major Chester and now I was in line to do two more year of "square bashing", or worse, doing National Service. "Look" said Uncle, seeing my dismay. "There is another chance. They told me that the Regent Street Polytechnic offers the same London Degree but teaches it externally in the School of Commerce. Let's get over there straight away!" Five minutes later we were jumping off a bus at Oxford Circus and wending our way through a maze of little back streets towards the College sited in Little Titchfield Street. To my overwhelming joy we discovered that there were two places left. I enrolled on the spot. He rang Aunty Gladys to say that we would be late back. That night we dined in style at the Middle Temple, where he spent some of his time, working as a Barrister, for the Factory Inspectorate. Never had wine tasted sweeter. I was intoxicated by the thought of becoming an undergraduate. Uncle Norm had saved the day!

It was agreed that I would lodge with my Uncle and Aunt and Cousin Linda in Coulsdon on very generous terms, and travel up to London every day to go to college. My County Major award from East Sussex was not a full grant, but just about covered the cost of my keep and season ticket with a little over to spend on books and entertainment. I vowed to do as many fruit picking and potato harvesting jobs in the holidays as I could, to eke out my slender budget, although, I knew that such work was seasonal and precarious. Mum and Dad were pleased to hear that, against the odds, I was set to be one of an elite group of three percent to study for a degree in the 1950's. The first part of the BSc Econ course included a wide variety of social science subjects such as Political Thought, Government, History, Psychology and Sociology, as well as Economics -- studied over two years, before candidates chose their Special Subject for Part two of their Finals. Uncle had achieved a First in Philosophy at London University before studying for an MA in Theories of Psycho-analysis under the Christian Philosopher John MacMurray. He seemed almost as excited about the course as I was and looked out a bundle of his old notes. "I can help." He enthused "We can have great discussions!" I showed him the daunting University Book List I had picked up at the Poly. Uncle was undismayed. "You won't need all of these, Boy! Anyway, I am sure you can get some of the textbooks second hand from the College Bookshop or from Foyles or Pools in Charing Cross Road. You'll need to take lots of notes in lectures -- develop your own type of short-hand -- write them up afterwards to get the ideas clear in your mind. That's the trick!"

A couple of days later I was saying goodbye to my Aunt and Cousin Linda in her green checked uniform, ready for school, and then walked down the road to the station, with Uncle Norm, to catch the 8.15 am travelling to London Bridge. In one hand I held a brand new brown leather briefcase. In the other I carried a rolled-up copy of The Manchester Guardian. I said goodbye to Uncle at Bank Station and caught the tube to Oxford Circus. I headed up Regent Street, towards the main Poly building. When I saw the outline of Broadcasting House in the near distance I turned to the right and walked down a variety of small streets, passing factories devoted to the rag trade with workers pushing racks of dresses across the road and elegant models hurrying to work.

When I arrived at the School of Commerce there were groups of students sitting on the steps outside happily chatting away. They were a colourful lot, and a couple of Indian girls immediately stood out in their bright saris I also caught the intonation of lots of different accents and realised that many of them came from a variety of different countries. I entered the foyer to check on the time of my first lecture, and five minutes later I was sitting in a crowded class room listening to Dr Stephen Cotgrove talk about the Social Structure of Modern Britain. I saw that there were some mature students present, notably a Mrs Enid Wistrich who insisted on telling us that she engaged on writing some obscure thesis about Family Law. There were also some students like Ted and Doug who had already completed their National Service and seemed more self-assured than the rest of us. In addition there was Ted's mate, a very large and amiable African Student called Mr Ocorodudu. The Sociology classes contained more women than men, and I noticed a talkative Greek girl named Miss Roncarlier, nick named Ronky, sitting next to a very pretty girl called Lucy. In this first class the I Lecturer was very respectful of people's different views, although he explained that the following seminar was the correct forum for discussion. Everyone was referred to as Mr, Miss, or Mrs and it was a pleasant surprise to be treated in such an adult way. When the formal lecture began I started to scribble furiously trying to record the bare bones of the argument in my bizarre spelling.

At lunch time I queued up for fish and chips in the crowded canteen in the basement, and got talking to a variety of students who seemed very friendly and well-motivated to learn. A few of them shared flats or had digs near the Poly, but most came from further afield, and quite a number lived with their families or, like myself, commuted in from outside London. A few confided that they would have liked to have gone to LSE, and maybe regarded the School of Commerce as second best. But, as time went on, I had no such regrets and grew to love the institution and the kindness and respect that most of the teachers showed towards their students, many of whom came from working class or ethnic minority backgrounds. The College was not too stuffy and undergraduates shared some of the table tennis and sports facilities with clubs like the London Harriers and local societies, who attended on an occasional basis. The institution was no doubt, less exclusive than the likes of University College. The library was small and cramped, but we learned to use the other facilities provided by London University and I soon found myself spending time studying in the Goldsmith library at Senate House.

After the first week I started to become more accustomed to the routine of college life. The time table seemed pretty heavy with formal lectures followed by seminars, where students delivered academic papers dealing with the subject under review, and we discussed tutorial issues. On Monday afternoons, there was a double period on the Principles of Economic Theory, delivered in the Main Hall by Mr Ruddock. He droned away for what seemed like hours in a boring monotone and drew numerous "Supply and Demand Diagrams" on a variety of black-boards. His delivery was like the rat-a-tat of a machine gun and we barely had time to copy down one diagram before it disappeared in a cloud of chalk dust to be replaced by another -- equally obscure. In desperation a group of us took to imbibing a pint of cider at lunch time as an antidote to the tedium to follow. This, of course, proved totally counter-productive. Economic theory was not my strongest suite and after a frustrating couple of hours trying to master "indifference curves" in "Stonier and Hague" -- regarded as the economic bible for the course, I was none the wiser.

The next day I chatted to a student called Dereck, who had appeared equally mystified in the class. He said that the only one who had understood it was a boy called Stuart, who was a bit of a boffin, and we agreed to chat over the problem with him at a nearby café. A Chinese girl called Lily asked if she could come, and we all met up at lunch time. The café was friendly and informal, (rather like the one run by my Uncle Les and Aunty Doris -- in another part of Town) it specialised in good cheap meals, and it became a favourite haunt of mine. Stuart had been educated at Dulwich College and was one of the few Public school boys, myself included, to attend the Poly. He was bright at Economics and very serious. His explanation was not much clearer than Mr Ruddock's, but what impressed me was the effort he put in to help other students. I suddenly realised that the years of competition and struggle for personal marks were behind me – at the Poly everyone seemed to want to co-operate. The next day we were back in the café talking and laughing too loudly. We were happy to be undergraduates turning our tongues around newly acquired academic phrases, talking animatedly amongst ourselves and to anyone else who would listen. Even the café regulars -- businessmen and shop girls, gave us an occasional indulgent smile – or we thought they did.

Although I didn't like the long commute to College I adapted better than I expected to reading books on the train, screening out the chatter of other passengers, as best I could, in order to concentrate. I even unconsciously imbibed some of Uncle Norm's "city slicker routines" – learning to stand at strategic parts of the platform where more passengers were likely to alight, and you could quickly dive into the carriage to grab a free seat. At home Uncle Norm was full of enthusiasm. He liked talking about the Psychology Modules in my course, and loved the excuse to chat about the Theories of Psychoanalysis espoused by Freud, Adler and Jung. He was equally at home with political theory and we had long discussions about the ideas of Plato, Hobbes, Hegel and Marx. He liked nothing more than an excuse to rifle through his old notes, and hold forth on any subject relevant to my studies -- and some which were not. "All part of your general education Boy!" he would say.

He liked DIY and we took a trip together to the wood-yard in Coulsdon to buy hardboard and wood strips to make a makeshift table tennis board, which we designed to fit over the dining room table. The whole family had endless fun with this -- with an animated Aunty Gladys, spooning balls over the net, and often stonewalling herself to victory – while the rest of us smashed the balls around the room in frustration. Like my Dad, Uncle was an accomplished amateur Artist. He painted portraits and still life studies directly on to the canvass. But his beautiful landscapes were sometimes copied from slides he had taken of the Gower Peninsular and other seascapes. Many of his paintings included busy scenes of foreign markets. One painting always fascinated me -- I think it was intended to be allegorical. It featured a war scene of a bombed house on fire in the background, with a beautiful bowl of primroses on a window ledge in front. It used to hang in my Granny's flat, opposite the basement where Norm and Gladys lived at 13a Buckingham Road in Brighton, and I first saw it as a small boy. He always had a picture on the go in the backroom and he let me try doing a painting in oils of some geraniums in a blue vase.

Uncle was full of surprises and one evening he appeared with a puppy. Linda was overjoyed. But Aunty was more circumspect. "It's got very big paws" she said. Sure enough it grew into a large Welsh sheep dog. It was a loveable intelligent dog but it was frustrated by being confined to a small suburban garden. Although, we took it for regular walks and let it run free in Banstead Woods, its loud barking led the neighbours to complain. Norm had to take it to the vet to be "de-barked", and poor "Taffy" spent the rest of his life croaking his disapproval as if he had a heavy head cold.

Uncle loved Art Galleries and we would meet in London, to visit the Tate and National Galleries. We also went the Theatre and I can remember going to see the original productions of "Look back in Anger" and "The Entertainer" with him at the Royal Court. When I asked why he never took Aunty. He said that -- "It was a bit too 'avant garde' for her!" I don't know how Aunty would have reacted to the brutal machinations of Jimmy Porter. However, I would have described her as slightly unworldly, rather than prudish. The White sisters had not led completely chaste lives. Aunty Alice claimed to have had an affair with the actor Robert Donat, and later lived with "Uncle" Morris who was an amateur conjurer, who was an active member of the Psychic Research Society. Aunty Emmy, who was nominally a spinster, lived with a property developer on the Costa Brava, while Aunty Gladys had divorced her first husband to co-habit with Uncle Norm. Aunty probably just liked Hollywood movies more than "kitchen sink drama", and Uncle made sure he went with her to the pictures at least once a week. He was also a good Dad, and regularly took my cousin Linda to dancing classes and concerts in Croydon, when I lived with them.

Uncle's background in the Congregational Church never left him, and he regarded his role as a barrister, working for the factory inspectorate, as an extension of his "Christian Socialism". He saw his job as defending the rights of workers against bad employers, who had cut corners ignoring safety regulations. He sometimes got me to bring back pieces of Meccano from home so he could make models of poorly guarded factory machines, which had caused accidents, to help his prosecutions. I occasionally went along to see him perform in court, and remember him being a brilliant advocate. He also volunteered for Prison Visiting. He took this work very seriously and old lags would sometime came and stay while they were "finding their feet in the outside world". He was very trusting and the ex-cons had great respect for him. There was never anything stolen or bad behaviour.

Mum and Dad were sometimes rather critical of Aunty Gladys. Mum regarded her Sister in Law as: "A goodtime Charlie" who had required her beloved brother to: "Take her to the pictures even when he was revising for his Bar Exams!" Dad who liked his tummy and looked forward to a "Good Tuck-in," complained that the Sunday

Roast in Coulsdon "always tasted of gas!" There was some truth in these assertions, and a slight acrid smell did seem to hang around the cooker at 16 Woodmansterne Road. Aunty could not hope to compete with my Mum's passion for cooking. Nevertheless, I found her a lovely person who cared deeply for my Uncle and Linda and provided me with the best digs I could hope for. She was a good foil to my Uncle. Whereas, he was the action man, always enthusiastic to embark on some new idea, she would provide practical advice and support. Uncle loved to reach out to other people and kept an open house so that friends and sometimes, casual acquaintances, would be asked back and often offered a bed for the night at short notice. Aunty never stood on ceremony. Camp beds would be erected in quick time, or extra cushions arranged on the setee and a scratch meal would be rustled up, from left-overs in the pantry, while Uncle held-forth about nuclear disarmament or John Mac Murray's theory of personal relationships.

Sunday tea-time could often be chaotic, rather hilarious occasions. Aunty's sardine sandwiches and coconut pyramids would be prominently displayed together with an iced sponge cake. For reasons of economy, this would usually be decorated with a few orange segments, left over from the contents of a tin which had previously been added to the jelly, rather than crystallized fruit which would have had a longer shelf life. This strategy worked alright in a freshly baked cake. However, it was not so successful when portions of the sponge were served up a week or so later and it was seen that the decaying fruit had scored green skid marks on the iced surface and dripped down the sides. Fortunately, Aunty always seemed oblivious of such culinary faux pas and, they were indeed of no consequence, amid the jollity of most of these occasions. Her capacity for self-deception was legion. On one occasion she handed me a jam sandwich as I was rushing out of the door to catch the London train. In Aunty's eyes this piece of cuisine might have been viewed as an exciting experiment, but I found such an item rather disgusting. However, not wishing to offend her, I wrapped it in my hanky and stuffed it into my pocket, meaning to dispose of it as soon as possible. I, of course, forgot all about it. I returned home in the evening and had a sudden sinus attack while sitting at the tea table. I pulled out my hanky, oblivious of its dubious contents, and blew a thick red stream of sticky strawberry and crumbs across the room!

Before marrying Norm, Aunty had been involved in the Citizens Advice Bureau, and she continued to be heavily engaged with community work and her local church. In addition to Prisoner Support, Norm's Christian Socialism led him to do voluntary work with youth clubs and help with adult literacy classes. Their friendship with a variety of groups in the community, encouraged a wide circle of people to pop in at tea time. I think that Norm sometimes underestimated the effect of his charismatic personality. There was no doubt that women particularly were vulnerable to his charm. Linda was friendly with a boy called Terry who seemed to have attacks of serial giggling, and was always immaculately turned out in his Sunday best. Hazel, his mother, was also done up like a Christmas cracker. When she came to collect him her nylons seemed to crackle with static electricity. After being offered a cup of tea, she would often stay for hours -- mesmerised by Uncle's talk of Art, Christianity and Peace and Aldermaston Marches...

Uncle was always a great one for innovation, and halfway through my stay with them the family acquired a television. I think we all became rather addicted for a time, and we would sometimes have our supper on trays in the backroom – supplicants to the flickering box in the corner. Uncle even became a fan of the Lone Ranger (An American Cowboy series shown on the BBC). "Hail Silver!" He would shout, as the familiar white horse with its masked rider rode across the screen. We also liked the new "Tonight" current affairs programme fronted by Cliff Mitchelmore which was seen at the time as having a new "zany" approach to news coverage. Linda and Terry, and Hattie, another of Linda's friends, liked the "Blue Peter" programmes and spent hours under the "telly", curled up with Taffy, making spaceships out of old lavatory roll tubes and strips of coloured paper from Woolworths. As the Rock and Roll revolution took off they became seduced by a new programme called "Six-five Special," a fore runner of "Top of the Pops". It was introduced by Pete Murray and Jo Douglas and we all sang along to the theme tune – "Six-five Special's coming down the line! Six-five Special's right on time!" The programme went out live, and featured groups of "hand jiving" teenagers screaming adoration at a succession of pop star idols and Elvis look-a-likes. The show even included an indulgent vicar astride a motor bike dressed in "ton-up gear," and a celebrated interview with Adam Faith and his views on God!

For a time on Saturday afternoons we were terrified by watching the first episodes of a ground breaking Si Fi horror called Quatermass and the Pit. The series starts with the unearthing of a mysterious capsule from outer space in Hobbes Lane in Knightsbridge. And images of the devil, as well as aliens and poltergeists, serve to build up the suspense. Somehow, the black and white pictures viewed in a darkened room -- somewhat distorted by the effect of the patent magnifying glass, Norm had just fitted to the twelve inch screen, stimulated our collective fear of the unknown....

My first term at Regent Street Poly went like a dream. I loved debating ideas on politics, philosophy, sociology and psychology. Although, I found micro-economic theory rather dry and utilitarian I enjoyed Keynesian economics and the approach of social economists. I was a serious student and worked as hard as I could, sometimes late into the night, laboriously correcting my spelling mistakes and copying out final draughts of workman like essays and notes for academic papers. I started to feel more at ease with myself and began to contribute to discussions in seminars -- refusing to self-censor myself for fear of my stammer. I started to look forward to my lunchtime meetings with Lily, Stuart and Dereck. I noticed that Lily now spent less time with Bazil, the boy she had palled up with at the beginning of term, and had now taken to waiting for me to come out of lectures. She was in striking contrast to the rather dowdy girls my Mum had thought suitable for me at home. She wore a brightly coloured sarong, tight at the waist with a high collar with mid-calf slits at the side. She was very petite with a ponytail and a kiss curl hanging to one side. She was bright eyed and excitable -- at ease in the cafe with us three boys. She came from Singapore and had worked in a bank in Britain, studying 'A' levels at evening classes before being accepted on the degree course. She was doing the same Money and Banking option as Stuart, and was finding some of the course hard going, as English was not her first language. She talked very fast and, to begin with, pronounced my name as "Mite".

We asked her to slow down, and by the end of the week we all seemed more proficient in understanding her Chinese patois. She was interested in what we had to say, asking us to explain certain parts of lectures she had found difficult. Her apparent deference flattered our egos, mine particularly, and I often spent time explaining ideas to her about political theory or sociology when the others had left to attend different classes.

One evening we were late returning to the School of Commerce. Lily said she wanted to buy some note paper from the College shop and we walked together up the deserted back stairs to find that the shutters had already been put up. Suddenly, in what seemed like an act of glorious spontaneity, we were in each other's arms. Her body felt warm and subtle as we kissed. "You are such a lovely girl" I said as I pressed her close. We walked back to Oxford Street tube station, but instead of going straight home I rang my Aunty to say I would be late back. We walked in the other direction and went into the Cameo Poly News Theatre to watch a couple of hours of British Movietone and Disney Cartoons in the back-row. And to engage, in what Uncle Les, might have called, an "Act of Spooning". After I had kissed Lily goodbye and walked back to the tube station I heard a news vender parrot out his usual Cockney refrain –"Star News and Standard!" I bought a paper and hurried through the barrier feeling, in some way, that I was part of the fast moving London scene depicted on the BBC's "Tonight" programme. There was a spring in my step, and the smile on my face seemed to suffuse my whole being. A couple of days later Lily bought me a London University scarf and I wore it draped casually around my shoulders -- an ostentatious badge of my undergraduate status and my loving friendship with her.

Over the next couple of years we were pretty much inseparable. Lily introduced me to real Chinese food and we occasionally ate in Soho in a restaurant owned by one of her relatives. She had a flat in Craven Terrace near Regents Park, and we used to take boats out on the Serpentine, and row to one of the tiny islands in the middle and lie, locked together under the trees in our own special "Camelot". Lily liked musicals and romantic films such as "South Pacific". Not all the films had a happy ending and one -- "Love is a Many Splendored Thing"-- which featured a romance between a female Chinese doctor and American reporter estranged from his wife ends with the Chinese girl being ostracised by her own community. Lily's obsession with the film may have been prophetic. At the time, inter racial relationships were something of a rarity. Although our love was cocooned by the tolerant and optimistic values of university life, we were aware that even, in the environs of Hampstead -- once we had strayed away from Parliament Hill and walking on the Heath -- many of the adverts for bedsitters, in the windows of newsagents, often carried the caption "No Blacks or Coloured".

Lily liked to shroud herself in mystery. She was older than me, although by how much was difficult to calculate since she said that Chinese people counted their age from the moment of conception rather by their birth. She was clearly more worldly wise and financially independent than me. Although she had saved money from working to fund her course, it was likely that her extended family paid some of her living expenses. She hinted at riches in the Far East, and that her mother was one of the wives of a rich potentate but was too far down the pecking order to share in much of his wealth.

Politically Lily was on the left and shared my critical views of Harold Macmilian's populist appeal to the "Affluent Society". However, she was more enigmatic in her view of foreign affairs, hinting at her support for "Uncle Ho" in the aftermath of the French defeat in Indo-China at Dien Bien Phu. Lily sometimes talked excitedly about taking me on a great holiday to meet her family in Singapore, but I soft peddled on this suggestion on the excuse that I should have to save up to fund my own passage for such an expensive trip. The 1950's was still patriarchal. Popular Culture demanded --"That a man's gotta do what a man's gotta do!" Carol Smith had regarded her glittering engagement ring as a passport to deferential marital bliss. Lily clearly saw me as her beau and here I was, a penniless student, not even a year out of a monastic boarding school -- naïve about the ways of the world. I took Lily down to see Uncle Norm and Aunty Gladys in Coulsdon. We had a lovely time and they were kindness itself. I also took her for a meal at the London restaurant run by Uncle Les and Aunty Doris. They put on a good show, with Uncle Les cracking jokes and spouting rhyming slang in a fake Cockney accent. A few weeks later, however, I was shocked, and angry, to hear Aunty Doris, talking to my Mum and Dad about our visit, refer to Lily as a "Yellow Nigger!"

I often went back at weekends to see my new home on Ashdown Forest. Mum had objected to its original name which was "The Brown House" which summoned up unfortunate memories of

Hitler's Black Shirts. She had re-christened it "Kilvrough," after a stately home on the Gower Peninsular where she had attended dances as a young girl. The adoption of this high sounding name did little to lift my sprits about the house, but I set about helping Dad in the garden. He had cornered off a section of the field and I helped him erect a chicken coup and dig in the posts and lash up the wire netting for a run. We also used a petrol-driven rotavator, he had acquired, to plough up land ready to plant fruit trees and blackcurrants and loganberries. The relief of no longer having to pay for my school fees was apparent, and Dad proudly showed off a new second-hand Vauxhall 10 he had bought from his friend Brady, who ran the garage at Ringles Cross. He had secured a good mortgage deal from the Bank, and had commuted some of his pension so there was enough money to pay for us to be connected to mains electricity and to install central heating. A new black and white television stood proudly in the front room next to the open fire place. I bought hardwood and strips of wood and constructed a copy of the makeshift table tennis table I made with Uncle Norm. I designed it to fit over an old gate-legged table. When the family came for Sunday Lunch we often played outside on the patio -- the garden echoing to the happy cries and laughter my Mum liked to remember from her youth at the original Kilvrough Junior House in Parkmill.

On these happy occasions the men, myself included, would sit in front of the fire reminiscing about the war or engage in political debate. Uncle Les and Dad would puff away at their Manikin cigars -- periodically sipping their whisky -- with Uncle Norm, sitting slightly to one side, with a glass of cordial. In the late afternoon, after tea we would all gather around the piano singing a mixture of romantic ballades and hymns – any catchy tune which could be summoned up, as my Mum's agile fingers danced over the keyboard. Uncle Les fancied he had a good bass voice and Dad was quite a good baritone. Sometimes, we would all fall about in laughter as they attempted to sing Victorian classics like "Come into the garden Maud!" The evening would usually end with us all singing Men of Harlech and chanting "Cymru am Byth!" ("Wales Forever!") Mum loved these family get-togethers and, she liked showing off the new spacious house and garden. Like many families at this time we embraced the rise in post-war living standards. But in Mum's case new carpets and fur rugs, and occasional family visits, could never compensate for the loss of day to day contact with her friends in Pound Green, and the sense of isolation she felt at Herons Ghyll. Uncle Norm sensed the deep sadness of his sister, and confided in me that he thought that both Frank and Vera were romantics whose dream of the "good life" in Ashdown Forest would end in tears. My parents, however, stoically defended their decision. Mum said that she would --"Rather die than live in a town". Dad thought that things would be better as soon as he retired in a couple of years time. He took on more of the household chores and cooking, which was unusual for a man at this time. He also made an attempt to teach Mum how to drive, which was only abandoned after the car careered off the road -- narrowly avoiding a collision with a signpost.

My concern about my mother's health may also have partly been a projection of my own feelings at this time. I enjoyed living with my Uncle and Aunt during term time, and loved life at the Poly. In the second year of my course was making good progress with my studies. I enjoyed studying Sociology and Psychology and, with the encouragement of Uncle had read some of Sigmund Freud's original writings on Psychoanalysis. My life in London seemed new and exciting, in contrast to my rather humdrum existence in the holidays. Part-time work was extremely difficult to find, and the stints of potato harvesting and fruit picking, I undertook, were poorly paid. I did my best to put my back into helping Dad with the garden -- mixing concrete for the base of a new greenhouse, mowing the two large lawns, and cutting logs for the fire. I even sank a flower pot into the centre of the formal lawn and made a "Clock Golf Course" so we put some of the old clubs Mum had acquired at an auction to good use. However, like her, I felt isolated from my old life in Pound Green. Ian had left school to work in the City of London as a Trainee Accountant and the Lyle family had moved to Sevenoaks, where his father had taken over managing a pub. I missed my new student friends, and wrote Lily long passionate letters from my rural exile. When I asked if she could come for Christmas there was a great deal of prevarication and hand-wringing. "What will she think?" my Mum said. "You're not in a position to get serious with any girl ...... aren't you leading her on?" My protests were swept aside, and in the end I asked an American boy called Paul Culp from Texas, who had nowhere to go at this time of year, to come. Mum cooked some lovely food, but the visit was not a great success. Somehow, I felt that the presence of a stranger in the house, at the time of the year when charity was supposed to be the order of the day, had been resented. It was almost as if Mum, deprived of my company for long periods at boarding school, now wanted to covet me all to herself.

A few weeks later I decided to tell Mum and Dad the real truth about Harper's College I had hidden from them for so long. I really felt that the ghosts of the past needed at last to be exorcised. But when I formally sat them down in the dining room at Kilvrough and tried to tell them about homosexuality and paedophilia in the institution, they flatly refused to believe me. Initially I felt angry, but later I was smitten with guilt. They had made a huge financial and emotional sacrifice to send me away. For them the end had justified the means. Who was I, as a greenhorn disciple of Freud, to dig up such a quagmire of sad memories? I should have let bygones be bygones.

The end of my second year at the Poly coincided with my twenty first birthday, and it was arranged that I could ask my friends Dereck, Stuart and Lily to the party. None of my old mates from Pound Green could come, but Mum, to my great embarrassment, invited a girl called Jane, who I had never met before, to join in the celebrations, together with uncles and aunts and cousins from all sides of the family. I had asked Lily to come a day early to help set up the party, and Dad and I collected her from Eridge Station. On the way home, she sat in the back of the car holding my hand and balancing a big box of Chinese lanterns on her lap. She talked excitedly about her plans for the party. Mum met us at the front door. Her welcome was genuine, but in truth Lily's overnight stay was a challenge to her puritanical views about no sex before marriage. The two old cottages that had been knocked into one, to form our house, had a passageway upstairs with connecting bedrooms, and I had insisted on Lily sleeping in the room next to mine, rather than be confined to a more remote corner of the dwelling. This had elicited more fears in my Mum's mind about me – "leading Lily on..." Mum and Dad saw themselves as being enlightened. Dad read the "New Statesman and Nation" and Mum had always railed against racial prejudice -- defending the rights of Black GI's during the war. The reality of their only child's romantic attachment to a bright and attractive Chinese girl was, however, a challenge to their "taken for granted view of the world". The "Permissive Society" had yet to arrive, and the 1950's represented a tight conventional world of chaste courtship and engagement. Change was in the air, and jukeboxes had just begun to thunder to the beat of Bill Haley's Comets playing "Rock around the Clock" and Elvis Presley singing "Love me Tender" but, as Philip Larkin later reminded us -- "Sexual intercourse began in 1963 – between the end of the Chatterley ban and the Beatles first LP". Britain in 1959 was still a world of rigid moral certainties where homosexual offences were punished by imprisonment; unmarried mothers could be confined to mental hospitals -- or be pressurised into having their babies adopted; and hanging was still the ultimate punishment for a capital offence.

After lunch I showed Lily our garden and two acre field and we then walked up the bridle-path leading to Ashdown Forest. Many of the trees, in this part of the wood had been cut down in the Napoleonic Wars for ship-building, and for the production of charcoal for gunpowder. We looked across an open stretch of moorland towards a clump of trees called Kings Standing, and the pylons of the old Radar Station, I remembered from my childhood. It was a lovely hot summer day and we lay down on a patch of ferns under a gorse bush. The heavy scent of talc from its yellow buds hung in the air as I drew Lily towards me in a close embrace. Five minutes later we were rudely awakened from our revelry by the sight of two eyes staring at us from behind the bushes. Shocked and embarrassed, we struggled to our feet and a youth blundered clumsily away down the woodland path. It was alarming to think that even, in such a deserted place we were subject to the prurient gaze of the outside world.

We walked back home and hung Lily's Chinese lanterns and candles around the garden. We chatted to Mum and Dad and I rang Stuart and Dereck to discuss their travel plans. Dereck was surprised at my ignorance of pop records and said he would bring lots of his own singles together with a sound system. He said his mum would run him down and would give Stuart a lift as well. We agreed that she would stay for the party and they would all return home the same day. Lily dressed in a different sarong for supper, and Mum hinted, rather unkindly, I thought, that she "must have a big laundry bill". Undeterred, Lily talked animatedly about working in a bank and her undergraduate course. She laughed a lot and did her best to make nice remarks regarding their house and garden. She talked about our visits to Chinese restaurants and Chinese New Year celebrations in Soho. She chatted a little about her extended family in Singapore, and also did her best to ingratiate herself with my Dad by saying that:" She had great respect for older men!" Finally, we said good night. Mum had reluctantly relented on the connecting bedrooms but, nevertheless, gave me a long hard stare as we mounted the stairs. Lily, of course spent the night with me. But Mum's gaze had done its trick, and we had a largely fretful night – our ears attuned to the sound of creaking floorboards and the midnight knock on the door.

The next day was fine, and after breakfast Lily and I carried tables and chairs out into the garden and did our best to help Mum make jellies, trifles and jam tarts. We also found some old bowls and a jack, in one of the outside sheds, and laid them out on the lawn by the pond for people to play with. In addition, we carried a set of clubs out to the other more ornamental lawn, in case anyone fancied a game of Clock Golf. Dad busied himself sorting out trays of glasses and drinks, and stuck up a notice telling people to park in the field. Dereck's mother arrived at about 12 O'clock with the two boys, and they set about arranging the speakers and turn table. She seemed a larger than life character with a large feathered hat and painted nails. Dereck – dressed, yellow checked suit with a fur collar, introduced his mother with an elaborate theatrical flourish. I hardly recognised him from our lunchtime meetings at the Poly. "This is my mater!" He boomed. His voice and manner were totally camp. I suddenly realised, in a split second, something I had failed to con in the last two years –Dereck was as queer as a coot!

After Two 'O clock the guests began to come thick and fast. A girl arrived in sensible shoes and an "A Line" plaid dress, I had never seen before, who I assumed to be Jane. I quickly steered her in the direction of Stuart. Soon uncles and aunts from both sides of the family arrived and, it was great to see my cousins, Linda and Allen and Pam with her fiancée Malcolm. Dereck and Stuart got the music going and the party started to swing. Dad, who was always rather retiring on such occasions, covered his shyness by taking people on tours of the garden. Others guests enjoyed ping-pong on the patio, and some liked playing bowls and Clock Golf. As the alcohol started to take effect people began to dance -- led by Dereck stomping around with his mother, while I smooched in a quiet corner with Lily. Mum had made a terrific effort, and was relieved that things had gone well. The sound of laughing and dancing, echoing around the garden, had meant that her dream of garden parties at Kilvrough had come true – a last hurrah -- at least for one day of the year. After the party was over and we had said goodbye to all the guests, Lily and I lit the Chinese lanterns and danced amongst the flickering shadows on the back lawn.

The next morning we were up early, with Lily's cases all packed in the car heading for Eridge Station. When we arrived, Dad stayed in the car and I went with Lily on to the platform. There were tears in her eyes –"When shall I see you again Mite?" She whispered. I knew that my lack of finances would make it difficult for me to travel up to London in the holidays. I knew also, that what I said was totally inadequate "I'll write" I said "I'll see you at Senate House, when the results come out...."

The next few days after the party seemed very dull. I was completely broke, and my efforts to find casual work in Herons Ghyll proved unproductive. Any suggestion that I might spend some time with Lily in her London flat, caused a moral panic and I was reminded of my duty to establish my credentials as a breadwinner before entertaining any ideas of formal courtship. Mum returned to the theme of me leading Lily on, and said I was too young to get serious with any girl. There were—"Plenty of fish in the sea"-- the implication was that I should take time to sow my wild oats – anywhere it appeared, apart from the environs of Craven Terrace, would do. I felt sad and confused, and wondered if I was being encouraged to follow the same path of dalliance trod by Uncle Les in the late 1930's. I knew I had to get away, and rang up the Students Union in Bloomsbury to arrange to work in an International Student Farm Camp in Suffolk. A couple of days before I left, we went on a family outing to Uckfield Cinema to see "Whisky Galore" – the first in a series of Ealing Studio hits. Afterwards, in the car park, we bumped into a girl called Miss Ginger who worked in Dad's bank. I had never met her before-- but I gathered from casual snips of conversation, I had picked up previously, that she was regarded as something of a vamp. Dad offered her a lift home, and as soon as I got into the back of the car with her she squeezed herself against me and started to rub her thigh against mine. I froze inwardly, and refused to yield to her strenuous efforts. I thought of Lily, and felt a sharp pang of sadness well up inside me -- as well as a resolution to leave home as soon as possible.

The next Monday I travelled to London and caught a train from Liverpool Street to Witham. There was a tractor and trailer waiting, and I joined seven or eight other students, mainly from overseas, for a bumpy ride to Tiptree. We were housed in an old barn, and slept in bunk beds on straw palliasses. There was a brick building with youth hostel type facilities for washing, and a canteen with a bar at one end. We would earn our keep, and a small amount of spending money, by picking fruit in the fields, and working in a couple of canning factories. The other students were a sociable lot, and I soon made friends with boys and girls from a variety of European and Eastern European countries, as well as some from Britain. The Camp was run by an older student from Israel called Aron together a girl called Maria from Slovenia, who served the food and looked after the bar in the evening.

The following morning we were up early, shaving in lukewarm water and snatching a quick breakfast, before boarding the trailer to be towed by tractor to the Wilkins Jam Factory. Here we had to quickly don a green overall and scoop our hair back to be contained in a net. Our main job was to stand beside a white conveyor belt and pick out all the bad plums, which danced before our eyes for hour after hour after hour, and collect them in buckets besides us. The machinery was noisy, and the din was made worse by highly amplified pop music which blared out of the speakers above our heads, designed to boost the output of the resident workers. The fruit had the sweet smell of putrefaction and attracted wasps. When we asked where the rotten fruit was destined, we were told that it would be shipped down the road to the Kingsmere Factory, where it would be mixed with pulped turnip, and other leftovers for sale in Woolworths. There was a short lunch time break, when the conveyers were turned off and we ate our sandwiches and poured the dubious contents of our buckets into larger vats. We sat down outside on wooden pallets, rubbing our eyes in an effort to expunge the lingering image of dancing plums engraved on our retinas. We watched the factory workers, mainly young girls, jive to the rock music which still blared out of the loudspeakers, until the hooter sounded and a supervisor herded us back for the afternoon shift. The same monotonous process was repeated each day for the next week. The only change was that some days we worked at the Kingsmere Factory, helping to process the detritus we had already dispatched to them. Here the conditions were even more primitive, and we had to open large tins of various fruits, to be mixed together for one of the firm's product lines of Mixed Fruit Salad. Some of the tins were blown, and produced some welcome comic relief when we punctured them with a tin opener, and they went off like a fire extinguisher, disgorging putrid liquid in all directions! Strawberry Jam was another Kingsmere brands destined for Woolworths. It was almost completely artificial, and made from pulped turnips plus the leftovers from the Wilkins Factory, with added colouring matter and artificial pips made by an old crone, sitting in the corner, feeding bits of wood into a special mincing machine. One afternoon there was a great panic, when it was learned that the Inspectors were coming for a snap check. The "Pip Lady" was spirited away into a backroom, and we were issued with white hairnets and overalls. The brooms were out, and the whole factory smelt of stale Dettol. Supervisors were suddenly on hand, to watch us spooning regulation amounts of fruit into the tins of mixed salad, which passed before us on the conveyor belt. We heard, the next day, that the inspection had not gone as planned, and that rodent pee had been detected in the strawberry jam!

On some days the schedules were changed, and we were dispatched to work on different farms. This mostly involved picking fruit, cutting out dead canes from long rows of raspberries, and general weeding. It was a lovely hot summer, and it was good to be out in the open air. But the work was tiring and repetitive, and students often worked with friends from their own country, so they could chat to someone familiar to relieve the boredom. The English contingent was fairly relaxed, and we gradually edged along the rows, leaving little clumps of unearthed weeds as we went. The Germans, however, saw the task as a test of will for the Fatherland and blitzkrieged up the line with weeds flying in all directions! The war had been over for fourteen years, but national stereotypes, it seemed, still abounded. In general, however, all the different national groups got on well. Some farms were near to the Blackwater Estuary and we often swam together at lunch time. In the evening most of us would visit the local pubs in lovely villages like Tolleshunt Knights. We would walk back to the camp in the moonlight, along the lanes, which meandered through flat fields of wheat. On dark nights, our way was often lit by glow-worms shining from beneath the hedgerows.

Sometimes, back at the hostel in Tiptree, groups of students would put on spontaneous concerts, with Israeli and Polish students usually doing the best singing and dance routines. On some nights, I drank at the bar in the camp and talked to Maria, who was studying to be an English Teacher and came from Ljubljana in Yugoslavia, and another girl called Anne, who had been educated at Bedales – which at the time had the reputation of being an expensive "Freedom School". I recall that her experience of A. S. Neill type education, seemed to have left her just as confused about life as my sojourn in a more authoritarian institution. I also had long exciting discussions late into the night with a variety of other students about politics and world peace. Although I missed Lily, and wrote her regular letters, and rang my Mum and Dad, to check on things at home. However, there was no doubt I was enjoying my summer in the Essex countryside. Deep down, however, I harboured worries about what I would do if I had failed the first part of my Finals.

The Results Day coincided with the beginning of my third week at the Camp and I hitch-hiked into Witham with Maria and a small group of other students. I was relatively green to the technique of procuring lifts and I noted, with a wry smile, that it was the girls who did the thumbing while, the boys hid in the shadows, only appearing at the last minute, when a car had been loured to the kerb-side. I said good bye to the others, and caught the train into London. I arrived at Russell Square, and saw a group of my old friends standing anxiously outside a big notice board next to Senate House. At this time in the 1950's, no course work was submitted for first degrees, and everything depended on exams at the end of the course. In the case of the BSc Econ course, Part One of the Finals was judged on eight three hour examinations, sat at the end of two years. Part Two, which mainly determined the class of your degree, required candidates to sit five more three hour exams in their specialist area, were sat a year later. The stakes were, therefore, very high and students who failed Part one, would leave after studying for two years with nothing to show for their troubles. Although the teaching was good at the Poly, because we were external candidates, our lecturers were not privy to setting, or marking the exams, and we were denied the tips, and inside information students at LSE might have received. It was, therefore, harder for us to get a good class of degree.

I saw Lily looking worried and immediately embraced her with a big hug. At eleven 0'clock sharp, a clerk from the university appeared and pinned a long list to the notice board. The results were worse than we expected. I had survived, along with some of my friends like Ray, Bazil, Stuart, Doug, Lucy. But Lily had failed, together with Dereck, John, Ronky and some others. Lily, who had worked so hard, was inconsolable. She wanted to be as far away from the others as possible, and we sat on a bench in the corner of Russell Square. I put my arm around her but nothing I could do would quench her bitter tears of sadness. I tried to talk about the options she may have -- like doing a correspondence course -- or seeking help and advice from tutors, in the parts of the degree she had found difficult. But my words sounded hollow. I knew nothing about the Money and Banking part of the degree she had failed. And I also realised that, in reality, I knew little of her financial situation, or the support she might receive from her extended family in Singapore. She was too upset to eat anything and seemed anxious to escape from the medley of other students as soon as possible. In the end I walked her back to Tottenham Court Tube Station and we said our sad farewells.

Later I rang my Mum and Dad from Fenchurch Street Station to tell them that I had passed. My money ran out soon after I had pressed button "B" and I had no time to elaborate on Lily's sad fate. I got back to the Camp at Tiptree just in time for the evening walk to the pub. It was a beautiful night and the glow worms were winking in the hedgerows. The camaraderie was as good as usual and my friends bought me a pint for passing. More pints followed, and I came to realise that I was developing a liking for Suffolk beer. The taste of the amber liquid seemed to enter my soul -- almost as if it was passing judgement on the bitter sweet events of the day.

I worked the usual factory and farm shifts for the next three days, but when I returned on Thursday night I found a telegram message from Uncle Norm. Poor Dad had suffered an appendicitis and been rushed to hospital. It was imperative I return home immediately. I rang my Mum, and discovered that he had already had the operation and was recovering in the local hospital. I arranged to meet her in Uckfield in time for the evening visiting session, and caught the train back to Sussex the next day. When I got to the ward Dad was sitting up in bed looking surprisingly chipper -- happy to be the centre of attention. "I'm a tough old bird!" he said. And went on to recount that, under the anaesthetic the nurses were surprised to hear him babbling away in Italian. I wondered to myself whether the redoubtable Chalkie White had featured in his musings, and that if this was the case, it might have been just as well if his utterances were in a foreign tongue. We were both relieved to see that he had come through the operation so well and we left him happily sucking grapes and reading his Agatha Christie paper-back at the end of the visiting time.

We caught the bus back to Herons Ghyll and I fed the chicken and collected the eggs. I also lit the boiler and carried buckets of coke into the kitchen and pumped water into the header tank in the roof, while Mum got the supper. She was pleased to have me home. And indeed, I wondered how she would have coped on her own without my help. I missed my friends at the Farm Camp, and I was worried about Lily, but I also appreciated that at times like this, it was necessary for me to shoulder my family responsibility. I realised that when Dad came home he would be in no fit state to resume his heavy gardening routine, so the next morning I started to cut back the heavy foliage, which separated our garden from the encroaching forest, and used Dad's new Tarpen electric hedge trimmer to saw away at some of the very tall hedges. In the afternoon, we visited Dad again at the Cottage Hospital and bought some food back for the evening meal. Dad was released a couple of days later, and came home to convalesce, and for the next few weeks I continued to do all the heavy work around the house and garden.

Towards the end of the holiday I received a phone call from Stuart asking me if I would like to come on a short holiday with him to the Gower Peninsular. It was organised by the National Union of Students, and – this was an amazing coincidence – we would stay in the original Kilvrough Junior House, where my Mum had danced away the midnight hours in the 1920's. Although, Dad was now a good deal stronger, I debated whether I should go. But my parents, knew I had to return to College in a week's time, encouraged me to have a final fling before the beginning of term.

I met Stuart at Paddington Station, and we joined a party of students and other young people boarding the Swansea train. The NUS had combined forces with the Association of Boys and Girls Clubs and some of the holiday makers were youth leaders. I had been on lots of family holidays to the Gower, and knew all the good places to visit. On the journey down, Stuart and I poured over an old ordinance survey map of the area, planning trips to all the beautiful places I had known as a boy. When we arrived we found that the grandeur of Kilvrough, remembered so romantically by my Mum, had been diluted somewhat by the addition of youth hostel facilities. However, it was still a very imposing building, with spectacular views over Pennard Burrows, towards Three Cliffs Bay and Crawley Woods, and the broad sweep of Oxwich Bay. Stuart was keen on walking and natural history, and we spend our first days exploring as much of the beautiful peninsular as we could by walking along the wet sand at low tide, past a rocky cliff called Big Tor and Nicholaston Burrows, to a little church hidden in the trees which covered Oxwich Point. We also walked from Parkmill to Cefn Bryn, the highest point on Gower, where you could see sea on both sides of the peninsular, and look west to the majestic sweep of the Rhossili Downs, and across to the cockle beds near Penclawdd. We found a large megalithic monument called the King Arthur Stone, and I took a photo of Stuart perched on top with my Brownie Box camera. Our ability to explore the rest of the area was limited a little by the limitations of the local bus service, but we did manage to have lovely swims -- battling the big breakers at Rhossili, and a walk over the majestic cliffs as far as the causeway leading to the rugged point of Worms Head.

Towards the end of the week, the weather changed and we were forced to wrap up warm and explore nearer home. By this time we had teamed up with some of the others at the holiday centre, and we struggled through the rain as far as Shepherds – a local store and tea room in Parkmill where we sat around drinking coffee, and rubbing our hands to get warm. Stuart buried his nose in a local guide-book he had just bought, and announced that there was an inland pre-historic cave we could visit nearby at Parc le Breos. Not everyone was persuaded by his Public School zeal, but a girl called Margaret, and a boy called Jeff who were both youth leaders, decided to come with us. We walked up the road together, our heads bent against the icy downpour. After half a mile we turned off, and followed a path through a small park flanked on the left hand side by tall cliffs of rock partly hidden by undergrowth. Stuart marched purposely ahead, guide book in hand, and then we all saw it – a dark diagonal cleft in the cliff, partly obscured by bushes. We climbed up a scree of rocks and managed to find sufficient hand holds to crawl inside. Margaret produced a torch from her rucksack, and we could see that the cave ran steeply uphill opening up further on like the nave of a church. A small ray of natural light shone down from a small hole high above us. I was impressed, I had been coming to Gower for years and been on expeditions with my Dad and Averil ("Aunty"Ethle's Niece), to see a variety of prehistoric caves like Paviland and Minchin Hole, but this one was new to me. We poked around for a short time, looking vaguely for old bones or any other signs of the marks made by its ancient Neanderthal occupants. When we came out, the rain had stopped and the park was bathed in watery sun light. As we started to walk back Stuart, still clutching his guidebook suddenly bounded forward. "Look". He shouted triumphantly, "Here's the tomb of the giant who lived here 2000 years BC!"

The next day was our last, and because the weather still looked very changeable, the four of us decided to explore the local area. Stuart was still focused on caves and said we should try to find some interesting ones with natural chimneys at Pobbles Bay. We walked over the dunes and then clambered down the cliff path and made our way over the stepping stones that crossed the stream, which meandered through Three Cliffs Bay. When we reached the iconic cliffs themselves the tide was coming in and spilling through the natural arch in the rock. We looked back, and saw wild horses paddling in the river nearer to the shore, and the stark outline of Pennard Castle on the high dunes above the bay. It was a beautiful dramatic scene. Rather than retrace our steps, we decided to wade through the water under the arch and take the seaward route to Pobbles Bay. But the water was deeper than we expected and spilled over the bottom or our shorts while Margaret had to hitch her dress into her knickers. We finally paddled ashore and made our way around the next rocky promontory and into Pobbles Bay. We discovered the caves almost immediately, and had good fun trying to inch our way up the chimneys to the top of the cliff. In the end the task proved too arduous and we decided we would have to climb up the cliff from outside. When we came out of the caves we saw that the tide had come in quicker than expected, and this was our only option unless we wanted to swim back home! We managed to clamber up the cliff relatively unscathed. When we reached the cliff path Jeff and Stuart wanted to go on and explore a cave at the top of Big Tor further on towards Oxwich despite the strong wind that was beginning to blow in from the sea. In the end, Margaret and I decided to walk back to the centre at Kilvrough on our own. To begin with our route was fairly straight forward, but we then came to a fork in the path. One looked as if it would take us on a big loop to the main road leading to Parkmill. The other path appeared to take us back the way we had come and looked more direct. Margaret said she wanted to visit the ruins of Pennard Castle before she went home so we opted for the shorter route. We followed a steep sandy path leading through ferns and gorse down to the beach. When we got there however, we found that the tide was in, and what had been a lazy stream had turned into a raging torrent, so it was impossible to take a short cut across the bay. It the end we managed skirt around the other side of, what was now a river, by navigating marshland and scrubby tree roots. We then had to ascend another precarious path through the sand-dunes to the Pennard Burrows. The path was so steep that, in some cases, it was one step forward two steps back. By this time there was a full gale blowing causing the sand to lash against our bear legs and arms and sting our faces.

 Finally we struggled into natural ditch beneath the walls of Pennard castle which afforded us some protection from the wind and rain. Margaret cuddled up to me and I felt the warmth of our two bodies mix. Our struggle against the storm had seemed like some kind of baptism. Or at the very least, part of a plot from a romantic short story, or a scene from "The Famous Five". I pulled her closer and she responded, to my great surprise by giving me a French Kiss. We lay together wrapped around each other, for a few more minutes before the howling gale got the better of us, and we made our way back to Kilvrough. On arrival we hung our macs up to dry and changed out of our wet clothes. I bought Margaret a drink, and we sat at wooden benches, waiting for Stuart and Jeff to return, and excitedly telling anyone, who would listen, about our day's adventures. I felt mixed emotions. Part of me was elated that I had followed my Mum's advice and played the field. But I also felt guilty at betraying Lily. In the straightened world of the 1950's -- when girls in Noel Coward type plays -- once kissed in the garden, would burst through the French Windows triumphantly announcing their engagement to an indulgent Mumsie and Daddy! I wondered about the consequences of my mild flirtation. I needn't have worried. Margaret told me quiet firmly that she was already -- "spoken for". She would, of course, be happy to be my Pen Pal.

On the way home I left my heavy suitcase at the cloakroom in Paddington Station and went to see Lily in Craven Terrace. She seemed overjoyed to see me and we spent a beautiful afternoon together. Our conversation was easy and we felt totally at ease in each other's company. I asked her about her plans for the next year and she said she was determined to re-sit Part One of the Finals although she was rather vague as to how this was to be accomplished. I told her that I had to get back to Sussex to see my Mum and Dad, but that I would take her out for the whole day as soon as I resumed my studies at the Poly. She trembled in my arms as I left, and I felt sadness well up inside me as I kissed her goodbye.

A couple of days later I was catching the 8.15am train with Uncle Norm with a bulging brief case full of new files and Sociology books for the last year of my degree. It was good to be back at the School of Commerce, but it was sad to think that Dereck, and John and some of my other friends were now awaiting their call up papers for National Service. While girls like Lily and Ronky faced an uncertain future. The survivors, like Ray, Bazil, Stuart, and others were anxious to do well. Change was in the air, and Lucy, the beautiful English Rose in our Sociology group, who always looked so untouchable, suddenly took up with Demitrius, a mature Greek student – much to the chagrin of some of the English boys who had been too frightened to date her. Doug set up a special tutorial group where we all helped each other with essay writing and examination technique. Because of the limitations of the Poly Library, we were allowed to access some of the books we needed for the course by studying in the Reading Room of the British Museum. I still occasionally had lunch with Stuart in our old café, but it was never the same without the languid drawl of Dereck's voice, or Lily's excited chatter. As time went on, I spent more and more time studying in the Goldsmith Library at Senate House or sitting in the great Round Reading Hall of the British Museum, with Ray and Doug and other students from the Poly, amongst some of the old men with grey beards, who seemed to model themselves on Karl Marx. We were amazed that the flunkies delivered rare books to our places with the same deference they displayed to visiting professors and other academics.

I used my season ticket to travel up to London from Coulsdon on my first free Saturday. I met Lily at Charing Cross and we caught a boat up the Thames to Kew Gardens. It was a lovely bright day with just the first hint of autumn colouring the leaves in the trees. We had a lovely time walking around the gardens and, scaling the heights of the wrought iron walkways in the old Victorian glasshouses. On the way back the eddying ripples at the back of our boat caught the last of the evening light mixed with blush of neon from some of the public buildings we passed. We held each other others hands tight -- both wishing that the day would never end.

As the year progressed, I settled into a routine at College. I enjoyed specialising in Sociology for the second part of my finals, and had lots of long discussions with Uncle Norm about Marx and Hegel and different sociological theories. I had little idea what I wanted to do for a career but I enjoyed studying, and harboured vague ideas of continuing my studies after the course finished. A few bright students were sometimes hired to teach 'A' level and conduct undergraduate seminars at the Poly and even LSE. Ray, Doug and I all hoped that we could somehow prolong our existence in the hallowed halls of academe, with the help of part-time work of this kind. Towards the end of our last year the Government abolished National Service. Doug had already done his time, but Ray and I were overjoyed -- despite the fact that part-time teaching was difficult to obtain and there were virtually no grants for post-graduate degrees.

At last the first day of the finals arrived, and we all trooped into a great examination hall with all the other London University students. I had a streaming cold and the invigilators put me in a corner away from the others. At the end of each three hour exam my desk was surrounded by a heap of sodden tissues. I was in a highly nervous state, and for some unaccountable reason, wrote my 'A' Level exam number on my first script, only correcting my error at the last moment when the papers were being corrected. I had put a big effort into my revision programme, even absenting myself from my cousin Pam's wedding, which was held a couple of days before the beginning of the exams. At the end of the week it was all over. My fountain pen was back in my inside pocket and the aching fingers of my right hand could finally rest. My head was still spinning with facts, but there was nothing more I could do. I felt an odd feeling of anti-climax. Outside the examination hall everyone was swapping names and addresses. It was very sad saying goodbye to friends I had known for three years realising that I would probably never see some of them again. Later on I walked over to the Student's Union's office in Endsleigh Street with Ray. He said that that they were promoting an amazing holiday offer, subsidised by the government in Yugoslavia, where you could go to an international camp where political seminars would be held in Marxist-Leninism and Tito's Third Way. The trip would last 15 days, and include a train journey right across Europe to Rijeka and a boat trip down the Adriatic to Dubrovnik, where we would live in tents outside the city's ancient walls. Food would be provided as part of the deal. The total cost was £28 and Ten Shillings. I had never been abroad before, and the offer seemed too tempting to refuse. Ray and I paid our deposit on the spot. Later in the day I took Lily to see the film Marjorie Morningstar -- a 'rite of passage' story about a Jewish girl who challenges the conventions of her family in the pursuit of romance.

The next day Mum and Dad journeyed up to Coulsdon to collect all my stuff. We had lunch, and a good family get together, but it was sad to realise that this was the end of an era and that would meaning moving back to Sussex which seemed so far away from my friends and associations in London. Norm and Gladys had been so good to me, and I felt quite emotional as we said our goodbyes to them and my Cousin Linda. On the way home, Dad confided that he would retire at the end of the year. He had now completely recovered from his operation, and was looking forward to being with Mum during the day, and developing part of the field as a small holding. He also promised that he would teach me how to drive. He was as good as his word and a week later I had my provisional licence and we had attached 'L' plates to the old Vauxhall. We chose some quiet roads, and I started to practice basic procedures like hill starts and double de-clutching in the little lanes between High Hurstwood and Hadlow Down. Dad had never had any formal lessons and had simply "Got the knack of it!" in the 1920's when he had bought his first car and had to drive it home. However, he was a good teacher, and taught me the mechanics of driving very well. After a few weeks he seemed pleased by my progress and encouraged me to put in for the test." No harm in trying" I bought a copy of the Highway Code and swotted up my road signs and practiced my three point turns.

Ten days later, I was taking the test at East Grinstead replacing Dad at the wheel of our old car and opening the passenger door for the tester to sit beside me. He was a miserable looking individual wearing a green cap pulled down over his eyes like a stable boy. He spoke like a Dalek "Proceed with the test" He intoned. I exaggerated the twist of my neck to indicate that I was looking in the rear mirror, and engaged first gear and let in the clutch. We eased away from the kerb and I breathed a sigh of relief. After a couple of hundred yards the tester asked me to turn left into a minor road. I indicated that I was about to turn and gripped the gear lever tightly as I double de-clutched to help break my speed. Suddenly the top of the gear stick -- which was simply a rubber ball secured by a small nut, came away in my hand -- I panicked and hit the kerb. "I've failed!" I said. But Green Cap was undeterred. "Proceed with the test" he growled as he watched me frantically trying to screw back the top of the gear lever. Although my confidence was shot to pieces, he forced me to do the rest of the test, even the emergency stop, all the while scribbling furiously at the check list in his hand. When we finally skidded to a halt back at the Test Centre he threw the book at me. I didn't try for the test again for another four years.

The next day my passport came through and I was packing my case for my first holiday abroad. Mum and Dad were quite supportive, and said I deserved a break for all the hard work I had done. A couple of days later, I was boarding a train at Victoria Station with Ray and a group of other students. After crossing the Channel, we boarded a train travelling through Lille to Paris, where we transferred to a sleeper train which took us on an exciting trip through Strasbourg, Munich, Salzburg, and Ljubljana. I can remember being struck by the beauty of the mountain scenery, and the impressive churches and chateaus which clung to the hills, or were sunk deep in the valleys. When we reached the port of Rijeka we boarded a small boat packed with excited locals, many carrying baskets of fruit and chickens in cages. The trip down the Adriatic took twenty-four hours, and we made frequent stops at some of the pretty islands – a few little more than a shelf of rock with a lone minaret, or small house shimmering in an azure sea. We also visited the ports of Zadar and Split, on the way to the ancient walled city of Dubrovnik. I was amazed at the beauty of some of the local girls, taking trips between one island and the next, whose white dresses and bare arms and legs, contrasted with the black peasant costumes of many of the older women. I also marvelled at the purity of the evening light and the reflections of white buildings and red roofs dancing in the sparkling water.

We arrived at the seaside resort of Lapad, and transferred our things to the tents, which were already pitched in the grounds of a hotel. We were then issued with meal tickets and told we could use them at most restaurants in Dubrovnik. Ray and I, and most of the others, then caught a lovely old double-decker tram along the sea front to a stop outside of the City walls. We walked through the main gate, and found ourselves in the main street. The lights were lit, and the sound of music filtered out of nearby cafes. Flocks of excited holiday makers and locals, most dressed up for the occasion, were promenading along the length of the central avenue. We passed by a fountain and a medieval old Franciscan Apothecary shop, and headed towards a tall Bell Tower at the end of the boulevard, and then followed a labyrinth of small streets towards the port. We found a café that would accept our tokens and sat around in a circle under a big umbrella and had a meal of goulash washed down by good local wine. We were all smiling broadly. If this was communism, then I think that most of us would have voted for more of it!

The next day after breakfast, served in the hotel, we sat outside under some trees in the garden for our first session of political indoctrination. The Yugoslavian students and card carrying members of the local party were a little older than most of us. They spoke quite good English and even managed a few jokes. The message was to reject the authoritarian regime of Soviet Communism, and the unbridled Capitalism of the USA, in favour of "Titoism" which offered the best of both worlds. No one could really object to this message of a benign "third way" – especially after we had been plied with free glasses of Slivovitz after the contribution of each speaker! Each afternoon we were allowed to do our own thing, and Ray, myself, and another boy called John Mountsey -- who spoke with a strong Yorkshire accent, and was studying Physics at University College -- spent the rest of the day exploring the old city wall of Dubrovnik, and swimming off the nearby rocks. John vouchsafed the he thought the English girls on our trip were a prissy lot –"Not a patch on those Yugoslavian wenches!" In an era of pre-political correctness we all heartily concurred.

For the next ten days the holiday followed a predictable pattern. Each morning we would be woken by an announcement over the Camp's Loud Speaker System of the day's events -- followed by a burst of "All say Romantica!"-- a Yugoslavian pop song of the time. Part of each day was usually given over to political seminars -- with the rest of the time being free for our own activities, like visits to the lovely old port of Dubrovnik, and trips to the Island of Locrum, with its peacocks and stunning views of the Dalmatian Coast. One evening, we were all bussed to a big open amphitheatre to see a play put on by a local dramatic group. Another time, we were encouraged to engage in a big political rally. While sometimes the trips seemed to have no obvious political message, like a visit to Mostar – a famous bridge which guarded the passage over the Neretva River and was a beautiful example of Sixteenth Century Islamic architecture. On some occasions the political message didn't always coincide with our everyday experience. Yugoslavia, at this time, was anxious to market its own version of Coco Cola and also, its own revolting brand of cigarettes – a poor man's Gauloise. These were heavily advertised, with big hoardings -- sometimes erected in the shallows of beautiful lakes. This didn't seem to chime well with the official party line which attacked the iniquities of Western commercialism.

Near the end of the holiday we were all given a heartfelt memory. A group of partisans took us to a remote prison where Nazi guards had regularly executed anyone they caught participating in the Resistance. The method used was particularly sadistic. Prisoners were strapped to a wall at the end of a long corridor. Then all the doors, which were heavily reinforced with steel studs, would be closed. The guards would then take turns at firing through the doors, with the terrified prisoners sometimes experiencing long periods of agony waiting for the final bullet to strike home.

When we returned to St Pancras Station we all agreed that we had had the holiday of a life time. Now the magic had stopped and we were at a crossroads, waiting for our exam results to come out -- facing an uncertain future. We all vowed to keep in contact. Although, I had kept up my correspondence with Lily and recent sent her a funny account of my driving test debacle, I felt guilty about the holiday I had just enjoyed and my period of exile in Sussex away from London. I left my luggage at the station and caught the tube to Queensway. I walked to Craven Terrace and rang the bell of her upstairs flat. There was no reply and I scribbled a short note to her on a scrap of paper and pushed it through the letter box. I was sorry to have missed her, but I still harboured the vague hope that I might return to London soon, and be back at the Poly doing some kind of research or part-time teaching, so that I could give her more constant support. As I turned to walk back up the street, a Chinese man suddenly loomed out of the shadow of a doorway and angrily confronted me. "You stay away from her you understand!" He shouted. "She not want you anymore!" My protests were to no avail. And our angry exchange caused another Chinese man to appear from an adjacent garden in support of the first. I had little option but to walk away. My family, fearful of my contact with the mysteries of the orient, had sometimes, joked, half seriously, about Triad Gangs taking me out. But I suspect that what I had encountered was either possessive rage of a new boyfriend, or members of Lily's extended family, finally closing ranks to protect one of their own against the dalliance of a less than constant boyfriend. I felt emotionally bereft by the experience; and had great difficulty coming to terms with the loss of such a treasured relationship. I of course, made great efforts to contact Lily. But my letters remained unanswered. Although I never said anything at the time, I was inclined to blame my Mum's ambivalent attitude towards Lily. But this was unfair. I was green about the gills, and five years in a single sex boarding school had done little to prepare me for the emotional demands of adult love. A year later, when I rented a room in London, and had a regular income, I speculated as to whether things would have turned out differently, if I had met Lily at this time. Given the conflict of interests I faced in 1960, I even gave myself airs and graces by quoting the Bard – "The time is out of place – Oh cursed sprite that I was ever sent to put it right!" However, one can always over romanticise regrets about the past. In truth, I had been over absorbed by my own problems and interests in my last year at university. I had dallied too long with Lily's affections and paid the price. Deep down, however, I vowed that that next time I fell in love - I would follow my instincts regardless, and brook advice from no one.

Chapter 6
Organisation Man

My degree result came through in the middle of august 1960. I discovered that I had been awarded a 2.2. I was relieved to have passed, but saddened that this grade of degree would make it difficult for me to pursue an academic career at university level. I discovered later that Doug was the only student in my year at the Poly to get a 2.1. I discussed the possibility of doing teacher training with Mum and Dad but they were strongly of the opinion that I should now get a job and stand on my own two feet – the Sunday Papers featured lots of job adverts for graduate training schemes in big companies. Why didn't I try for one of them? I said I had no inclination to join the ranks grey suited suburban executives I had commuted with for the last three years. Instead I fell back on an earlier dream I had harboured in my teens -- that of being a journalist. I started to explore the possibility of graduate entry and training as a cub reporter. I soon found that it was more difficult than I expected. Most trainee journalist served an apprenticeship after leaving school at 16 on a local paper and the few graduate places available seemed to be reserved for high fliers from Oxford and Cambridge or were recruited because of family connections. In desperation I opted for nepotism. Dad had handled portfolios of stocks and shares for a client in the bank who was well connected in the newspaper world, and I sent off copies of my stories and articles in my old school magazine for his perusal. Mum was more dubious about my journalistic ambitions and was worried about the effect unsocial hours would have on my delicate constitution! I told her that, thanks to my five year exposure to the "kill or cure regime" at Harper's College, I now enjoyed very robust physical health. But I did harbour secret fears of whether I was really fitted to the fast moving life of a reporter phoning in copy to meet deadlines if my stammer cut in. In the end I received a nice letter back from Dad's friend saying that I had undoubted writing ability but that the only vacancy they had was working in their city desk on stocks and shares. They would be happy for me to come for an informal chat to see if I might be suitable. I was in a terrible dither as to how to respond. I had hated anything to do with the money and banking aspects of my degree and had always avoided doing these questions in the exam. Furthermore, working in the City seemed to be a betrayal of all the socialist ideology I had imbibed over the last three years. Dad, wisely counselled -- that if I stuck it for a bit I could move to something more interesting in the field of journalism. I rejected his advice, and wrote a letter back saying that finance wasn't an area of interest for me. I bought a copy of the Times Educational Supplement the same day and put in for a job lecturing in Social Studies at Brighton Technical College. To my great surprise I got a phone call three days later asking me for an interview.

The next week, somewhat bemused, I was sitting in front of a panel of lecturers and local dignitaries – a rooky graduate with no teaching experience. I felt I had nothing to lose and prattled on about how I might apply my knowledge of Sociology, Politics and Applied Economics to the needs of HND Engineering students. I even attempted a few jokes and raised a couple of laughs. I was politely thanked for my efforts and asked to retire to the visitors' area, where

I would await the result with other nervous looking applicants who were being interviewed at regular intervals. I discovered that almost all of them had teacher training or previous teaching experience. Finally, in the late afternoon, the Principal appeared, and a gaunt looking individual wearing horn-rimmed glasses was summoned to the inner sanctum. A few minutes later he reappeared. "I have the pleasure to announce that Mr Simkins has accepted the appointment". He intoned. "Thank you for your attendance, it was a strong field of candidates and err", he paused, "We would like a quick word with Mr Strange". He laid a light hand on my shoulder and I was steered back into the Committee Room. The Chairman, who was a Local Counsellor rose to greet me. "Thank you for coming back" He smiled encouragingly, "We thought you would like to know that you put up a very good performance and we liked the ideas you put forward for our Complementary Studies Programme. The problem is that you would be younger than most of our students and you haven't had any previous teaching experience. Our advice to you is that you gain some industrial experience if you want to Lecture in a Technical College. We might well be interested in employing you in a couple of years' time".

I liked the atmosphere at the Brighton Tech and returned home to look through the jobs pages in the latest edition of the Times Educational Supplement in the vague hope that another college might have need of my social science skills. There was nothing. Summer was coming to an end. The evenings were drawing in and I was desperate to get away from home and start to lead my own life. I turned again to the Observer and Sunday Times which were still stuffed with advertisements placed by firms for graduate traineeships. I applied to join a two year scheme at the Headquarters of the Electricity Generation Board in London. Probationers would be given experience in General Administration, Consents (dealing with the sites chosen for new power stations) Wayleaves (planning permission for the routes taken by overhead lines) and Public Relations. If their face fitted they would be offered a permanent post at the end of the training. I sent off my application with a heavy heart knowing that I had no intention of becoming a bureaucrat in a large organisation. I felt I was selling out on all the socialist ideals I had imbibed over the last three years. My motives were purely instrumental : To earn enough money to live in London and keep contact with as many of my university friends as I could and to gain "industrial experience," which might help me eventually get a job lecturing in Further Education.

Ten days later I was being grilled by a group of black suited executives at the Headquarters of the CEGB. Fortunately, in 1960 there were no preliminary IQ or Personality tests, which would have probably caused me to fall at the first fence. And I was asked in general terms about how my knowledge of economics and government, featured in my degree course, might contribute to the planning procedures of a nationalised industry. I parried the questions as best I could, tried to look as earnest as possible, and truthfully affirmed my support for nationalised industries as opposed to private enterprise. A few days later I received an official letter confirming my appointment and setting my salary at the princely sum of £715 p.a.

Dad was pleased. "You'll be starting where I left off!" He exclaimed, grinning broadly. But I knew I had sold the pass. I also knew that I had run out of options. There was already a carpet of autumn leaves littering the ground outside Kilvrough, and the branches of the trees in the bridleway leading up to the glade of ferns, where Lily and I had once lain, in Ashdown forest were now bare. I was anxious to be away. Mum and Dad lent me enough money to survive the first month. I bought a dark suit for £10 from John Colliers. Before the week was out I was back in London walking down the Finchley Road looking at the small ads in the windows of tobacconists shops for bed-sitters, retracing the steps which Lily and I had taken eighteen months earlier.

The faded cards had not changed. The messages of "No Pets", "No Coloureds," "No Irish", "No Children" were as stark as ever. But, looking back, it was amazing that in 1960 one could find basic accommodation for as little as £5 a week a few tube stops from the centre of London. In the end I opted to look at a vacant bedsitter in Greencroft Gardens. I followed the directions and walked down the Finchley Road past the North Star Pub, and turned right at a big department store called John Barnes into Goldhurst Terrace. This road was boarded by a Jewish Delicatessen on one side and a garish looking night club called "La Cage D'Or" on the other. From here the road led downhill to Greencroft Gardens which was lined by trees flanked by large four storey Victorian Houses on each side. I rang the bell of number ninety and a woman in her thirties wearing a housecoat showed me a small room on the third floor. Its best feature was a large bay window, which afforded a good view of the street outside. Apart from that, the facilities were minimal comprising a single bed, a table and chair, a couple of shelves, one gas ring, and a gas fire. Both were fed on demand from a shilling in the slot meter. There was a wash basin, but no refrigerator or any means of keeping food fresh. The wall paper was beige, decorated with faded rose buds. The bathroom and lavatory were shared with other tenants on the same landing, and was dominated by a huge gas geezer with a winking pilot light, which looked as if it might explode at any minute. The room reminded me of the pinched little garret occupied by the ill-fated Mr Morrison I had visited four years earlier. But I was anxious to have a room of my own. "I'll take it" I said, and handed over the £20 demanded for four weeks rent paid in advance which also served as a deposit.

The next Monday I was walking up Oxford Street ready to begin my first day's work at the CEGB. As I swung my briefcase on my arm I mused that it now contained nothing more exciting than a newspaper and a pack of salami sandwiches I had bought earlier at the Delicatessen in Goldhurst Terrace. I remembered that, as little as three months ago, it had contained folders of radical sociology notes on Karl Marx, C.Wright Mills and Herbert Marcuse and a copy of William H Whyte's Organisation Man. I wondered why large companies were so interested in recruiting social science graduates at this time, who were likely to have a mindset critical of their world view, unless they intended to knock the subversive shit out of them in the first few weeks of their initiation. At five to nine I turned into Winsley Street and entered the ground floor of Waring and Gillow, which was a Department Store specialising in upmarket furniture, and waited for the lift to descend to take me to the fifth floor offices of the GEGB at the top of the building. I was joined by a number of other black suited Board men, many carrying furled umbrellas, and some even wearing bowler hats. The lift finally arrived and someone pushed the metal lattice door aside so we could all crowd in. The button was pressed and the whole contraption began its creaky ascent. When we reached the top floor, a voice brayed out from somewhere in our midst. "Well done Curruders! -- up in one this morning, you are a good driver!"-- Which meant the lift had had an uninterrupted ascent. There was a collective grunt of approval from the group. The same little ritual was enacted each morning during my sojourn in the Consents and Wayleaves Departments. Sometimes it was "Bad luck Tomkins -- Stopped at three and four today. You are a bad driver!" followed by mirthless snigger from the assembled suits. At the end of my first week I groaned inwardly as the same stale verbal exchange took place yet again. With horror I glimpsed the grey years stretching ahead of me and vowed that my stay in the organisation would be a short one.

On the first morning, one of the clerks, James Sparkes ("He's a live wire in the Electricity Board!") introduced me to the Head of Department -- a Mr Fenton. He was a large man with a rubicund face. His body was loosely contained in a pinstripe suit. He spoke with a broad Wiltshire accent and looked rather like an overgrown farmer's boy. "Sit down" He said. "We've 'ad quite a lot of you lot through recently". By this I assumed he meant Graduate Trainees. "Two bright ones from Oxford and Cambridge" I noted that Regent Street Poly didn't bear a mention. "Listen" he continued, "I want you to shadow me. I'm about to write an important letter about planning permission for the site of a new coal fired station. I am going to talk in general terms about my proposals and want you to take notes and draft a reply for my signature". Without more ado he launched into a quick-fire soliloquy full of bureaucratic jargon and references to local planning regulations. I was taken off guard and only managed to grab a writing pad, from an adjacent desk, on which to take notes, halfway through his delivery. At the end he handed me a large red file. "You can follow the previous correspondence in this. Let me have a draft reply in time for the afternoon post -- A top copy, and two flimsies". The session was abruptly terminated and I found myself outside his door, cradling the file in my arms and clutching my inadequate scribbled notes. James Sparkes kindly came to my aid and showed me a crib letter which contained the standard reply for the set of circumstances Mr Fenton had outlined. All I had to do was to write a draft letter and get it typed up for the great man to sign. The "flimsies" referred to were carbon copies to be kept on file.

Later that day, I was introduced to a Miss Dove, a severe looking grey haired woman in her fifties who dealt with Parliamentary Questions, and was given a desk in her office. She stood in the entrance to her room, as if prepared to defend her territory. Although her greeting was pleasant enough, I sensed she resented any invasion of her privacy. I walked in and laid my file on the desk immediately opposite hers, and dumped my briefcase under the coat stand behind me. The room was small and smelt of dust. It was lined on three sides with four-draw kaki coloured filing cabinets, which looked as if they had been left over from the war. There was a clock on the wall behind Miss Dove with a minute hand which, as the weeks went on, I watched every afternoon as the hands slowly crawled towards Five O'clock and I could make my escape. There was a small window to my left, underneath stood a long table piled high with files. The office was claustrophobic. It was difficult to directly view the street outside without moving mounds of paper. I felt cut off from the real world. On fine days the room would become very stuffy and I would be allowed to open the window a crack for ventilation, allowing faint sounds of humanity to drift in. But this only served to reinforce my desperate sense of isolation.

On my first morning I made an attempt at polite conversation. "How long have you worked for the Board Miss Dove?" I asked : "Since Vesting Date."-- came the abrupt reply, rather like the programmed response of a robot. While I was trying to get my mind around whether she meant the original date, when the electricity industry was nationalised in 1948, or the formation of the GEGB in 1957, I was interrupted by the rattle of a trolley in the corridor outside. "Tea" She announced, and rose up from her seat like a battleship in full stream. As she waddled past me out of the room, I noted that she was heavily corseted with the mark of the stays clearly visible through her grey skirt. When she returned, cup in hand, her back reminded me of a gigantic turtle. Her body was so constrained by the carapace of the under garment, which lay beneath, that her neck and arms appeared to move independently of the rest of her body. When she sat down, it seemed to me, that her neck sunk back into its shell and her face partly disappeared behind her raised tea cup.

I got on with my task of writing the planning letter for Mr Fenton. I followed James's advice and crafted a reply based on previous correspondence. I found some of the English rather archaic and altered trite phrases like "Thank you for the letter of the twenty-first inst ..." I had it typed in the Typing Pool and duly knocked on the Great Man's door, half an hour before the post was due to be dispatched. He took it from me wheezing and tut tutting as he scanned through it. In his hand he held a rubber stamp bearing the words "Fenton Approved". Any letter passing out of his office had to receive his purple seal of approval before being dispatched." Damn it

"He groaned "You've altered the introduction!" My draft was "corrected" back into Edwardian English and I had to run back to the Typing Pool for them to deal with the final version.

Later that day I felt the need to identify my existence to the rest of the organisation and wrote my name on a card and slotted it into a metal holder on the door of my office, next to Miss Dove's' name. The following morning it had mysteriously disappeared! I decided to remain anonymous for the remaining period of my secondment to the Consents Department. Over the next few weeks my relations with Miss Dove deteriorated still further. She seemed totally humourless and communicated almost entirely in bureaucratic jargon. Instead of saying she was going on holiday, she would -- "Indent for Leave". Parliamentary Questions, about planning consents for the building of new coal fired and nuclear power stations, directed to the Minister of Power, which might have been interesting to research, were referred to as "PQ's". Instead of consulting the engineers themselves about the latest developments, Miss Dove usually sort information from the dusty files in our office. When these failed to suffice I was dispatched to the registry deep in the basement where thousands of ancient ledgers were housed in great metal cabinets -- in the hope that some obscure statistic or planning decision would mollify the Minister's request, or help him play for time at the dispatch box.

Things came to a head when I attempted to smoke. Apart from an occasional cigar at Christmas with Dad and Uncle Les, which I sucked rather than inhaled, and a few Yugoslavian fags, imbibed with my friends on the Dalmatian Coast a couple of months previously, I had no form in this area. However, most people seemed to smoke in the CEGB and offices were often shrouded in a blue haze. I felt vaguely that I was in need of a new macho image. In addition, my isolation in my bedsit in Greencroft Gardens, had encouraged me to identify with existentialist literature and the world of Jean Paul Sartre and Colin Wilson. Phenomenology, mixed with my sadness at the ending of my relationship with Lily --- combined with reading radical sociological books, like William H. Whyte's Organisation Man, which talked about of the life cycle of executives in big American companies, and how they became more and more dependent on the firm they worked for. On a lighter level, I had read Kingsley Amis' first novel "Lucky Jim" and I may have unconsciously identified with the character of James Dixon -- a junior lecturer who feels an outsider in a provincial university, and reacts against the institution with disastrous and hilarious consequences. I saw the film version, and in quiet moments, even hummed its catchy theme song "Oh Lucky Jim! How I envy him!" I had also begun to write a first novel, pretentiously called "Saturday Night and Sunday Morning Hampstead version", and imagined myself struggling against feelings of ennui induced by my work. Life was boring and humdrum at the CEGB. Surely a fag or two would help me get through the day? The next morning at tea break I produced a packet of Woodbines from my jacket pocket and proceeded to light up. My attempt to inhale engendered a mild fit of coughing, but I persisted, exhaling puffs of smoke towards Miss Dove. She grunted a sigh of disapproval, but nothing was said. I busied myself writing a couple of letters for Mr Fenton's stamp of approval and took them to be typed. When I returned I found that Miss Dove had built a huge barricade of files across the middle space separating our two desks. Lines had been drawn for the cold war which was to exist between us!

I was determined not to let the organisation grind me down and made an effort to contact as many of my old university friends as I could. I wrote Lily a long letter and a poem about my new nine to five life style, but received no reply. I also contacted Ray Gordon and found that he was living in a shared flat in Belize Park. Like me he was desperate not to lose contact with our mates at the Poly, and we both hoped to find a back-way into teaching in FE. He said that Stephen Cotgrove was exploring the idea of running an evening tutorial for ex-students thinking of doing research for a further degree, and we agreed to attend the first session. It was good to see Doug and some of our other friends. Dr Cotgrove was quite encouraging, and we each talked about different areas of research we might pursue. Ray and I had no interest in any kind of statistical Durkheimian type of investigation, and so opted for studies requiring participant observation into areas of everyday life. It was suggested that I might get a job in a Public School to further my interactive study. However, the very thought of returning to a total institution, I had only escaped from three years earlier, filled me with horror. Strangely enough I never considered doing a similar study on the CEGB which could have given my life at the Board more purpose. We agreed to write up our initial ideas and research methodology, and return for another discussion in a few weeks time. Then we retired to the pub, lecturers and students alike, together with the Registrar of the School of Commerce, an affable Cockney called Mr Beard. We all engaged in boozy banter and the atmosphere was a world apart from my daily contacts at work. Ray and I talked to Doug who said he had a friend doing research at LSE who was also giving a series of lectures on Sociology for the Workers Educational Association. He thought it would be good experience for us to see him perform, and the see the kind of students the WEA attracted, if we aspired to teach in Further Education. Doug handed us the application forms and we both signed up for a course of ten lecturers starting in the New Year.

The year was drawing to an end, and Miss Dove informed me that as Christmas Day and Boxing Day fell over the weekend we would not return to work until Wednesday 29th of December. New Years Day would be worked as usual. New recruits like me were entitled to ten days annual leave a year plus statutory holidays. I would accrue an extra day of holiday, with every additional year of service up to a maximum of fifteen days a year. I groaned inwardly at the loss of my lovely long university holidays. My beautiful voyage down the Adriatic seemed a distant dream. But Miss Dove was quite chipper. Her spectacles glinted above the top of the barrier of files. "I intend to indent for three additional days between Christmas and New Year to extend my leave"-- she informed, me before sinking back into her shell.

The Office Christmas party was held on Wednesday 22nd of December 1960. There was a staff whip-round for the cost of wine and nibbles and the big tables in the large Board Room were moved to one side. Chairs were arranged around the walls and someone has rummaged in a filing cabinet and retrieved a few strips of bunting left over from the previous year. These, together with a few balloons hung limply from the ceiling. James Sparkes had brought in a turn table and some records which had been connected up to a loud speaker system. After work I treated myself to a pub meal and read the Manchester Guardian until the party started at 7.00pm. When I pushed back the lift door on the fifth floor of the Winsley Street Building, I heard music coming from the Board Room and saw that some of the girls from the Typing Pool had changed into party gear. Some were wearing little page girl hats, while others sported very full skirts bulked out with voluminous frilly petticoats. A few had hobbled themselves in very tight pencil skirts. Some board men had smartened themselves up with freshly ironed shirts with cuff links and neck wear skewered in place with shiny tie pins. I noticed that Chambers, one of the two Oxbridge Graduate Trainees, had also prettied himself up for the occasion. I scuffed my black shoes around the back of my trousers in the hope of raising a shine, and stuffed the tails of my drip dry shirt further into my trousers in the vain hope that I would pass muster for the occasion.

In the Board Room the lights had been dulled and someone had attached a rotating mirror ball to the ceiling which reflected shafts of coloured light in all directions. Some of the Board Men, who were usually so conscious of status demarcations, had thrown caution to the wind, and were already lumbering around the floor -- quick stepping with their secretaries or girls from the Typing Pool. However, while their partners still deferred to them by using their surnames, the pinstripes addressed them in a more familiar way. Conscious of the fact that, despite hours of compulsory skipping at Miss Punt's Dancing Classes, I still lacked any sense of co-ordination -- I avoided the melee in the middle of the room and followed Chambers to a table in the corner, where we helped ourselves to a glass of punch. He was a year ahead of me on the training course, and I asked him how he was getting on. He exuded confidence -- "I'm just about to start my period in Administration". He volunteered. "That's where they separate the men form the boys. I'm fairly confident they will put me on Grade Five when they make a permanent appointment". "But do you like the Organisation?" I persisted. But his answer was drowned by a burst of laughter from the dance floor. I helped myself to another glass of punch and ear wigged in on quite an interesting conversation between two engineers, who seem to have wandered in from a different party, about St Christopher Hinton and the post-war "Atoms for Peace Nuclear Power Station Programme". Eventually I felt the need to relieve myself, and walked up the corridor to the gentleman's toilet. On the way back I noticed that the party seemed to have spilled out in to a number of other offices. Here some Board Men appeared to be in the middle of rediscovering their Neolithic ancestry. Jackets had been discarded, shirts were unbuttoned, girlie hats were prized asunder and frilly bums were spanked as the GEGB executives pawed and fondled their way to oblivion, while the girls looked either startled or elated and sometimes a mixture of both at the same time. I was briefly reminded of the end of term Christmas Concert conducted by Raymond Basset and Tarty which had played on the idea of role reversal, three years previously. Tomorrow, I surmised, we would be back to "One top copy and two flimsies, and a cup of tea please Miss Pew!"

The innocent world of Regent Street Polytechnic and Lily Kong suddenly seemed light years away and I felt profoundly sad. I retraced my steps back to the main Board Room. I was already slightly intoxicated, and I started to indulge myself by imagining that I was the outsider in the organisation. For one night only I would be Jean Paul Sartre and Lucky Jim combined. Fortified by alcohol I would fearlessly defend my existence against the CEGB. Cocktails had been mixed for an important group of dignitaries who had toured various Departments bestowing Christmas cheer and boosting morale. They had now left and a row of discarded drinks remained on a shelf. In a moment of madness I started at one end and finished at the other, draining each glass as I went. Suddenly, it felt as if a great door was being slammed shut inside my brain. I remember very little about the rest of the evening. I have a vague impression of wandering around the whole of the Winsley Street Building, and being at a variety of different parties – my appearance at each, engendering either sighs of concern or gales of laughter. More frighteningly, I can recall the squeal of brakes and the hooting of horns as I blindly staggered across Oxford Street. And later, a very squalid scene where I threw up in a crowded tube train, and saw group of strap holders reeling back to avoid being engulfed in my vomit. I failed to get out at Finchley Road and ended up in an engine shed at Stanmore.

I was awakened the next morning by a friendly guard to discover that my front half was enveloped in an evil smelling deposit. My head throbbed. I looked at my watch and saw that it was 6.30 am. I went into automatic pilot and realised I had just enough time to return to Greencroft Gardens and scrub myself down ready for work. Back at my bedsitter I changed into another drip dry shirt and did my best to scrape the rest of the detritus off the lapels of my suit and applied a dab of "Old Spice", in the hope this would neutralise the unsavoury odour filtering up to my nostrils. By 8.30 am I was back in the lift heading for the fifth floor – except that it stopped at levels three and four. "I say Strange! You are a bad driver this morning!"-- came the syncopated response. This time, however the humour sounded a little more genuine. "I say old chap" came a voice from an anonymous bowler hat, "You had quite a night of it last night!"

The next evening I was relieved to be on the train with a big suitcase full of washing heading home for Christmas. Dad met me at Eridge Station and chided me for bringing all my dirty linen home. "Your mother's not up to it these days". He said. "You ought to get used to going to one of those washerette places". I felt guilty. He was quite right. By way of recompense, I handed back half the money he had lent me. "I'll give you the rest next time if that's OK?" He gave me a broad smile and seemed pleased -- Dad always liked you to pay your debts.

When we arrived home there was a cheerful log fire burning in the lounge and Mum was ready to serve a big supper in the dining room. She looked tired, but was very pleased to see me. She gave me a long hug and then drew back holding her nose. "There's a funny smell coming from that suit of yours". She exclaimed. "I thought they were teaching you how to supply electricity, not to roll around in the sewers, in that old Board of yours?" I said nothing. "We'll see what we can find for you in the January sales won't we Frank?" I was dispatched upstairs to change into my old Harpers College Jacket and a pair of thread-bare corduroy trousers. My John Collier suit, together with the mound of washing I had brought home, was laid to soak in the bath upstairs.

Later Dad confided in me that we were going to spend Christmas Day in with Uncle Norm and Aunty Gladys and Linda. He hated turning out at Christmas, but Mum chimed into say that it would be a great family occasion. Les and Doris would be there. They had sold their café in London and had bought a Wool Shop in Coulsdon. We could see their new house and shop. She volunteered that Farmer Curd, who lived at Fairwarp, had just dispatched one of our cockerels and the three of us would sit down to a great spread in our house on Boxing Day.

The next day the weather turned cold and snow began to fall as we drove across Ashdown Forest on the way to Coulsdon. After East Grinstead we stopped to scrape the ice off the rear window. The snow had started to settle on the road, and when we attempted to drive on the rear wheels spun, and I had to get out of the car to give it a push to get us going. Mum was a little worried and wondered whether we should turn back, but Dad threw caution to the winds. "Fiddlesticks Sis". He enthused, using my Mum's family nick name, "We've got a shovel in the back and some old sacks to put under the wheels! We'll get through!" He looked at his watch – "Let's get going we don't want to be late!" An hour later, after a few skids, we slithered to a halt outside 16 Woodmansterne Road. "We've made it" said Dad "It's five to one -- we're right on time!" A triumphant smile played around his lips and I was reminded of the day, long ago, when he had stood under the white porch of our home in Pound Green, kitbag in hand – a survivor of the desert war.

Aunty Gladys had made a great effort and it was good to be at a family gathering with both my Uncles and Aunty Doris and my Cousin Linda. Mum hurried into the kitchen to see if there was anything to do to help. I saw Dad's nose twitch slightly as if he was checking for the smell of gas and stale cabbage, but he was prevented from following her by Uncle Les' offer of a Manikin cigar and the clink of glasses as Norm laid out a tray of pre meal drinks, and the men, myself included, all settled back to talk about politics and life in general. Aunty Doris, who had followed my Mum into the kitchen, was a rabid Tory, and Uncle Les was cross pressured regarding his political views. He often played the role of devil's advocate and, as a restaurateur, and now shopkeeper, he liked to represent the view of the small businessman -- weighed down by business rates and the cost of wages. He would wave his arms about to emphasise points and sometimes mimic leading politicians like Harold Macmillan and Hugh Gaitskell. At the end of his "performance" he would usually re-affirm his lifelong support for Labour. In contrast, Dad with his studious reading of the "New Statesman and Nation" liked to present the considered views of the well informed Labour supporter, while Uncle Norm staunchly defended the leftwing views of Michael Foot and the cause of CND.

Before long there were there we signs of activity and Mum appeared with a tray of warmed plates and vegetables, followed by Linda carrying a jug of gravy and a pot of cranberry sauce. Norm retreated to the kitchen and fetched in the turkey which he proceeded to carve at the head of the table. "It's a feast fit for a king!" He enthused, looking rather quizzically at my Dad, who gingerly raised his glass in salutation. "Well done Glad!" At this we all chorused our approval. And Norm proceeded to dispense portions of leg and breast and stuffing to the waiting plates which were ritually passed around the table. Napkins were unfurled from silver rings and crackers were pulled, and suddenly, amidst the bangs, curses, and laughter we were all adorned with funny hats, almost as if were pre-programmed to act out the part of the middle class family in the 1960's. The second course was a large Christmas Pudding made by one of Aunty Gladys's sisters and laid down a year before, encased in a large white earthenware pot bound by a white cloth -- before its boiling for today's feast. Uncle Norm carried it to the table, where Uncle Les doused it in brandy and struck a match. It then radiated blue flames, and flickers of light danced before our eyes. This effect elicited a collective sigh of contentment. Not everyone favoured Christmas pudding, and I noticed, that Aunty Gladys had thoughtfully added to the menu by baking a sponge cake with icing adorned with tinned orange segments which had slithered down its side leaving the characteristic green skid marks. I caught Dad's eye and he winked at me as he held out his plate for another helping of Christmas Pudding.

After the entrails of the meal were cleared away we all retreated to the backroom to watch the Queen's Speech. She spoke about the birth of Prince Andrew and Princess Margaret's marriage to Armstrong Jones as well as the independence granted to Nigeria and the terrible massacre of those marching against the Apartheid regime at Sharpville in South Africa. We all sat in a deferential semi-circle facing the television. Ardent Monarchists like Aunty Doris, whose father had worked for the royal household, and Republicans like Uncle Norm -- who would probably opted for Buckingham Palace being turned into a rest home for retired trade unionists, fell silent. I can remember that my Mum cried in 1951 when the news of George V1's death was announced on the Home Service. Fifteen years after the war the Royals were still given credit for their public duty during the blitz and the idea of a New Elizabethan Age fitted well with the belief that the British Empire would gradually morph into a Commonwealth of free states linked by culture and tradition bound by monarchy --despite fears of the H Bomb and the bloody Verwoerd government in Pretoria. The Tories had recovered from the Suez debacle and Harold Macmillan had just secured a resounding election victory on the back of rising living standards and a naked appeal to a "New Middle Class" to embrace the fruits of affluence. However, the main elements of the post-war settlement remained, and Keynesian Economic Policy still ensured the worst excesses of a free market economy were properly managed. The maintenance of Full Employment remained a priority contributing to a general feeling of wellbeing.

After the broadcast Aunty Gladys produced cups of coffee and tea, as an antidote to our feelings of torpor induced by the heavy meal we had just imbibed, and it was suggested that we go on a short walk to visit Les and Doris' new house. A frost had set in and it was very cold outside and we all wrapped ourselves in our warmest clothes. The women wore fur coats and the men donned overcoats. Linda was forced to wear extra cardigans and a woolly pixie hat with ear muffs. The pavement was very slippery and I noticed that Mum, already out of breath, leaned heavily upon Dad's shoulder for most of the walk. I tried to throw a snowball at Linda but the frost was so sharp that it powered in my hand. The road, which glistened under the street lights, was a sheet of black ice.

My Uncle's new home was very similar to his brothers' -- one of the thousands of three bedroom pebble dashed semi's which had spawned along the railway line from East Croydon to Tattenham Corner to serve needs of commuters at the beginning of the twentieth century. Les said he had plans to keep chicken in the back garden in the same way that he had, when he and Doris had first set up home in Woodingdean in East Sussex and I wondered, to myself, how his new suburban neighbours would take to the idea. He also wanted to pull down a decrepit old asbestos garage, adjacent to the house, and put up a new ferro-concrete version. He was going to send off for one of the kits advertised in "Exchange and Mart" and Norm and I agreed to help him assemble it up as soon as it arrived. After a cup of tea and a mince pie and a quick inspection of the house, led by Aunty Doris, we again donned our heavy coats to face the cold conditions outside. The weather had deteriorated and an icy wind blew the snow straight into our faces. As we slipped and slithered on the frozen pavement it became clear that my Mum, who was wheezing and coughing, would never be able to make it down the steep hill to the centre of Coulsdon to see Les and Doris's new shop. Uncle Norm looked alarmed. He laid his arm on my Dad's shoulder. "Look boy" he said gently "the weather's getting worse, no sense in risking it – why don't you and Sis stay the night, we can put you up in the spare room and Mick can doss down on the camp bed". But Dad would have none of it. "It's very kind of you Norm" he said but we have to get back to feed our chicken and the cat – best if we leave now before it gets any worse". Further entreaties proved useless, and five minutes later we were in our Hillman Minx saloon with the engine revving and the wheels spinning and the family pushing to free us from the frozen snow which impeded our progress. Suddenly we were away -- careering down the steep hill leading to the main road with Dad struggled with the lever on the steering column, in an attempt to engage a lower gear to help break the car. Cars that had failed to get up the hill, had been abandoned, and lay at odd angles sticking into the road. They loomed out of the darkness like white phantoms, as Dad wrestled with the steering wheel and ground the gears in a desperate effort to avoid collisions. On one occasion we grazed against another car being pushed up the hill. We slithered to a stop and Dad got out of the car expecting the worse and was mightily relieved when the other driver agreed it was a "knock for knock incident" and waved us on. Dad whistled through his teeth --"Phew that was a close one!"

The conditions were just as treacherous when we reached the main road leading through Coulsdon, and we were lucky that most other motorists had decided to stay at home. We stopped at the turn off for the A22 to clear the ice off the car windows. When we tried to get going again the back wheels spun round and I had to jump out to push. In the end I made a track of old sacks before we could gain enough traction to get up the hill. The rest of the journey was something of a nightmare, but somehow we got through. We parked the car at the bottom of our drive, which was blocked by a snow drift, and Mum hurried in to put the kettle on while Dad and I locked up the chicken. He was pleased that we had won through against the odds. "Wouldn't want that fox to take our chickens for his Christmas dinner would we?" He mused, as we struggled to slide the bolts home of the coup door. I murmured agreement, but part of me would have like to have stayed at Coulsdon sharing the warm, if chaotic, family atmosphere which Norm and Glad always seemed to generate around them. I looked up at the grey sky, and then across at the bleak emptiness of Ashdown Forest. As we retraced our steps through the snow the stark outline of Kilrough loomed before us, flanked by high ornamental hedges which each year Dad struggled harder to tame. Icicles hung from the guttering and the wind caused the briars from the climbing roses to lash against the upstairs windows.

We entered the house by the backdoor and were thankful to kick off our wet shoes and warm our hands on the cup of tea Mum had made for us. She looked exhausted but endeavoured to put on a good face as she handed round a tray of welsh cakes. "You and Dad can get the cockerel from Farmer Curd's tomorrow and we'll get it in the oven nice and early with roast potatoes and all the trimmings". She said, "We'll have a great Boxing Day, just you wait and see …"

Later I pumped the water to feed the header tank and played with Twinkle our cat, then, I went up the backstairs to my bedroom. The gale continued to blow outside. It was almost as cold as the dormitory in the Headmaster's House at Harpers College and I wrapped myself in an extra blanket from the airing cupboard. Eighteen months previously I had lain in the same room in Lily's joyful embrace. Now I was a CEGB apprentice manager. A bachelor facing an uncertain future -- It wasn't until the small hours that I fell into a fitful sleep.

I awoke the next morning to the sound of Mum coughing and reaching up phlegm in the bathroom. I knocked on the door to see if there was anything I could do to help. "A cup of tea would be nice" she whispered "And check the boiler's come on. There's eggs and bacon in the fridge you can start making breakfast if you like. Remember Dad likes his fried bread -- there's dripping in the bowl by the tea caddy …" He was already up and I met him on the stairs carrying a stepladder. "Just thought I'd check on the water tank," he said," last time there was a cold snap the whole damn lot froze up and we had a hell of a job with the water system". I went down to the kitchen and started to prepare breakfast. Dad never varied in his demand for two courses -- starting with either Kellogg's Corn Flakes or Porridge, sweetened with a heavy dollop of Lyle's Golden Syrup, followed by a big fry up, which would frequently require added mushrooms and tomatoes and well done rashers of streaky bacon, plus the egregious fried bread! Mum opted for a bowl of Grape Nuts, which she said was good for her bowels, and toast and marmalade. I made some cups of Nescafe Coffee and noticed that the old square bottle of Camp Coffee with a picture of an Indian Prince, which had fascinated me as a child, had been faithfully transported from the Hollies. It must have remained unused for years but I was pleased that it had been kept as a talisman from the past – unlike my lovingly preserved collection of my old Eagle Comics which Mum had donated to a children's hospital, I ruefully remembered, while I was away at Harpers College.

After breakfast Dad and I walked up the road to Farmer Curd's farm to collect our Christmas bird. His cottage lay amongst a group of ramshackle farm buildings by the turning for Fairwarp which ran over Ashdown forest towards the radar pylons at Kings Standing. He met us at the door with the plucked and gutted chicken already prepared for the oven. He had just come in from milking and still wore his chequered cloth cap. His weather beaten face and hands bore the signs of years of toil against the elements in a harsh environment. There was a distant look in his eyes which seemed to hint at some tragedy and I wondered, momentarily, if he was old enough to have experienced the horrors of the First World War -- or maybe lost a son in the Second World War. He offered us his festive greetings in a thick Sussex accent while his wife, dressed in black, hovered in the shadows behind him. There was no attempt to ask us into the cramped parlour beyond, and we quickly negotiated the deal and headed for home. I sensed that the friendly relationship, Mum and Dad had enjoyed with Farmer Ford and his wife and family would not be replicated in Herons Ghyll. On the way back Dad confided that Farmer Curd was a "bit of a Gypsy who steered rather close to the wind". Apparently, he had secreted a load of bricks the Council had dumped on the verge opposite his farm, to use as hard core for road maintenance, to build an extension to his cow shed under cover of darkness.

Later in the day we all sat down to sumptuous Christmas meal and raised a toast to one another in Burgundy wine. Dad talked about his ambition to grow grapes and make his own wine. He had bought a Canadian rotavator and had plans to cordon off a corner of the field next to the chicken run to grow soft fruit. He would begin by growing loganberries on trellises and plant lines of black currants and raspberries and fruit trees. Mum was going to make lots of jam and bottled fruit. They were going to put up a sign by the entrance to the drive to attract passing motorists interested in their produce and Dad thought they might get a contract to supply the Ribena Factory with fresh currants. I murmured my approval but I wondered how Dad, who already struggled to cut the gigantic box hedges and cope with the garden, would manage this extra labour.

We lit a roaring log fire in the front room and Dad and I settled down to read the News Chronicle and the New Statesman while Mum had a rest upstairs. Later I had a game of Chess with him. After tea we all played Rummy and later watched a Maigret drama on BBC.

The next day we were all up early to get ready for our trip to the sales in Tunbridge Wells. When I went downstairs for breakfast Dad had already been up in the roof to free the frozen stopcock to allow the water to run freely in the bathroom. He looked pleased with himself -- "I've put the hurricane lamp up there – that should take the chill off!" Later, when we got in the car, I noticed Mum had put on her best dress and powdered her nose. She was looking forward to an outing. She laid a hand on my shoulder ---"We might go to that posh tea shop in the Pantilles" she said, "You can have beans on toast like you always do." She was determined to mother me. I knew how much she had missed me when I was away at boarding school and, despite her grand talk about Kilrough and fruit farming, I knew how much she missed her social life in Pound Green. I was prepared to indulge her for this one day at least. Part of me, however, felt detached. Deep down I still resented the way my mother had tried to manipulate my relationship with Lily at my 21st birthday party. I was pleased that I was now living my own life in London and was determined to be my own man.

When Dad pulled the starter a low groan was heard beneath the bonnet. "Damn it!" exclaimed Dad "Battery's a bit flat. Can you give us a swing Mick?" I took the starting handle from under the seat and swung the engine as hard as I could while he fiddled with the choke. Finally the car burst into life and we were away – wheels skidding, as we made our journey past the "Crow and Gate" pub towards Crowborough -- heading east. Trudging around the Sales in Tunbridge Wells was not my idea of a great day out and I relapsed into a kind of mental trance and we wandered around what seemed like an endless number of Department Stores with Mum fingering pairs of gloves and funny hats. Finally, we alighted on a Gentleman's Outfitters and I stood, like a silly mannequin, while Mum did the talking. "He'd like a best suit." She said, pointing at me. "Have you got one his size in the sale?" There then followed an embarrassing measurement of "Young Sir's" inside leg, waist and chest measurements. Finally the obsequious shop assistant produced a green worsted suit that looked as if it had been personally tailored for Bertie Wooster. I was ushered behind a curtain and persuaded to try it on. When I emerged I was conscious of the thick tweed itching my legs and arms. My nose twitched and I stifled a sneeze. "I don't think ... I began. But Mum was beaming adoringly at me. "He's a Management Trainee at the Electricity Generation Board." She announced to the whole shop. "Do you think it is suitable?" "Oh Yus Ma'am "came the unctuous reply from the assistant, and my protests were brushed aside. Five minutes later I had written the cheque and I was standing outside Mum's favourite tea shop clutching a large brown paper parcel. I harboured a sinking feeling that I had made a terrible mistake but I went on to act out the part that Mum expected me to play. Inside the café while Mum and Dad delicately forked their portions of carrot cake, I ate my baked beans with great relish and said that I had had a wonderful meal. Later in the evening Dad dropped me off at Eridge Station for my return to London clutching my new suit and a bag of clean clothes. Christmas had come to an end.

The following Wednesday I was back at work wearing my new suit. There were sniggers in the lift even before the button had been pressed and Ralph Foreman, Mr Fenton's number two, asked if I had just returned from my country retreat? Miss Dove was still on holiday and I was grateful to have the office to myself, but later when I was called to take notes at the feet of the great man he chided me for still wearing "holiday gear". Later, when I took stock of myself in the toilet mirror, I decided that this pantomime grouse moor suit would actually look better on the florid Fenton than myself, and vowed never to wear it again.

That evening I wrote another letter to Lily suggesting that we meet up at Trafalgar Square to celebrate New Year's Eve together. When I arrived at 7.0clock on the 31st of December I remembered that I had stupidly failed to mention which area I had selected for our meeting, and was forced to keep walking around the square in a hopeless quest to find her. My regular beat around Nelson's column attracted the attention of various homosexuals. Some old Queens took my curt rejections as a "hard to get courting strategy" and simply redoubled their efforts, forcing me to run from the scene and seek sanctuary in a News Theatre. After a session of gung-ho British Movietone reports of the Royal Wedding and Nigerian Independence celebrations, followed by Tom and Jerry Cartoons, I emerged to find the streets already crowded with revellers. I bought a copy of the "Star" and retreated to a snack-bar. I felt sad and dispirited and rather foolish. I was in no mood to celebrate the birth of a New Year, but a part of me was determined to put the naivety of my country upbringing behind me. I wanted to be a fly on the wall and dispassionately witness these traditional celebrations at the heart of London. Nevertheless, when I emerged from the bar I was ill prepared for the scene I witnessed. Semi-clad revellers were dancing in the fountains and drunks were throwing up around the square. While most people were determined to have a good night out, and were joining in the singing of "Old Lang Sine", some had had their inhibitions dulled by alcohol and were randomly embracing complete strangers -- declaring them to be their lifelong buddies. The neon lights from the advertising hoardings, surrounding the square, cast flickering reflections over the crowd and added a surreal feel to the whole proceedings. I realised I had to get up early for work the next day and made my way towards Leicester Square tube station, only to find it closed and surrounded by a great mass of people. I eventually walked as far as Oxford Street and caught a late night tube back to Greencroft Gardens. The evening had been a complete failure -- but I contented myself with the thought that I had notched up some "real life" experiences, to leaven my rather abstract diet of existentialist reading, which might provide good raw material for my novel about bedsitter life in Hampstead.

The beginning of 1961 ushered in no great change in the routine tasks I did at the CEGB and I continued my humdrum work concerned with the acquisition of new sites for power stations. Then one day in March I was summoned to a planning meeting with Mr Fenton and Ralph Foreman. The great man started with a rather pompous preamble. "The Consents Department has been awarded the great privilege of organising a very important International Conference on the Future of Nuclear Power to be held at Berkeley Castle in Gloucestershire". He announced. "The delegates will be bringing their wives -- and you." He glared at me – "will be responsible for organising their entertainment together with a Lucy Webster, eh from the Powell Duffren travel people." He looked at me quizzically --"You'll liaise with her for the three days of the Conference. She'll need the names of the delegates' wives, and all their special requirements, so you better get on to Administration and get all the gen." He gave me a dark look -- "I don't want this buggered up! – understand?"

Three weeks later the three of us were sitting in a CEGB chauffer driven car with our travel bags and briefcases bulging with conference paraphernalia. Over-night trips from the office were regarded as a great perk and we all had our green travel expenses forms (colour co-ordinated to depict our rank and level of remuneration) tucked inside our bags. The great man, however, liked to give the impression that expensive meals, bought en route, were the product of his own largesse. Halfway down the A303 heading towards Gloucestershire, he hollered through the hatch separating us from the driver-- "Turn left at the next junction, will you Samuels and follow the signs to the Roebuck Inn." He leaned towards us in a conspiratorial way, his little piggy eyes already narrowed in expectation -- "I think you'll like the superb Crepes Suzette they serve here." Five minutes later we were walking through the white swing doors of a smart restaurant and being ushered to our places by an attentive waiter. I noticed, with a pang of shame, that Samuels had suddenly disappeared, either to the Public bar, or to eat his sandwiches alone in his cab. I had no idea what Crepes Suzette was so I simply followed what the others ordered, ending up with a rather bloody steak for my first course. When the second course arrived, served personally by the head waiter, Mr Fenton could barely contain himself -- raising his arms in salutation as the flames flickered upwards and the smell of burning liquors filled the air between us.

We arrived at Berkeley Castle late at night and I went straight to my room and fell asleep almost immediately. After breakfast the next morning I sorted out the lists I had compiled of the delegates wives and then helped Ralph lay out all the Conference pre-prints in the Long Drawing Room for the nuclear research scientists to read at the beginning of the Conference. His wife was pregnant and he sometimes disappeared to ring home to check on her confinement. I prayed that she would hang on until the end of the week as I had no idea how I would cope if he disappeared and I was left holding the can. The castle was a warren of different turrets, battlements and keeps and I frequently got lost trying to navigate its many rooms and connecting passageways. But I had to admit that it was an absolute gem. It dated back to the 12th Century and had been continually occupied by the Berkeley Family for the last 800 years. It was very well preserved and was one of the March Castles built to resist Welsh invasions with a defensive outer wall cut with arrow slits to deter attack.

At eleven 0'clock a fleet of coaches arrived carrying the conference delegates and their wives and I helped usher them to their rooms. After lunch it was arranged that while the nuclear engineers were engaged in the plenary session of the conference, their wives would go on a coach tour of the castle grounds and surrounding countryside bordering the banks of the River Severn. In 1961 the boundaries separating the roles of men and women were as solid as the class segregation which had divided farm labourers from the country gentry in Pound Green. No one questioned the scene, when at the end of the meal, the male engineers and scientists were directed towards the long drawing room to collect their conference papers and their ladies were led to the outer courtyard to be briefed about their afternoon's entertainment. Freed from the grind of their domestic responsibilities at home, they were in holiday mood. They were dressed as if for a party. Some, whose eyes sparkled with the effect of good table wine, even gave me a coquettish look as I endeavoured to marshal them towards their waiting transport. In order to enhance my official role I had acquired a Tannoy loud hailer and was nosily blasting out the message that –"All the wives of delegates should proceed to coach five!"

Lucy Webster was standing in the car park, clip board in hand. She was dressed in blue uniform like an airhostess with a little peaked cap held at a rather rakish angle atop an abundance of blond hair. "Hello", she said, "I'm Lucy, you must be Mike. Are you coming for the ride?" "Well ..." I hesitated, thinking of the conference documents I was supposed to be collating "Go on" she smiled and gave my hand a quick squeeze "I could do with some help!" After herding the conference wives on to the coach, I dutifully followed her to the vacant seat behind the driver. We toured around the six thousand acre Berkeley estate, stopping briefly to see deer grazing on a sun topped hill, and then headed off to drive through the Vale of Berkeley ending with visits to lovely little hamlets on the bans of the river Severn. On the outward drive, Lucy had conducted the proceedings well, with a good knowledge of local history coupled with a few well-honed jokes. She was a professional who did her job well, whether she was talking about the arrow slits in the battlements of Berkeley Castle, or nesting sites for white fronted geese, or stories of ghostly apparitions on lonely marshes. On the way home she relaxed and put her microphone aside. A warm spring day was coming to an end and the sun turned red as it sunk behind the hills. The effects of a good lunch and the steady motion of the coach had caused some of the company wives to drift off. Lucy slumped back in the seat and I felt the warmth of her body next to mine. "Tell me about yourself?" She murmured you don't look like a typical Board man to me?". This seemed like an open invitation for me to rattle on about bedsitter life in Kilburn and my attempts at writing. She laughed when I told about my bid to smoke in Miss Dove's office and my unspeakable behaviour at the CEGB Christmas Party. "It's early days," she said – "You don't think you might turn into a Boardman one day?" This provoked me, as she knew it would, into more personal revelations about studying at Regents Polytechnic, and my views on politics and life in general, and more thumbnail sketches of "Characters" in the CEGB. "Ah" she sighed, when I had finished, "You are very young ..." She linked her hand in mine and I felt the outline of a ring on one of her fingers and the thought suddenly struck me that she might be married or engaged. I had no time to consider the matter further as the coach ground to a stop in the courtyard of Berkeley Castle and she reached for her microphone to tell her charges about the arrangements for the rest of the evening.

At Dinner I noticed that Ralph Foreman sat next to Lucy Webster and paid her a good deal of attention. He expanded at great length about his up and coming role in the organisation, while, at the same time hinting at a "Man about town Joie de vivre" denied to the other pinstripes. Later at the bar, he confided in me –"That he fancied that Lucy Webster something rotten!" The role of the "concerned expectant father" was laid aside, and late night liqueurs were deployed in the pursuit of his carnal goal. I expected great revelations the next morning. But nothing was said. At breakfast he sat apart from Lucy and later, before the beginning of the big morning conference, he was back at the phone in the lobby with a new round of earnest enquiries about his wife's condition.

Later in the morning I was out in the car-park again with my tannoy directing the wives to the coach where Lucy awaited to escort them to the Peter Scott's Wildfowl Trust in Slimbridge. Ralph Foreman had ruled that I should not accompany her as my services were urgently required for the correlation of pre-prints for the scientists and engineers to discuss.

The Conference finished the next day and the Delegates and their Wives were spirited away in their coaches and I could lay my loud speaker aside. The Conference memoranda had been filed away and our bags were packed ready for an early departure the next morning. I was in my room filling in my expenses form when the phone rang. It was Lucy Webster. "I'm just compiling my returns for the cost of entertaining the wives and I wondered if you would like to come to my room so we could compare figures" "Oh", I said, caught unawares, "That's a shame I've given all my figures to Mr Fenton". "That's a pity", she replied, it would have been very nice to see you ..." there was a long pause and then she hung up. Looking back all these years since, I am amazed at my naivety. At the time, I told myself, that I didn't want to be part of a cynical power game played away from home by married couples, but I also reasoned that if my puritan conscience remained too censorious I would never amass any raunchy material for my Hampstead novel.

When I returned to my bedsitter that evening I found a letter from Maria Jarbensek saying that she had started teaching English at a school in Ljubljana. She was visiting friends in England and would like to see me. I wrote her a long airmail, all about my life in the CEGB, and said I would love to see her. It was good to be reminded of another world outside the organisation.

A few weeks later I was moved to the Wayleaves Department, which dealt with acquiring land for the erection of pylons and the routing of underground power cables. It was good to get away from Miss Dove's office, but the routine of writing bureaucratic letters to be stored in pink files was much the same. I was now allowed to dictate letters to a secretary from the typing pool, who would attend my office to take shorthand. On more than one occasion I caught myself saying -- "One top copy and two flimsy's thank you Miss Pink". And wondered if Lucy's prophecy of me morphing into a Board-man was coming true. Not long after I started my job, I received an official memo saying that because of the popularity of mini-skirts all the desks in our offices reserved for visiting stenographers would be fitted with "Modesty Panels" to discourage the prying eyes of young clerks. The Generating Board really did want to own you body and soul! Graduate trainees were a relatively new innovation and were seen by some as "Johnny come Latelies" defying laws of seniority and incremental progress. On one occasion James Sparkes drew me aside in the canteen. "Married men", he confided, stood a better chance of promotion. He nodded towards Rosie, who worked in the Basement Registry, and had recently announced her engagement --- "That's the kind of girl for you ..."

During my time in Wayleaves the Organisation and Methods Department of the GEGB decided to utilize the floor space in its Headquarters building more efficiently. Induction meetings were hurriedly convened for staff addressed by Time and Motion boffins, armed with flip charts and slide-rules, droning on about efficiency and human motivation. Office partitions, we learned, would be removed over the weekend and we would all enjoy the benefits of "open plan" working. Such revelations were received in stunned silence by the assembled clerks and executives. Privacy and personal office space were indicators of status. The following Monday there were heated arguments over the ownership of potted plants and paperweights, and whether the names on the door to the new main office should be ranked alphabetically or in terms of seniority. As I began a frantic hunt for my lost files I wondered how Miss Dove in Consents was dealing with her new "freedom". In truth I did sympathise with her, as one of the symptoms of my (yet un-diagnosed dyslexia) was a problem concentrating when other people were talking. I seemed to have a compulsive desire to earwig on other people's conversations to the detriment of my own thought processes. The strategy of retreating to the lavatory, as I had at Harper's College to revise for my A Levels, was not an option, and for a short period I tried wearing ear muffs. After I was teased into capitulation by my fellow clerks I took to the occasional use of ear plugs, despite a notable decline in my response time for answering the telephone.

A couple of weekends later I met up with Maria and we had a lovely day wandering around Hampstead. Later, I cooked her a fry-up, and we lay on my bed for hours in an intimate embrace. It was good to talk and laugh with her and share my ideas with someone so sympathetic to my view of the world. I sensed that she still carried a candle for Ayron, the organiser of the Camp in Tiptree, and I wondered if she had visited him during her stay in England.
At this time I also met my cousin Diane who had flown over from Australia to "Do Europe" in three weeks. It was good to see her. She had kindly bought a Kodak Movie Camera for me in Aden, which Uncle Norm, who loved gadgets, later used to film Linda and myself acting out a comic turn in the grounds of Kilvrough. I took Diana for a meal and a whistle-stop tour of the West-end and Soho. But our meeting was brief, as her Tour Company whisked her around "Little old GB" in three days flat before she embarked for the Continent.

I also visited Uncle Les in Coulsdon to fulfil my promise to help him build his new garage. I arrived to find him and his man Doug and Uncle Norm poring over plans in the driveway outside his house. Some large stone blocks had been bolted to reinforced concrete beams which had been designed to bear the main weight of the structure. The whole erection was supported on one side by a couple of car jacks and leaned over at an odd angle. "Why is it jacked up like that?" I asked. "We can't get it to fit any other way ..." muttered Uncle Norm. "It's not right". I persisted. ""You'll have to unscrew the whole lot and start again!" The brothers looked dumbfounded. "What the hell for!" they chorused. "Because the whole damn lot's upside down!" I yelled. It was true. Once we undid the metal bolts and turned the lateral beams the other way up, the structure lay flat on the ground and we were able to screw it together quite easily. At the end of the afternoon we were fitting the metal clips which held the corrugated asbestos roof panels in place, and ready for high tea at Uncle Norm's. Les and Norm looked at me with a new respect. The Boy had done well. At the time I attributed my insight to my love of model engineering. But much later in life I learned that Dyslectics were often good at spatial awareness.

A by-product of the new open plan working at the organisation was an opportunity to socialise with a greater number of CEGB staff. I was befriended by a middle aged divorcee called Dora Brown, who said I looked as if I could do with a good meal. She persisted in asking me home for the weekend. Having stood up the beautiful Lucy, I was in no mood to accept, and invented a busy itinerary of social engagements to keep her at bay. She was friendly with a young Irishman from a different Department, who had the habit of popping in to see her for a gossip when we were all packing up to leave in the evening. Damien was a good conversationalist, with a well-developed sense of humour. As time went on I was gradually drawn into contributing to their banter. He was very critical of office routine and bureaucracy and I sensed he was something of an outsider – a fellow comrade in arms even? One Friday evening Dora left early and he stood by my desk. He was full of quips and zany anecdotes about life in general. When the small hand of the clock finally pointed at Five O'clock and I got up to reach for my brief case. He said, "Fancy coming for a meal?" As I had nothing special planned for the evening, I heard myself say – "Sounds like a good idea."

We walked down Winsley Street and turned off into a maze of smaller streets where there were a variety of pubs and eating places. Damien seemed very familiar with his surroundings and we entered a restaurant of his choice. I deferred to his menu suggestions and we eat a good meal washed down by a large quantity of red wine, while he continued his patter of funny stories. I balked at him paying the bill and said that we should go halves. But he waived my objections aside. "You can pay next time mate!" He said. When we got up to leave I was surprised when he started to help me on with my coat and I prized it from his grasp. "I can do that!" I exclaimed. While he laughed – "You should not be so touchy mate. It's just part of my old world charm!" He quipped. I told him I should get back to Finchley Road. But he feigned a sense of outrage – "Gwad the night is young! Do you know that? You'll be sure to come back to my place for a nightcap – it's just around the corner!" It seemed currish not to comply, and I followed him a couple of blocks along the street. Finally, we entered an old tenement, which had been converted into flats, and through an entrance leading onto a flight of steps. I followed him up the stairs, "Chez Moi!" He announced, flinging open the door on the landing which revealed a huge double bed surrounded on three walls by lurid film posters and homo-erotic pictures. Damien took my arm and pointed to one of Spartacus flexing his mighty muscles. "Now what do you think of him Boyo?" He whispered in my ear. Finally the penny dropped. I wrenched myself from his grasp. "I'm sorry", I yelled, "But you have made a terrible mistake!" I didn't wait for a reply and ran down the stairs and out into the night.

Over the weekend I had another look at "Saturday night and Sunday Morning Hampstead Version" and decided it was self-conscious pretentious crap. My over indulgence with the world of Existentialism was getting me into a lot of trouble. The novels of Francoise Sagan and Jean Paul Sartre were laid aside, in favour of readings from George Orwell's "Lion and the Unicorn" and "The Road to Wigan Pier". I contacted John Mountsey and we went along to Endsleigh Street to sign up for an NUS sponsored holiday –"Canoeing down the River Wye" in the summer. John was studying an MSc in Radiation Physics at University College London, and we later went to the Saturday Night Union Dance. John's dancing skills were no better than mine and we failed to "pull" any girls but we had a good laugh and I felt strangely cleansed by the experience.

The following Wednesday I met up with Ray Gordon at one of Stephen Cotgrove's MSc Seminars and we agreed to sign up to attend a WEA course on "The Social Structure of Modern Britain" given by Dr Alan Little, one of Doug's friends who was an up and coming lecturer at the London School of Economics.

I was now almost halfway through my graduate training scheme and, as I was very unlikely to accept permanent employment with the Board I, therefore, thought it would be a good idea if I gained a little background experience in some of the caring professions. So I signed up to do Voluntary Social Work at the "East London Family Service Unit" The Unit was housed in a couple of dilapidated buildings in

Valence Road in the East End and the approach to it lay under railway bridges and poor lit streets. At first sight it looked rather like the set of "Six Five Special" Programme, much loved by Uncle Norm, with trendy "ton-up" vicars and youth workers playing ping pong and chess with a variety of kids. The professional social workers, however, appeared to be well versed in Freudian Psychology and attributed outbursts of violent behaviour, manifested by some of the youths, to the trauma of deep repression. Teenagers, found hammering their helpless victims into the ground were dispatched to what was called the "Rumpus Room", where such deviants were encouraged to break things as much as they liked. The theory, explained to me by Agnes, was that the release of such frustrated energy on inanimate objects would purge their psyches of the aggression previously visited upon their rivals. I thought such theories to be naïve in the extreme, as there were plenty of opportunities for kids growing up in such a harsh and deprived environment to smash things up without an official sanction to be yet more destructive. But I kept my council and asked Spike, who was about to lay into a fat girl called Brenda, if he would like another game of table tennis? Volunteers were encouraged to take some of the youths on visits designed to broaden their horizons. A trip to the West-end referred to as "Going up West" by the kids, was much prized. And so it was agreed, that Sandra, who was another volunteer, and I would take a small group of kids to the West-end the following Saturday.

We met a group of boys and girls at Waterloo Station and brought them tickets for the short for the short tube trip to Charing Cross. Although I had become inured to bad language at Harpers College – the expletives trilled from the throats of middle class adolescents seemed tame compared to the earthy rendition of their Cockney cousins. As we entered the train, parties of well healed passengers, up from the country for a day's shopping, or theatre trip, reeled back in horror as infantile Bill Sykes and Nancys yelled lavatorial abuse at one another. Efforts to quieten them, from Sandra and myself, fell on deaf ears, and the other commuters gave us scornful glances as if we were their errant parents We were both relieved when we reached Charing Cross. And we could steer our boisterous charges up the steps and along the Victoria Embankment. We stopped to look at Cleopatra's Needle and then walked on to see the massive cranes working in St Catherine's Dock, and then headed up White Friars road into Fleet Street and Ludgate Hill. When we stopped for a rest on the steps of St Paul's Cathedral. We could see that some of the children were quite tired. Henry had his head in his hands and was wheezing heavily. "I'm worn out!" He wailed "When we's going to eat?" "Yus" the others chorused "When we going to eat!" I conferred with Sandra. Fatigue had its advantages and the kids now seemed a little easier to handle. "Tell you what." I said brightly "If you are good in the Cathedral, we'll take you to a Lyon's Corner House on the way home." They kept their side of the bargain and when we trooped inside they stood in awe, gaping up at the vastness of the great dome above us. Later we shepherded them up Newgate Street to Holborn Circus to the Strand and into the same Lyons Corner House where, four years earlier, I had planned my academic future with Uncle Norm.

We ordered sausage and mash all round and took our plates to a large round table in the middle of the café and sat down. Then, without warning, Sadie grabbed hold of a large plastic dispenser, moulded in the shape of a gigantic tomato. Before we could stop her she gave it an almighty punch and a fountain of red sauce shot up to the ceiling and rained down on to some of the inhabitants of the adjacent tables. I jumped up immediately and heard myself say – :"We're terribly sorry, eh, we're on a trip from the Valence Road Family Service Unit". "Bloody lunatic asylum more like!" growled a disgruntled customer behind me. Sandra flushed bright red and looked as if she might have a panic attack. Thankfully, Bertie, relieved the tension by letting out a burp and pronouncing that the meal was the best he had ever had, and the rest of the kids chorused their approval.

On the way back to Waterloo Station we chose not to risk confining the kids to the carriage of a crowded tube train. And we decided to cross the Thames by way of Hungerford Bridge, using the pedestrian walkway which ran alongside the railway-line. Halfway across, Bertie suddenly pulled down his breeches without warning and, before we could stop him, stuck his bum over the parapet and dispatched a large turd into the fast flowing water below – eliciting ironic cheers from the other kids. "What the hell!" I cried. But Bertie was unrepentant. "I got anal frustration Mister" he yelled and we all fell about laughing to hear him echo the Freudian jargon of the social work team at Valence Road.

The next Saturday I met John Mountsey at Paddington Station and we joined a group of university students with rucksacks all heading for the NUS holiday on the River Wye. While we waited on the platform for our train to arrive John and I chatted to some of our holiday companions. Many of them had scouting backgrounds and some had been on tough outward-bound courses. Even the female students nurses, who we glad eyed, seemed more at ease with tent toggles and orienteering than any thought of a holiday romance. Our fears that this was going to be a tough no nonsense holiday were heightened by the arrival of our group leader. Peter Manley Toms was a raving extravert, with a large orange beard, and a booming voice which echoed around the station concourse.

When we arrived at Ross on Wye we were picked up by a minibus and followed by a large transporter laden with canoes and camping equipment and headed for a camp-site on the banks of the river. We were then issued with two man tents and Peter Toms, and another leader called Jeff, pegged out our pitches. "All canvasses must be pitched in line!" He ordered. As we struggled to erect our tent in the pouring rain, John whispered to me that he was glad that he had just booked for a week, while I thought ruefully, that my two week commitment had consumed all my holiday entitlement with the CEGB for a whole year. After breakfast the next morning, which we consumed cross legged sitting on the wet grass outside our tent, we felt a bit better and enjoyed the preliminary canoe training which involved us being able to right our capsized craft in an emergency. Peter Toms then departed to pick up another party of campers and we were left in the hands of his number two, and Hannah, our German Cook, who looked as if she might have a black belt in unarmed combat. We then packed up out wet tent and damp sleeping bags and stowed them in the front of our canoe. As we paddled away, and picked up speed when we hit the fast flowing water which ran under the bridges of Ross on Wye, I had to admit it was an exhilarating experience. Later the sun came out and the current slowed as we entered the beautiful Wye Valley, flanked by woods and small fields with cows and sheep grazing and sometimes wading in the shallows near the river bank. By late afternoon, John and I were surprisingly tired and our arms ached with the effort of paddling. We were grateful to make camp and even queued for a second helping of Hannah's indifferent goulash.

The pattern of the holiday for the next few days varied from short periods of intense excitement, when we had to navigate swift flowing rapids -- to days, when we followed the endless twists and turns of the river, which seemed to go on forever, and we were exhausted at the end of the day. On one occasion we beached the canoe by mistake on a shallow bank of pebbles, in the middle of the river. No amount of pushing with our paddles would shift our craft and John said—"Why not hop out Mike and give us a push?" I dutifully obliged, but stupidly chose the wrong side of the canoe. I was swept down-stream by the fast flowing current. I love swimming and found the experience quite exciting. I eventually grabbed on to an overhanging branch and hauled myself out, but just as I paddled ashore an eager boy scout standing on the bank suddenly embraced me, calling gleefully back to his troop leader that he had saved me! Not wishing to deprive him of his Tenderfoot Award, I went along with the deception as a gaggle of Cubs gawked at me from the river bank.

After six days we had just passed Symonds Yat and were roughly halfway down the Wye towards the holiday finishing point south of Tintern Abbey. As one of those staying for a week, John was due to be picked up the next morning, and we decided to make a night of it, and after pitching or tent, we took a footpath across three fields to a local pub. It was a very traditional hostelry with skittles and bar billiards. We asked about the local brew and in the end opted for their homemade scrumpy cider. When we carried the pints to our table we noticed that curds of extraneous matter seemed to be floating in the auburn liquor. We asked one of the locals and he said that all sorts of bits and bobs, including dead rats, were added to the fermenting apples to give the brew to give it "body". By the time we had drained our glasses our wits were already starting to dull and we ordered another round. By closing time, after a third pint, we were beginning to feel distinctly queasy, and when we stood up to leave, our legs refused to obey our commands. In the end we were reduced to virtually crawling out of the pub on all fours.

We headed towards the lights of our camp fire, but halfway across the first field I was seized by an appalling gastric convulsion and yellow bile seemed to flow from every orifice in my body. Poor John fared no better, and I heard him reaching violently from behind a bramble bush. Somehow we made it back to our tent. We awoke the next morning with very sore heads. I said goodbye to John and he was whisked away by mini-coach, with a group of others to catch the train back to London. Jeff was quick to notice the spare place in my canoe and I was requested to carry extra provisions. This was a rather silly decision, since even if my debilitated state, following my hangover, was disregarded -- it was unrealistic to expect one person to carry the weight of two with only one set of paddles for propulsion. I lagged behind everyone else, and was in danger of getting totally separated from the rest. Jeff had to frequently stop the flotilla of canoes to wait for me to catch up to the ironic cheers of the rest of the group. One the last day Hannah took pity on me. My extra cargo was moved to her canoe which was to be paddled by someone else. A larger lightweight wooden framed "Prout" canvass canoe was loaded with boxes of food in the front, and I was placed behind, with Hannah taking position in the rear. She was determined to demonstrate her physical prowess and we took pole position on the our last lap between Tintern Abbey and our pick up point at the Devil's Pulpit. She was a well-built girl and I glanced back on occasions to see her bulging biceps as she wielded her paddles behind me. Finally, we rounded the last bend in the river and saw the camp come into view "We're here!" I yelled, relaxing my concentration momentarily. Suddenly, there was a huge bang and we collided with a big boulder in the middle of the river.. The "Prout" canoe jack-knifed and we were struggling in the water with the cooking provisions for the evening meal, rapidly floating down-stream...

Six hours later, I was walking up the stairs to my room in Greencroft Gardens clutching a leather suitcase full of water logged pants and socks. The clothes I stood up in were wet and smeared with mud and traces of duck-weed. I found that my room was full of other people's possessions. Mrs Kemp, the landlady, had taken advantage of my fortnight away to boost her income by double letting my room.

My "tour" in the Wayleaves Department had come to an end, and when I returned to work, a day later, I caught the tube to Waterloo and walked through The Cut to the offices of the Board's Public Relations Department in Blackfriars Road. The Department had received the same going over from the Organisations and Methods Team as the other London Offices of the CEGB, and I entered a huge open plan office. I was introduced to the head of the organisation – a large man called Tommy Johnson. He occupied a glass box on a raised platform away from the hoi polloi, who sat in serried ranks of desks spread out below him. Those who worked in Public Relations often had a background in journalism – they were, in effect, poachers turned gamekeepers – whose main job was to monitor all news output to try to ensure that the CEGB received the most favourable coverage. Tommy Johnson liked to project himself as Editor in Chief and would always wear a white shirt and red braces. He could be frequently be seen in his glass box, with one phone clenched between his neck and shoulder, with another cupped in his other hand. He seemed permanently tethered to this instrument and sometimes, he would lean out of his box with its coiled cord behind him like a Jack in the Box on a spring. "Pailing!" he would yell to his Number Two. "Pailing I want you here now!" and his henpecked assistant would have to do his bidding. He was fond of claiming that he was a descendant of Dr Johnson and I wondered briefly, whether Boswell had to stomach such boorish behaviour from his famous namesake. I was also introduced to Brenda, another graduate from Oxford, who was busy proof reading Board material for publication. She said that the two of us might be involved in planning the forthcoming visit of the Queen Mother to Bankside Power Station. Later I visited the offices of "Power People", which was housed in a smaller room, and was introduced to its bearded editor -- a Mr Clover. I also met the Assistant Editor called Phil Greenman who had had a spell working on popular newspapers. He gave me a welcoming smile and said that we should go for a drink sometime. That promise was fulfilled quicker than I could have expected and at 12.30 pm I noticed that most of the male members of the Department decamped to the local Southwark pubs for an extended lunch hour. Tommy Johnson liked to be the centre of attention at these sessions, trading on the glory of his Fleet Street past. His great bulk seemed to effortlessly soak up the pints, leaving the rest of us far behind.

Although "Power People" looked like a newspaper, it was really a House Magazine designed to improve communications between various Departments within the CEGB. The scientists and engineers at the top of the organisation were always deferred to, and any speeches or statements they made were reported with a Pravda like reverence. I was given an assignment to interview some corporate boss. He was photographed behind an imposing mahogany desk with an impressive display of rising production figures hanging from a wall chart behind him. In my piece I did my best to add a little colour and texture to the rather boring speech he had just made to a committee meeting. But when Phil vetted it I was chided for not sounding more enthusiastic. My reference to the boss's well stocked library, was changed to the more clichéd –"Book lined office".

In 1961 environmental issues were just beginning to come on to the political agenda. Pressure Groups like "The Campaign for the Preservation of Rural England" were critical of the erection of electricity pylons, especially in "Areas of Outstanding Natural beauty". The PR Department suggested one or two rather barmy solutions. One was to paint the pylons the same colour as their natural background thus rendering them "invisible". This, of course, took no account of the changing seasons – and green masts gleamed like Wellsian fighting machines from Mars, when the leaves fell off the trees in the autumn. Blue pylons, marching over the tops of hills, might be invisible "against the sky", but a danger to low flying aircraft.

Digging trenches for the electricity cables to run underground was expensive, and we were leaned upon to come up with a slogan which would encourage the general public to accept the ugly pylons. In the end we made a short film featuring a newly-wed "Dolly Bird" perched on top of a washing machine, being embraced by her indulgent young husband. The backdrop featured a big picture of pylons striding over the English countryside. The caption read – "Don't you know that it costs ten times as much to bury these cables!" In a voice over a vocalist crooned a refrain from a popular song of this era -- "Love and marriage. Love and marriage! Goes together like a horse and carriage, that was told by mother – You can't have one without the other try, try and separate them --- it's an illusion …!" the price of conjugal bliss, it seemed, was ugly pylons in a National Park.

Phil Greenman prided himself on his knowledge of subliminal approaches in advertising. He told me that when he had previously worked for the Shell Company, it was advised by Freudian Psychologists, that drivers felt insecure when pump attendants served them with gasoline by injecting the nozzle into the petrol tank at the back of their cars. This approach from the rear, according to these gurus, promoted an unconscious fear of an unsolicited anal attack. They advised that the introduction of self-service pumps would free drivers from such nightmares. Once outside their cars they would feel liberated and less fearful of embracing new experiences. According to Phil, the company was advised to site the payment counter at the rear of their garages, thus creating a "lure" full of merchandise that would attract customers on their way to pay. Apparently, he said, consumer sales rocketed once these changes had been made on garage forecourts. Phil also was an inveterate gossip and once claimed that he had seen Clover coming out of a bookshop of ill repute in Charing Cross Road carrying a large brown envelop which, he deduced, must have contained illegal pornography. He also said that the CEGB had a secret account with a firm specialising in the production of anti-fart devices. These comprised of a suspender belt -- to which was attached a cord carrying a sweet smelling sponge. When worn by top Board-men, the sponge would hang neatly between their buttocks, thus neutralising the noxious effects of over indulgence of a VIP lunch at the top table.

The world of my childhood, I felt, was beginning to change. Although, representatives of the AA and RAC might still stand by their motor bikes and side cars deferentially saluting their members as they drove by. And Tom Smith continued to cut bacon to order, in the Pound Green Stores, while Grace cycled around the hamlet delivering groceries and taking orders. Entrepreneurs like Jack Cohen, were busy buying up little corner shops, and early supermarkets were beginning to "pile it high and sell it cheap". Shoppers started to be organised into malleable units of consumption as they were corralled through avenues of well packaged goods towards the checkouts and ringing tills. I thought of Vance Packard's popular book on the psychology of "Hidden Persuaders", I had read in my first year at Regent Street Poly, and mused that he had got it about right.

I enjoyed my work in Public relations much more than the clerical routine of Consents or Wayleaves. I liked working on "Power People" and even accompanied Mr Clover to the printers to see the edition "put to bed". However, the experience fell a good way short of real journalism and deep down I resented always having to put the best "spin" on some of the more questionable policies of the CEGB. The publication was weighted heavily towards the big wigs at the top of the organisation, and although we attempted to find human interest stories involving ordinary people in the lower echelons we found it difficult to elicit much popular response. Sometimes, we were even reduced to writing spoof letters to the editor from mythical characters like Sandra in Accounts or Jim in Despatch.

My involvement in the Queen Mothers visit to Bankside Power Station was hilarious, when late on in the planning, we discovered that the Palace required that her own special thunder-box with an ermine seat be plumbed in for her personal use.

Soon after our holiday in the Wye Valley, and the unfortunate incident with Mr Kemp, I joined forces with John Mountsey and rented a double bedsitter at Number 83 Greencroft Gardens. We paid five guineas each for a larger room with two gas rings. The property was owned by a Mr Manson, who was reputed to own seventy or so similar mansions in the neighbourhood. During this period Rachmanism was at its height and the property was divided into a variety of flatlets and bedsitters to avoid rent control. Some were very small indeed. As before, there was no fridge and the lavatory and bathroom were across the landing and shared by everyone on the same floor. We soon discovered that the gas fire was expensive and unequal to the task of heating the whole room. So I shared the cost of a big free standing paraffin stove with John, who was more fugal than me. He said that it would also double as a cooker to heat up his porridge in the morning.

In the August of 1961 John and I, and a variety of my friends from the Poly, attended our graduation ceremony at the Albert Hall. Mum and Dad came up from the country for the occasion, and I hired a gown and mortar board from Moss Bros. When I later bowed low to the smiling Queen Mum I wondered, briefly, if she had ever used the special loo that the CEGB had installed at such expense. As I left the stage, a representative from Moss Bros hauled the gown off my back and deprived me of my mortar board and rushed it away for the initiation of another student. Apparently, I had paid a cheap jack rate for the hire of my finery, and later, when my proud parents wanted to photograph me outside the Albert Memorial, I had to borrow Ray's gown and mortar board. Later, we walked in Kensington Gardens and by the Serpentine and I caught a glimpse of the island which, in what seemed another age, Lily and I had once called our own.

Over the next few weeks John and I settled into the routine of sharing our room at 83 Greencroft Gardens. Our cooking relied heavily on fry-ups for breakfast and supper. Although, I made some attempt to augment this by buying salami and cheeses from the Jewish Delicatessen which I passed on my way home from the Finchley Road tube station. John liked eggs and bacon in the morning, followed by his beloved porridge. Inevitably, it boiled over one morning and the odour of burnt oats, mingled with the acrid smell of burning paraffin, lingered for weeks after.

We continued to go to the occasional dance at the University College Union but, as before, our clack handed performance on the dance floor failed to elicit any lasting romantic attachments. We fared worse at "La Cage D'Or" at the top of our road. This was an expensive night club which seemed to attract playboys in open back limos. There were bouncers on the door, and you had to pay a club fee to get in – the cost of the drinks was exorbitant. The club had a reputation for attracting pretty au pair girls from well healed Hampstead homes. When we finally gained admission, we entered a kind of Dante's Inferno of flashing lights, thick cigarette smoke and loud music. Most of the girls seemed glued to their rich escorts, and the remaining wall flowers quickly discovered that we didn't have the readies, or inclination, to buy them the expensive cocktails that were on offer. They soon gave us the cold shoulder and we left early, chastened and wiser for the experience.

A few days later I received two letters which had been forwarded from home. One was from Psycho, who seemed keen to see the sights in London, and the other was from Margaret the Youth Club leader I had met in Gower. I arranged for Psycho to stay in our bedsitter for a couple of nights, dossing down on a sleeping bag in the corner of the room. I then contacted Margaret and fixed for her to come the following Saturday. I met Psycho at Paddington Station.

As I surmised "seeing the sights" was code for gong to a strip club – a "rite of passage" for sexually frustrated Public School boys. I calculated that it was four and a half years since I had last seen him and I was surprised that this was still top of his agenda. We caught the tube to Tottenham Court Road and threaded our way through a maze of small streets and into the heart of the red light district. Girls ogled us from shop windows and side alleys and I steered Psycho into a strip club featuring fan dancers, nude tableaux and striptease artists. The show started at what might be regarded as the "more artistic performances" with a teasing flurry of green fans fluttering over vital parts of the high kicking dancing girls, followed by traditional Can Can dancers and ending up with a seasoned woman, old enough to be Psycho's mother, gyrating before us in a sequined basque. As the drums rapped out their beat for the final act of disrobing, men of all ages stood up -- some surging to the front of the stage, yelling "Get 'Em Off! Get 'Em Off! Psycho stood gazing at the fallen curtain for some time after the show had finished. And I wondered whether this overt show of titillation had been any more liberating for him than Dr Matthews Sex lectures which we had attended in the Fourth Form at school? Later, when we sat in a Chinese restaurant, talking about life in general, I discovered that Psycho seemed just as depressed as I remembered him being at Harpers College. The mental wounds inflicted by the bullies, I feared, had marked him for life.

The next weekend I met Margaret at Finchley Road Tube Station, and we went back to have a meal together at the bedsit. It was two years since our brief encounter in the sand dunes of Three Cliffs Bay in Gower, and I was surprised how haggard she looked. She told me that her engagement to her Italian boyfriend had not worked out and his serial dalliances had made her seriously depressed. Her health had deteriorated, and she had succumbed to a serious gum disease requiring the extraction of some of her teeth. I felt sorry for her. I was surprised at her frankness. In the early 1960's when girls like Carol Smith were happy to tie the knot in their late teens, jilted women sometimes felt abandoned and stigmatised. We drank Merrydown Cider late into the afternoon, before I walked her back to the tube station. When the doors of the carriage slid open I gave her a kiss and offered to be her Pen Pal again. As the train roared away I felt guilty for not doing more....

At the start of the university year John returned from his extended holiday from Guisley, his home town in Yorkshire, to study for his MSc in Radiation Physics at Imperial College. He seemed quite chipper, and announced that he had met a girl from Ottery St Mary in South Devon, who he was keen on. Its hard work courting at long distance", He said "So when she comes up to London"-- he gave me a knowing look, "I want some privacy so I can get right down to it!" Being of a practical disposition John had acquired a couple of large curtain rods from a junk shop which, when cello-taped together, just about stretched across the side of the room, precariously balanced from a shelf in one corner to the picture rail on the wall opposite. We then experimented hanging an array of blankets and eiderdowns on this improvised rail, propped up in the middle with a sturdy pole. By the time Jennifer arrived, we had perfected our routine, and come nightfall, the couple were safely tucked away underneath their awning, preparing for the onset of their nightly nuptials.

Over the next few weeks we gradually got to know one or two of the other residents in the house. There were two girls on the ground floor called Penny and Susan. At the time, career girls were just beginning to break away from living at home with their parents and renting flats in London. The popular press nick-named them "Bachelor Girls". These two girls fell into this category – although Susan had a regular boyfriend and wore an engagement ring. Penny was an attractive girl with auburn hair who was always smartly dressed. John and I had introduced ourselves, when we bumped into them on the stairs, outside the bathroom. Later, when we wanted to know them better, we deployed the subterfuge of borrowing cupfuls of sugar or pats of butter from them, when we ran out of supplies. We discovered that Susan's beau was correct, to the point of idiocy, and never seemed to stay the night, while Penny didn't seem to have a gentleman caller.

The only other person we got to know was an old lady called Mrs Krech who occupied a tiny room scarcely bigger than a broom cupboard. I would sometimes meet her on my way back from work at the Delicatessen, and walk slowly down the hill with her, while she chatted non-stop about her life and troubles. She was a survivor of the holocaust and lived on a tiny pension. She always looked on the bright side and told me that she was waiting for reparations to come through from the German government. Then, she said she would be able to afford a proper room of her own.

One cold weekend in December, when John was away visiting his girlfriend in Devon, I was awakened in the middle of the night by the sound of terrible screaming and the smell of smoke and burning flesh. I dashed on to the landing and then down the stairs to the next. A tiny figure, with virtually all her clothes burnt off her back, was writhing in agony in the stairwell. She was surrounded by other tenants on the same floor who were desperately trying to douse the flames. The cause of the fire was immediately apparent. Mrs Kretch, in an effort to keep warm in her tiny room, had lit her potable gas fire and the flexible pipe had somehow become disconnected from the back of the fire and ignited – acting like a horrific flame thrower. Someone had already dialled 999 and the emergency services were quick to arrive. But, in truth, although we covered Mrs Kretch in towels and blankets, there was little we could do. The paramedics gently lifter her on to a stretcher and carried her to the ambulance, and the fire brigade hosed down her tiny room and disconnected the offending fire. Suddenly, it was all over. People stood around in small groups aghast at the tragedy which had so recently unfolded before our eyes. In the end there was nothing more to say. One by one the tenants made their way back to their rooms. As I turned to go I saw Penny, her face transfixed with terror, standing in to doorway to her bed sitter. "Come on" I said" You can't stay here on your own". And she followed me up the stairs to my room. She was sobbing uncontrollably, and I took her in my arms. The room was freezing cold and we soon retreated under the blankets of my bed. We held each other in a tight embrace all night. The next day was a Saturday and I was pleased I didn't have to go to work. At breakfast time I offered her a fry up and a bowl of John's porridge, but neither of us had much of an appetite, and we ended up sharing a couple of slices of bread and marmite, and a cup of tea. Later, the news filtered through that Mrs Ketch had died of third degree burns and Penny again sobbed quietly in my arms. Outside the snow lay thickly on the road and the pavements were icy. Neither of us felt any inclination to venture out, and Penny stayed for the whole weekend. I learned that she was a trainee buyer from Harrods, and took her role as a "bachelor girl" quite seriously. Her focused career ambitions contrasted with my own dilatory performance at the CEGB. When I talked rather vaguely about my long term plans to write, or become a Sociology Lecturer, I fancy I must have sounded rather like a gauche undergraduate fantasying about the future. She was a sweet girl, and for a few months our chance encounter morphed into a boyfriend-girlfriend relationship. I visited her parents' home in Southend, and she came with me to meet Mum and Dad in Herons Ghyll. Mum was very taken with her and did everything she could to encourage the relationship. In truth, however, although I liked and admired Penny, I was not in love with her. We had some good times together, but I never experienced the overwhelming attraction I had felt for Lily or the jokey repartee I shared with Maria. I can remember lecturing her about politics, and to my eternal shame, I encouraged her to give up her traineeship with Harrods and work for the Co op. She, in contrast, was honest and generous to the end, giving me a folding screen, that I still have, which I used to project

8mm film shot with the Kodak movie camera cousin Diane had bought for me.

In January 1962 I started to attend a series of WEA lectures on the Social Structure of Modern Britain with Ray and Doug and others from the MSc Seminar group at the Poly, given by Alan Little from the LSE. The lectures were very well delivered, and we all felt inspired to follow in his footsteps. In March, Ray Gordon managed to secure some part-time lecturing work in a technical college, and a month later I got a letter from the WEA informing me that one of their lecturers had dropped out, and asking me if I would fill in at short notice. I jumped at the chance.

Five days later, after work, I was on a train to Reigate clutching my briefcase containing some hastily prepared notes on the "Sociology of Crime and Punishment." When I arrived at the station, and asked where the village hall was I found I had to walk a further quarter of a mile along a path over a ploughed field to reach a remote scout hut. I was met by a Lady Convener and informed that I was to lecture to the Womans Guild. "This is, err, Mr Strange "Our *Substitute lecturer*" she announced. "He will talk for three quarters of an hour, before our cake making competition, after this he will continue his talk and answer questions -- she then fixed me with a quizzical stare. "We will finish sharp at 9.30."

Suddenly, I was up on the stage with my notes perched on the lectern gazing into the eyes of bout twenty five elderly ladies, their spectacles glinting in the light, which shone from behind me. As I introduced myself, I suddenly noticed that they all had their knitting out, and as I launched into my preamble about theories of crime and punishment, the needles began to click and I could see some of their lips mouthing their pattern instructions. "Knit one, pearl one, drop one, stitch one...." I began to appreciate that any finely prepared Socratic discourse, contrasting the work of R.K. Merton, Albert

Cohen, Hermann Mannheim and Erving Goffman might fall on deaf ears. After half an hour I was desperately adlibbing, and contrasting Old Testament views of an "eye for an eye and tooth for tooth" with more modern ideas of deterrence. Finally, the hand of the clock at the back of the hall drew it round to 8.15 am and the convener raised her hand. "That's enough thank you Mr Strange". There was a sudden buzz of excitement from the ladies. Chairs were pushed aside, and extra tables were arranged on the stage. The members of the Guild then retreated to the back of the room to retrieve their cakes and one by one paraded them on stage. Once the winner was announced, bits of cake were passed around for our delectation, and we all relaxed.

Questions in the second half further lightened the atmosphere, although some of the ladies appeared unmoved by my criticism of theories of retribution in the first half, one even proclaiming that – "Hanging was too good for them!" Towards the end of the evening I attempted to steer the conversation towards the finality of using Capital Punishment where there might be a miscarriage of justice, or an appeal in the light of new evidence. We then discussed the murder of PC Sidney Miles shot by Christopher Craig in 1952, where Lord Justice Goddard ruled that Dereck Bentley, who was present at the killing, was guilty of "mentally aiding the murder". Both were hanged on 28th January 1953. This caused some of the ladies to have second thoughts about hanging. But when I raised the question of Ruth Ellis, who was hanged for the murder of her philandering boyfriend in 1955, most of the group still favoured the verdict. The age of Feminism had yet to dawn ….

Somehow I completed my assignment for a further seven lectures and ended the course on good terms with the Guild Members. They even presented me with a large slab of fruit cake which I took back to Greencroft Gardens. Lecturing to such a group had been a steep learning curve and I was grateful to the ladies for their forbearance.

In March 1962 I moved back to Winsley Street to work in the Administration Department. This was the last and most prestigious Department, and it was assumed that ambitious trainees like Chambers were expected to apply for permanent positions at the end of their training. Since I had no intention of spending the rest of my days in the CEGB I parried searching questions from my superiors, and vaguely said that I hoped to seek an appointment in Public Relations, while at the same time filling in application forms for lecturing jobs in Further Education. I am sure the Personnel Department harboured doubts about my suitability for any appointment, and on one occasion I was summoned, with another trainee, to sit a test which required the solving of a number of hypothetical management problems. The exam had to be completed in three quarters of an hour and was to be executed at speed. Something which I hated – to make matters worse, there was a noisy meeting going on in the next room and the invigilators persisted in chatting loudly through-out the exam. I had terrible problems concentrating and my spelling went to pot. I never received any feedback, but I am sure my result was dire.

Organisation and Methods had neglected to open plan some of the rooms reserved for management at the top of the Winsley Street building, and I found myself sharing an office with a senior executive called Redwood. He was a large amiable fellow in his middle fifties with a ginger moustache – very old school, with elaborate manners. He seemed to hail from another era, and often talked nostalgically about his university days. Like Miss Dove, he had been with the Board since Vesting Date, and I had the impression, in some way that life had passed him by, and that he was bored with the routine of his job. In a moment of indiscretion, I told him about my interest in writing and lecturing and my misgiving about pursuing a career in the CEGB. On occasions we would while away a whole afternoon together chatting about life in general --and he would flatter me by saying that I exhibited wisdom beyond my years!

Quite soon after I arrived in the Administration Department I was given a assignment dealing with planning permission for the location of a new coal fired station in Nottinghamshire. It was to be sited at Holme Pierrepont and was designed to draw cooling water from the River Trent. The engineers were excited about this "state of the art" design, which meant that coal from highly productive pits in Nottinghamshire would be pulverised near the mines, and conveyed, via a pipe line directly to the furnaces raising steam for the turbines driving the generators. This would increase the thermal efficiency of the new plant, which would be the biggest in Europe, with cooling towers rising to over 800 ft. The problem was, however, that the site chosen was in the middle of a Smokeless Zone -- In the Green Belt, close to an Area of Outstanding Natural Beauty, and in an area scheduled for the development of domestic housing. Not surprisingly, there were a large number of objections, and I was given to understand, that my task would be to analyse these arguments and advise the Board on the viability of the scheme.

This was the kind of academic analysis that I enjoyed, and I was determined to produce a well-argued report contrasting the economic arguments for the site, with the strong views raised by lobbyists against the plan. In 1962 environmental pressure groups were on the rise and there were strong objections from the Campaign for the Preservation of Rural England and the Friends of the Earth and the Wild fowl Trust – and many other groups concerned with the preservation of wild life. There were also powerful representations against the development from the Nottinghamshire County Council and the District Council, which strongly argued that the plan would have a deleterious impact on the quality of life and the health of the citizens in the area. As time went on, objections flooded in from near and far and there were even letters from pressure groups in Holland and Denmark, fearing that the pollution from the station's high chimneys and cooling towers would allow Britain to export acid rain across the North Sea.

A couple of weeks later, after I had dispatched copies of my report to members of the Board, I was summoned to a meeting to review my progress, or lack of it, on the Graduate Training Programme. The Boardroom table was surrounded on three sides with notable Board bigwigs while I sat at the far end. The Chairman lost no time in getting to the point. "What is the meaning of this?" He ejaculated -- And waved a copy of my Report in front of my face. I was somewhat in awe of the grim faces before me, but I was determined to defend myself. "It's the Report you asked me to write," I said. "I've looked at all the evidence and, although the Board had a strong economic argument for building the new station at Holme Pierrepont, the environmental and social arguments against are so strong that the CEGB should amend its plans and look for another location". An angry engineer interrupted me – "The Ministry of Power has never refused a major project of this kind. Who are you to question our experience and expertise?" There were grumbling murmurs of agreement from others around the table. I repeated my arguments, but saw that I was staring at a group of un- respondent stony faces and realised that I was unlikely to make any conversions. I simply said that we would have to wait and see what the Government decided. The Chairman brought the meeting to a close by asking me if I thought I had a future in the Board. Not wishing to burn my boats completely I said "I might apply for a position in the Public Relations Department." My last remark engendered an ironic cry of disbelief from the assembled Board Members, as I left the room.

That evening I sent off two more applications for teaching jobs in Further Education, taking care to compensate for my lack of Teacher Training, by stressing my industrial experience and work with the WEA.

Back in the office I had the impression that the Board had quietly given up the task of converting me into a "High flyer" like Chambers, and I was given a variety of boring low level tasks to complete. I began to notice that Redwood's behaviour was decidedly odd. He would come in the morning and deal with a few letters and memos at the top of his bulging in-tray. Then at lunch time he would disappear for long periods. He would later reappear in the middle of the afternoon -- belching beer fumes. He would then sit down and slump over his desk and begin to snore loudly. When the phone rang he would remain unconscious and but somehow had the capacity to yell lines of bureaucratic jargon at random into the mouth piece. His routine never varied. The mystery of his high grade now began to become apparent. Redwood had built his career around his inefficiency. It was difficult to fire executives in the CEGB, so one Department after another, had discovered how hopeless he was and contrived to move him on, by recommending him for promotion to a higher level in the hierarchy. This pattern of behaviour served him very well. He had risen to the dizzy height of a Grade 8 Secretary, and was happy to serve out his time in obscurity.

One day, however, his luck ran out. A very important meeting had been arranged to discuss high level CEGB policy requiring the attendance of top personnel from all over the country. The Company Secretary assigned to take the minutes was ill and the Chairman, unaware of Redwood's little problem, noticed his high grade and requested that he attend to take the notes. The meeting was held in the late afternoon and Redwood joined the group after the completion of his usual Pub ritual. Tradition had it that the Secretary showed due deference to the VIP's present and he sat at his own table away from the rest. The meeting lasted for a couple of hours during which important business was enacted and key decisions were made. At the end, however, all hell broke loose, when a comatose Redwood was discovered slumped over a completely blank notebook.

The Board was reluctant to admit the real reason for his rise to such a high grade and the Personnel Department came up with the idea that Redwood was suffering from a rare illness called "Obesity". He was retired from immediate effect with an enhanced pension. He was overjoyed by the outcome, and later wrote me a long letter telling me that he had now met a mature lady of his dreams and was happily living on a house boat on the Thames. At the time, I wondered whether putting me in the same room with him was a recognition by the Board of my own hopeless status -- like Darney, in Dickens' Tale of Two Cities, would I be the next for the guillotine? In the event I made my own escape.

A few days after Redwood's departure I received two letters asking me for interviews on the same day. One was at St Albans College of Building and Further Education, the other was at a FE College in Stevenage. I caught a steam train to St Albans and discovered that the College was a modern building, which had recently won an award for architecture. It stood in its own grounds and was close to the centre of the city. Before my interview, I walked down St Peters Street, which was crowded by stalls for the Wednesday Market, and past the Cathedral and down Fishpool Street, and into the lovely old medieval quarter of the City. The sun was shining and there were pretty girls in spring dresses. I felt that I could make a happy life in this place. At the interview the Chairman of Governors turned out to be the local taxi driver, and some of the interviewers were informally dressed in sports jackets and flannels. It was a lovely contrast with the grey conformity of the CEGB. I performed better than I expected, and made as much as I could of my industrial experience and my lectures to the Women's Guild. At the end of the interview, I had to admit that I had another at Stevenage College later in the afternoon.

I was requested to ring the College before attending this second interview, and when I did I was offered the job. I had an overwhelming feeling of relief and elation, and accepted on the spot. Stevenage was a rather austere New Town, and although I went through the motions of the interview at the College, my mind was made up. I returned to St Albans College just in time to shake the hand of my new Head in the Liberal Studies Department and sign on the dotted line. My new life was about to begin.

****

Postscript in 1963 The Minister of Power rejected the CEGB plans to build a new coal fired station at Holme Pierrepont.

Made in the USA
Columbia, SC
21 January 2018